NO   A

ANDREW HE

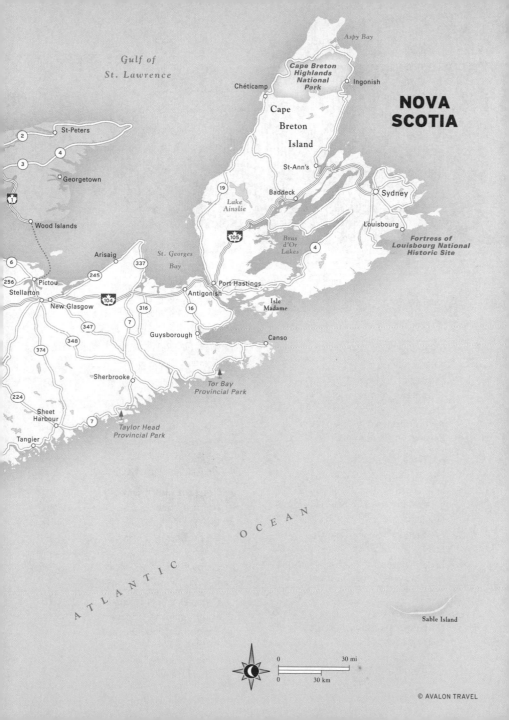

Gulf of
St. Lawrence

Aspy Bay

**Cape Breton
Highlands
National
Park**

Chéticamp   Ingonish

**Cape
Breton
Island**

**NOVA
SCOTIA**

St-Ann's

St-Peters
2
4
3
Georgetown
1
Wood Islands
6
256
Stellarton
Pictou
New Glasgow
347
374
348
224
Sheet
Harbour
Tangier
7
Sherbrooke

245
337
Arisaig

St. Georges
Bay

19
Lake
Ainslie
105

Baddeck   Sydney

Bras
d'Or
Lakes
4
Louisbourg

**Fortress of
Louisbourg National
Historic Site**

316
7
Port Hastings
Antigonish
16
Guysborough

Isle
Madame

Canso

Tor Bay
Provincial Park

Taylor Head
Provincial Park

A T L A N T I C   O C E A N

Sable Island

0   30 mi

0   30 km

© AVALON TRAVEL

Contents

Discover Nova Scotia **6**
Planning Your Trip 10
The Best of Nova Scotia 14
• Family Road Trip 16
Coastal Cruising 17
• The Currents of History 18
• Artists and Artisans 20

Halifax **22**
Sights 28
Recreation 41
Entertainment and Events 44
Shopping 48
Accommodations and Camping 50
Food 55
Information and Services 60
Getting There 61
Getting Around 63

South Shore **64**
Halifax to Mahone Bay 68
Mahone Bay 72
Lunenburg 77
Lunenburg to Shelburne 86

Shelburne and Vicinity 91
Yarmouth 94

Fundy Coast **98**
La Côte Acadienne 102
Digby and Vicinity 105
Annapolis Royal 111
Kejimkujik National Park 116
Annapolis Valley 118
Wolfville and Vicinity 121

Central Nova Scotia **128**
Halifax to Truro 132
Glooscap Trail 136
Sunrise Coast to Pictou 141
Pictou 144
Pictou to Cape Breton Island 147
Marine Drive 150

Cape Breton Island **158**
Port Hastings to Baddeck 162
Baddeck and Vicinity 166
Chéticamp 172
Cape Breton Highlands
    National Park 174

Ingonish and Vicinity. 178
The Northeast. 182

Background. 186
The Land 187
Flora and Fauna. 189
History. 194
Economy and Government. 199
People and Culture 201

Essentials 205
Getting There 206
Getting Around. 208
Recreation. 209
Accommodations and Food 215
Travel Tips 221
Health and Safety 223
Information and Services 225

Resources 228
Suggested Reading. 228
Internet Resources 232

Index. 235

List of Maps 242

DISCOVER
Nova Scotia

Enticing Nova Scotia is a like a picture-book painting, a spacious canvas splashed with brightly colored fishing villages, richly historic towns, uncluttered parks, and a melting pot of cultures that create a destination like no other.

Situated on Canada's east coast, compact Nova Scotia is Canada's second-smallest province (55,490 square kilometers). It is almost an island, encircled completely by water except at its slender, 15-kilometer-long border with New Brunswick. The 7,400-kilometer-long coastline—even without the colorful villages—is beautiful and varied.

Despite its size, Nova Scotia offers visitors a wealth of adventures. The initial focus for many travelers is Halifax, the provincial capital and home of the region's main airport. Here, you can combine historic attractions such as imposing Citadel Hill with walks through coastal parks and feasts of seafood fresh from local waters. But Halifax is just the beginning of your Nova Scotia adventure. Beyond the city limits, you can hike through national parks, bike along back roads, kayak the coast, and admire famously photogenic lighthouses. But the options don't end with the ordinary: It's also a place where you can feel the excitement of

---

Clockwise from top left: Shelburne Historic District; Mahone Bay; Lunenburg Harbour; boat shop near the LaHave River; Acadian church; tall ship in Lunenburg.

white-water rafting on a tidal bore, get up close and personal with the world's rarest whales, or feel the fresh salt air on your face as you set sail aboard a famous racing schooner.

Then there are Nova Scotians themselves, the friendliest folk you're ever likely to meet. Like they have for centuries, the vast majority of Nova Scotians continue to live an unpretentious and resourceful lifestyle, yet they are welcoming to visitors and generous to a fault. Conversation comes easily and humor abounds, especially over a few drinks. As a visitor, you will be encouraged to immerse yourself in their culture—to join in the dancing at a ceilidh (Celtic dance), to taste rappie pie, to watch artisans at work, and to raise a glass in thanks to the local king of beer, Alexander Keith.

Nova Scotia does have its touristy areas, but for the most part the province is waiting to be discovered. For you, the visitor, it will reveal itself slowly. You'll likely snap a picture of the lighthouse at Peggy's Cove, tuck into boiled lobster, and take in a few maritime-themed museums, but your greatest memories will be far from ordinary—ones that go beyond the scope of what a guidebook can recommend and instead revolve around adventures of your own making.

Clockwise from top left: Shelburne waterfront; Island Beach Co. in Halifax; Blue Rocks fishing shack; driving the Cabot Trail.

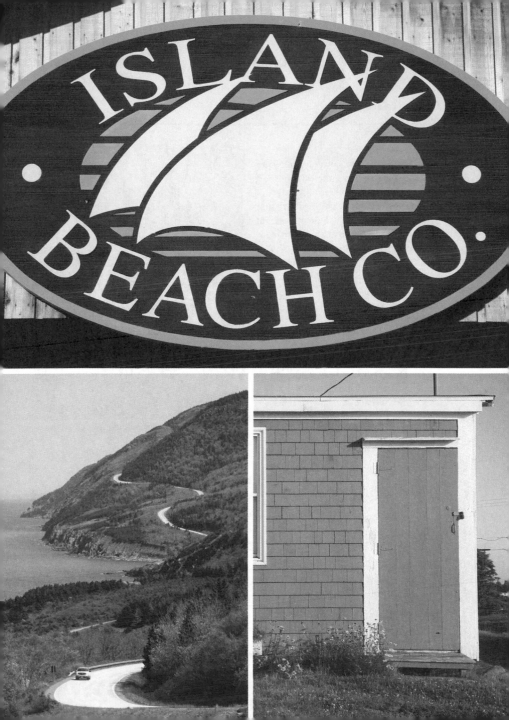

Planning Your Trip

Where to Go

Halifax

Blending the old with the new, Halifax is an excellent city to explore on foot—and there's a lot to discover. Below the modern high rises of downtown, the **hilly streets** are lined with **historic stone buildings.** Along the waterfront is the **Maritime Museum of the Atlantic,** as well as outdoor cafés serving **fresh seafood,** shops selling the work of Nova Scotian artisans, and pubs where traditional Celtic music is a constant.

South Shore

Many visitors head to the South Shore once they've visited the capital. They visit the lighthouse at **Peggy's Cove,** admire the trio of **waterfront churches in Mahone Bay,** and wander through the protected streets of **Lunenburg,** a UNESCO World Heritage Site. Further south are charmingly untouristy villages and towns, such as **Shelburne,** and **deserted beaches.**

Mahone Bay is famous for its photogenic churches.

© AVALON TRAVEL

one of Nova Scotia's many historic stone buildings

If You Have...

- **A WEEKEND:** In Halifax, visit the Maritime Museum and the farmers market and go for a harbor cruise.

- **ONE WEEK:** Add Mahone Bay and Lunenburg on the South Shore, and then Fundy Coast attractions such as Annapolis Royal.

- **TWO WEEKS:** Add a full week on Cape Breton Island to your itinerary, including golfing and exploring Cape Breton Highlands National Park.

Historic Gardens, Annapolis Royal

Fundy Coast

Bordering the powerful **Bay of Fundy** is a stretch of dramatic coastline as naturally impressive as the scattered townships are culturally interesting. Twice a day, **high tides** sweep into the bay. Birdlife is prolific along the shoreline, while whales find a food source in the plankton-rich moving water. Most important for seafood lovers, local fishermen bring ashore the **world's plumpest scallops** and **sweet-tasting lobsters** by the trap load.

Central Nova Scotia

Extending from the capital to Cape Breton Island, this region features the wonder of the **world's highest tides, dinosaur footprints,** and the **warm waters of Northumberland Strait.** Inland, **wineries,** restored **grist mills,** and **charming villages** make veering from the main highway an unpredictable joy. While the coastline along the **Marine Drive** is as rugged as the South Shore's, the landscape is more diverse, with long stretches of white-sand beach, windswept headlands topped by lighthouses, and fishing villages more practical than pretty.

Cape Breton Island

Cape Breton Island

Attached to the rest of the province by a causeway, this island is a world unto itself. The 300-kilometer **Cabot Trail** is a driving route that hits all the highlights—the upscale historic lodgings of **Baddeck,** the Acadian restaurants of **Chéticamp,** the hiking trails of **Cape Breton Highlands National Park,** and the beaches of **Ingonish.** With moose common through the highlands and whales frolicking offshore, the Cabot Trail also accesses some of the province's best **wildlife-viewing** opportunities.

When to Go

Summer revolves around outdoor activities such as hiking, biking, swimming, canoeing and kayaking, fishing, surfing, and just about anything you can do outdoors. **July and August** are especially busy. This is the time of year when school is out and the parks come alive with campers, anglers, swimmers, and sunbathers. If you're traveling during this time, you should book lodging as far in advance as possible.

Spring and fall are excellent times to visit Nova Scotia. While **May-June** is considered a shoulder season, in many ways the province is at its blooming best in spring. After the first weekend in **September,** there is a substantial decrease in travelers across the province. But **early fall** (Sept.-Oct.) provides pleasant daytime temperatures, reduced room rates, and uncrowded attractions. By late September, fall colors are at their peak, creating a mini-surge in visitors.

Officially, **winter** extends from late December to March, but in reality most attractions and visitor information centers, as well as accommodations in resort towns, start closing in mid-October.

Before You Go

Passports and Visas

To enter Canada, a **passport** is required of citizens and permanent residents of the United States. For further information, see the website http://travel.state.gov/travel. For current entry requirements to Canada, check the Citizenship and Immigration Canada website (www.cic.gc.ca).

All other foreign visitors must have a valid passport and may need a visa or visitors permit, depending on their country of residence and the vagaries of international politics. At present, visas are not required for citizens of the United States, the British Commonwealth, or Western Europe. The standard entry permit is for six months, and you may be asked to show onward tickets or proof of sufficient funds to last you through your intended stay.

Transportation

Visitors to Nova Scotia have the option of arriving by road, rail, ferry, or air. The main gateway city for **flights** from North America and Europe is the capital, Halifax. **Ferries** cross to Yarmouth from Maine and to Digby from New Brunswick, while the **main rail line** enters the region from New Brunswick and terminates at Halifax. **Driving,** whether it be your own vehicle or a rental car, is by far the best way to get around Nova Scotia, although some towns are served by bus. It is possible to visit Nova Scotia without your own vehicle (or a rental), but you'll be confining yourself to Halifax and then relying on public transportation and guided tours to travel farther afield. Driving is more practical, especially if you plan to tour along the coastline and pursue outdoor endeavors.

Driving is the best way to get around Nova Scotia.

The Best of Nova Scotia

Hitting all the highlights of Nova Scotia in one week is possible, but you're not going to see everything. In fact, you'll be covering so much ground, it may not seem like a vacation at all. This itinerary balances a little bit of everything—Halifax, the prettiest coastal villages, the two national parks, and the main historic sites—with time out for enjoying a glass of Nova Scotian wine over a feast of local seafood. This itinerary, like those that follow, assumes you rent a vehicle or have your own.

Day 1

Check in for a two-night stay at a downtown **Halifax** accommodation such as The Halliburton, a historic lodging within walking distance of Halifax's harbor front. Rather than start ticking off attractions, settle into the city by walking along the waterfront and soaking up the sights and sounds of the busy harbor. You'll see all manner of vessels tied up at the docks, and

plenty of places where you may want to eat dinner at an outdoor table.

Day 2

Start at the top, literally, by visiting **Halifax Citadel National Historic Site** and then take a stroll through Halifax's formal **Public Gardens.** It's now lunchtime, and the Italian Gourmet is ideally situated en route to downtown. Take a tour of **Alexander Keith's Brewery** on your way to the *Titanic* exhibit at the **Maritime Museum of the Atlantic.** Dine at the Economy Shoe Shop.

Day 3

Rise early for the one-hour drive to **Peggy's Cove,** famous for its photogenic lighthouse. Continue south to **Mahone Bay** for an early lunch and a walk through the many shops lining the main street of this busy waterfront town. **Lunenburg** is your overnight stop, and there's plenty of colorful seafaring history to soak up

Halifax Citadel National Historic Site

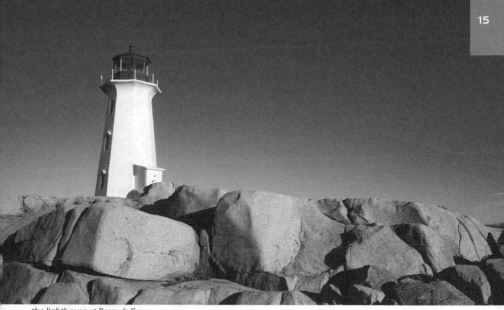

the lighthouse at Peggy's Cove

along the harbor of this town that UNESCO has dedicated as a World Heritage Site. Grand Banker Bar & Grill will be within walking distance of your room at the Spinnaker Inn (both have water views).

Day 4

Take Highway 8 to **Kejimkujik National Park,** which protects a large chunk of the forested interior. Rent a canoe for a paddle on the protected waterways. Continue to **Annapolis Royal,** where **Port-Royal National Historic Site** protects one of North America's oldest settlements. After dinner, watch the sun set across the Annapolis Basin from the grounds of **Fort Anne National Historic Site.** With reservations at the inviting Garrison House, you'll be within walking distance of everything.

Day 5

Drive through the apple orchards of the Annapolis Valley to Truro and take the TransCanada Highway across to **Cape Breton Island** and overnight lodgings at Baddeck's

restored Telegraph House. The **Alexander Graham Bell National Historic Site** is the main attraction, but the town also has a picturesque lakefront area and a good choice of stylish eateries.

Day 6

Today's destination is **Ingonish,** along the **Cabot Trail.** You drive the long way around, but that's a good thing, because the rugged coastal scenery between Chéticamp and Ingonish is more beautiful than you could ever imagine. (Though this also means that the 200-kilometer drive will take longer than you imagine.) Plan on feasting on lobster at Seascapes Restaurant and staying the night at Glenghorm Beach Resort.

Day 7

It takes a little more than five hours to reach Halifax International Airport from Ingonish. If you're on an afternoon flight, there's enough time to spend an hour or two in Ingonish. To play the revered **Highlands Links** golf course, you'll need to tee off early and fly out in the evening.

Family Road Trip

Trying to fit too much into your family travels will result in frustration for everyone. Because Nova Scotia is relatively compact, it is possible to spend at least two nights in each destination and still see the highlights of the province. It is especially important that accommodation reservations are made when traveling with children. Try to avoid bed-and-breakfasts, and instead choose motels with lots of facilities or cottage complexes with outdoor activities.

Here are family-friendly highlights from Nova Scotia:

ATTRACTIONS

- **Museum of Natural History,** Halifax
- **Hector Heritage Quay,** Pictou
- **Grand Pré National Historic Site,** Grand Pré
- **Shubenacadie Wildlife Park,** Shubenacadie

ADVENTURES

- **Harbour Hopper,** Halifax
- **Pirate Festival,** Mahone Bay
- **Riding the ferry** between Digby and Saint John
- **Whale-watching** at Pleasant Bay, Cape Breton Island

Grand Pré National Historic Site

ACCOMMODATIONS

- **Atlantica Oak Island Resort,** Mahone Bay
- **Dunromin Waterfront Campground and Cabins,** Annapolis Royal
- **Pictou Lodge Beach Resort,** Pictou

RESTAURANTS

- **Halifax Seaport Farmers' Market,** Halifax
- **Salty's,** Halifax
- **Murphy's,** Truro
- **Chowder House,** Neil's Harbour

Mahone Bay's Pirate Festival

Coastal Cruising

Like the province itself, this tour is defined by the ocean. So pack your swimsuit, sunscreen, and sandals, and be prepared to get some sand between your toes, as this tour circumnavigates the province without ever leaving sight of the sea. Summer is short in Nova Scotia, so you'll want to schedule this itinerary for July through early September.

Day 1

Don't worry: Even though you're flying into **Halifax,** you can see the city next time you're in town on business. Instead of heading downtown, make a beeline from the airport to **Marine Drive** and wash away the jet lag by taking to the waves of **Lawrencetown Beach** on a rented surfboard (if the water seems a little chilly, consider a long walk along the beach's golden sands). Stay in **Tangier** at Paddler's Retreat Bed and Breakfast.

Day 2

Grab a kayak from Paddler's Retreat and go for an early morning paddle, then go for a walk along the deserted beaches within **Taylor Head Provincial Park.** Continue north and take a boat tour to **Canso Islands National Historic Site,** which protects a grassy island that was the site of an 18th-century fishing village. Continue up the west coast of **Cape Breton Island.** You can't see the ocean from the lodge rooms at **Glenora Inn and Distillery** at Glenora, but after a few sips of whiskey and some good food, it won't matter.

Day 3

Watch the crab boats being unloaded at **Chéticamp.** Drive north on the **Cabot Trail** along one of the most spectacular stretches of coastal road you could ever imagine. The next section of road cuts across the interior, but you'll soon reach the water again. And this time, there are long stretches of sandy beach at **Ingonish,** perfect for sunbathing or swimming. Choose to stay at beachfront Glenghorm Beach Resort and dine on inexpensive seafood at the Chowder House.

fishing boats moored in Chéticamp Harbour

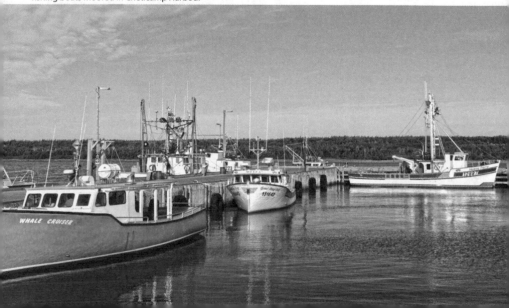

The Currents of History

While Nova Scotia's history dates back literally millions of years, this tour focuses on the last 400 years, from the arrival of Samuel de Champlain in 1605—which makes Annapolis Royal a sensible starting point for the tour.

BAY OF FUNDY

Make yourself comfortable at one of the many historic accommodations in **Annapolis Royal**, such as the Queen Anne Inn. From this lodging, you can walk down the oldest main street in North America to **Fort Anne National Historic Site**, which was the site of multiple turnovers between the British and French.

FUNDY COAST

Drive along **La Côte Acadienne**, admiring the old whitewashed churches and the resilience of the Acadian people who resettled here after the 1755 deportation from Nova Scotia. Allow a couple of hours for chatting about the importance of boat-building at the **Shelburne Historic District.**

SOUTH SHORE

Lunenburg will amaze you with its colorful nautical heritage and its downtown precinct protected as a UNESCO World Heritage Site. Plan ahead (reservations are essential), and you will find yourself with the wind at your back aboard the *Bluenose II,* a replica of the most famous schooner that ever sailed the waters of Nova Scotia.

HALIFAX

Plan on spending at least two days in the capital, resting your head at a historic accommodation like **The Halliburton.** Highlights include delving into Halifax's nautical history at the **Maritime Museum of the Atlantic,** wandering through **Halifax Citadel National Historic Site,** and visiting the graves of *Titanic* victims at **Fairview Cemetery.** Make sure your itinerary includes a pint of India Pale Ale at **Alexander Keith's,** the oldest brewery in North America.

Église de Sainte-Marie, La Côte Acadienne

CENTRAL NOVA SCOTIA

With more than a week, you can incorporate Central Nova Scotia in your history-themed itinerary, which should include **Pictou** and a visit to the *Hector,* a replica of a splendid sailing ship.

CAPE BRETON ISLAND

Best known for its namesake national park, the island is also home to the dramatically located **Fortress of Louisbourg National Historic Site,** an ambitious re-creation of a French stronghold destroyed by the British in 1760. For true history lovers, this attraction—along with Baddeck's **Alexander Graham Bell National Historic Site**—make the longer drive to the island worthwhile.

Customs House Inn

Day 4

Take the morning off to relax at nearby **Black Brook Cove,** where a trail leads over a forested headland and tame waves break across the bay. Have lunch at the Atlantic Restaurant, which overlooks its namesake. Don't gorge yourself too much, as you have an afternoon tee time at nearby **Highlands Links,** where the ocean is never far from view. Then soak up the resort-like atmosphere at the waterfront Inverary Resort in **Baddeck.**

Day 5

Take a boat tour at Baddeck and you'll pass by Alexander Graham Bell's waterfront estate (bald eagles are a bonus). The highway back to the mainland hugs expansive **Bras d'Or Lakes,** from where it's a two-hour drive to **Pictou** and waterfront accommodations like the **Customs House Inn.**

Day 6

Rise early to drive along the Sunrise Trail, which follows Northumberland Strait to the isthmus of land linking Nova Scotia to the rest of Canada.

There'll be opportunities at **Seafoam** and **Northport Beach Provincial Park** to swim or—for the not so brave—to walk through the shallow ocean water that is warmed by the sun. Drive around the Minas Basin to **ride the tidal bore** as it rushes up the Shubenacadie River south of Truro.

Day 7

Follow the **Fundy Coast** to **Digby.** Arrive in time for a lunchtime feast of Digby scallops at a harbor-front restaurant. Drive out along the narrow **Digby Neck,** where, after two short ferry trips and a stop at the **Balancing Rock,** you reach **Brier Island,** in preparation for a whale-watching trip the next day. Brier Island Lodge has the best water views on the island.

Day 8

Join a **whale-watching** boat tour into the **Bay of Fundy** for the opportunity to see finback, minke, and humpback whales up close and personal. Return to the mainland and sample Acadian culture by driving through the coastal fishing villages of Meteghan and Mavillette on

Artists and Artisans

Arts and crafts shopping opportunities are numerous in Nova Scotia. Quilts, sweaters, hooked rugs, porcelains, and wooden carvings are deftly mixed among the watercolors, oils, and sculptures in many arts and crafts venues. About 60 major art galleries are scattered across the province. The farmers markets are a source for local crafts; the major one is the Halifax Seaport Farmers' Market, while other summer markets are held at towns and seaports from Wolfville to Tatamagouche.

For a distilled taste of the province's fine arts and crafts, plan a visit to Halifax's Art Gallery of Nova Scotia. Quilts, porcelains, and wooden folk carvings are mixed among the watercolors, oils, and sculptures in the spacious galleries on Hollis Street, and the cream of provincial creativity is stocked at the museum's gift shop. The newest crafts developments are nurtured by the Nova Scotia Centre for Craft and Design, also in Halifax.

Beyond the ordinary, other homegrown products include delicate glassblowing from Halifax's Nova Scotian Crystal; furniture from Dominion Chairs; pewter products created in Mahone Bay and Pugwash; and Grohmann Knives, which sells its cutlery at its outlet in Pictou.

Nova Scotia is also the place for things Scottish. Tartans in innumerable clan variations are available by the yard in wool or blends; tartan apparel is stocked at shops in Halifax, Yarmouth, and Cape Breton's South Gut St. Ann's.

Studio Rally is an excellent arts and crafts resource. The free paperback book divides crafts producers by regions and towns, and an index lists the producers by medium. It's available at information centers, listed outlets, and online at www.studiorally.ca.

Mahone Bay is a hub of arts and crafts shops.

whale-watching, Bay of Fundy

La Côte Acadienne. Overnight at Whispering Waves Cottages, near Shelburne (be sure to order the lobster dinner, delivered to your room).

Lunenburg's harbour

Day 9

Wander through the shipbuilding precinct of **Shelburne** before starting the trip back up the South Shore to Halifax. This stretch of coastline is dotted with oceanfront parks—**Crescent Beach,** with its long stretch of white sand, is good for a leg stretcher. Continue to **Lunenburg** for an afternoon tour aboard a working lobster boat. Spend the night in nearby **Mahone Bay** at waterfront Fisherman's Daughter B&B.

Day 10

Spend the morning at your leisure in Mahone Bay. The main street, lined with fine boutiques, curves around the harbor to three photogenic waterfront churches. Drive along the old highway to charming **Chester,** where the natural harbor is filled with the curious combination of rusty fishing boats and million-dollar yachts. And yes, you will have time to stop for a picture of "the world's most photographed lighthouse" at **Peggy's Cove** before catching your flight home.

Halifax

Sights 28
Recreation. 41
Entertainment and Events 44
Shopping. 48
Accommodations and Camping. . . 50

Food 55
Information and Services 60
Getting There 61
Getting Around. 63

Halifax (pop. 390,000), the 250-year-old provincial capital, presents Nova Scotia's strikingly modern face wrapped around a historic heart. It's one of the most vibrant cities in Canada, with an exuberant cultural life and cosmopolitan

population. The tourist's Halifax is tidily compact, concentrated on the manageable, boot-shaped peninsula the city inhabits. Its prettiest parts are clustered between the bustling waterfront and the short, steep hillside that the early British developed two centuries ago. In these areas you'll find handsomely historic old districts meshed with stylishly chic new glass-sheathed buildings.

Halifax is more than a city, more than a seaport, and more than a provincial capital. Halifax is a harbor with a city attached, as the Haligonians say. Events in the harbor have shaped Nova Scotia's history. The savvy British military immediately grasped its potential when they first sailed in centuries ago. In fact, Halifax's founding as a settlement in 1749 was incidental to the harbor's development. From the first, the British used the 26-kilometer-long harbor as a watery warehouse of almost unlimited ship-holding capacity. The ships that defeated the French

at Louisbourg in 1758—and ultimately conquered this part of Atlantic Canada—were launched from Halifax Harbour. A few years later, the Royal Navy sped from the harbor to harass the rebellious colonies on the Eastern seaboard during the American Revolution. Ships from Halifax ran the blockades on the South's side during the American Civil War. And during World Wars I and II, the harbor bulged with troop convoys destined for Europe.

PLANNING YOUR TIME

Everyone has his or her own idea of how best to spend time in Halifax. History buffs will want to spend an entire week exploring the city's oldest corners, while outdoorsy types will want to hit the highlights before moving through to the rest of the province. Halifax has three attractions no one will want to miss, even if you have just one day. The first of these is the **Historic Properties,** a group

---

Previous: CSS *Acadia*, Maritime Museum of the Atlantic; Pier 21. **Above:** Public Gardens.

Look for ★ to find recommended
sights, activities, dining, and lodging.

Highlights

0   2 mi

0   2 km

Historic
Properties
Maritime Museum
of the Atlantic
Alexander Keith's
Brewery

Fairview
Cemetery ★

Halifax Citadel ★
National Historic Site
Public Gardens ★

Fisherman's
Cove ★
Point
Pleasant ★
Park

Halifax
Harbour

© AVALON TRAVEL

★ **Maritime Museum of the Atlantic:** If you visit just one museum in Nova Scotia, make it this one, which tells the many stories of the region's links to the ocean, from the *Titanic* tragedy to fishing the Grand Banks (page 30).

★ **Alexander Keith's Brewery:** Tours of North America's oldest working brewery go beyond describing the beer-making process, delving deep into Halifax's history and its most colorful characters (page 32).

★ **Point Pleasant Park:** On the southern tip of the Halifax Peninsula, this urban park is a favorite for walking and biking (page 33).

★ **Halifax Citadel National Historic Site:** Canada's most visited historic site lies atop downtown Halifax's highest point. It provides a glimpse into the city's past as well as sweeping harbor views (page 34).

★ **Public Gardens:** Strolling through these formal Victorian gardens is a morning rite for many locals (page 35).

★ **Fairview Cemetery:** Varying from three-digit numbers to moving family messages, the inscriptions on the headstones of more than 100 *Titanic* victims make this suburban cemetery a poignant place to visit (page 37).

★ **Historic Properties:** The oldest waterfront warehouses in Canada have been brought to life with an impressive restoration project and are now filled with bustling boutiques and restaurants (page 30).

★ **Fisherman's Cove:** If you're not planning to travel beyond Halifax, a visit to this historic fishing village will give you a taste of what you'll be missing farther afield (page 41).

Halifax

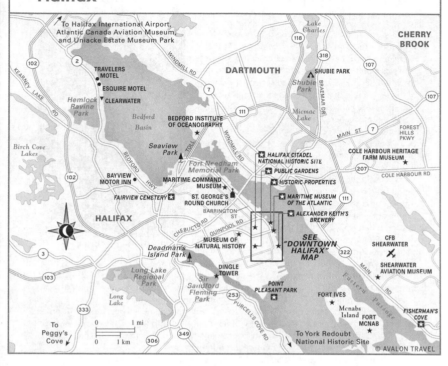

To Halifax International Airport,
Atlantic Canada Aviation Museum,
and Uniacke Estate Museum Park

CHERRY
BROOK

Lake
Charles

118

318

107

DARTMOUTH

TRAVELERS
MOTEL

ESQUIRE MOTEL

CLEARWATER

Hemlock
Ravine
Park

Bedford
Basin

Bedford

SHUBIE PARK

Shubie
Park

BRAEMAR DR

107

Micmac
Lake

MAIN ST

7

FOREST
HILLS
PKWY

BEDFORD INSTITUTE
OF OCEANOGRAPHY

Seaview
Park

COLE HARBOUR HERITAGE
FARM MUSEUM

HALIFAX CITADEL
NATIONAL HISTORIC SITE

PUBLIC GARDENS

HISTORIC PROPERTIES

207

COLE HARBOUR RD

Fort Needham
Memorial Park

BAYVIEW
MOTOR INN

MARITIME COMMAND
MUSEUM

FAIRVIEW CEMETERY

ST. GEORGE'S
ROUND CHURCH

MARITIME MUSEUM
OF THE ATLANTIC

111

ALEXANDER KEITH'S
BREWERY

HALIFAX

BARRINGTON
ST

MUSEUM OF
NATURAL HISTORY

Deadman's
Island Park

SEE
"DOWNTOWN
HALIFAX"
MAP

CFB
SHEARWATER

322

SHEARWATER
AVIATION MUSEUM

DINGLE
TOWER

Birch Cove
Lakes

Long Lake
Regional
Park

Long
Lake

Sir
Sandford
Fleming
Park

253

POINT
PLEASANT PARK

FORT IVES

Mcnabs
Island

FORT
MCNAB

FISHERMAN'S
COVE

To York Redoubt
National Historic Site

To
Peggy's
Cove

0   1 mi

0   1 km

© AVALON TRAVEL

of waterfront warehouses converted to restaurants and boutiques, while the nearby **Maritime Museum of the Atlantic** is the place to learn about the city's seafaring traditions. The third is **Halifax Citadel National Historic Site.** These three attractions, along with time exploring the waterfront, could fill one day, but you'd be missing one of Halifax's best known attractions—its **pubs and breweries,** including **Alexander Keith's Brewery,** North America's oldest, which is open daily for tours.

Since it's both a gateway for air travelers and the hub of three highways, chances are you'll be passing through Halifax more than once on your travels through Nova Scotia. This allows you to break up your sightseeing and to plan your schedule around the weather. If, for example, the sun is shining when you first arrive, plan to visit **Point Pleasant**

Park, the **Public Gardens,** and **Fairview Cemetery.** These spots and historic downtown attractions should fill two full days.

Across the harbor from downtown is the city of Dartmouth, where a seafood lunch at the fishing village of **Fisherman's Cove** makes a perfect getaway from the city.

HISTORY

The French learned about the area in the early 1700s, when local Mi'kmaq Indians escorted the French governor on a tour of what they called Chebuctook, the "Great Long Harbor," and adjacent waterways. But it was the British who saw the site's potential: in 1749, Colonel Edward Cornwallis arrived with about 2,500 settlers on 13 ships and founded Halifax along what is now Barrington Street. The settlement was named for Lord Halifax, then president of Britain's Board of Trade and Plantations. Early

HALIFAX

Halifax Links to the *Titanic* Tragedy

"My God, the *Titanic* has struck a berg." With these fateful words, uttered on April 14, 1912, by wireless operator Jack Goodwin of Cape Race, Newfoundland, the outside world first heard about what would develop into the world's best-known maritime disaster—the sinking of the unsinkable ship on its maiden voyage between Southampton, England, and New York City. On board were 2,227 passengers and crew.

headstone at Fairview Cemetery

At the time of the wireless transmission, the vessel was 800 kilometers east of Halifax. Three Halifax ships were promptly chartered to search for the foundering vessel. By the time the first had arrived, the *Titanic* was lying on the bottom of the Atlantic Ocean. More than 1,500 passengers and crew perished while 702 lucky souls, mostly women and children, were rescued. Bodies were brought ashore at Karlsen's Wharf (2089 Upper Wharf St.) and Coaling Wharf No. 4 (north of the MacDonald Bridge), neither of which is open to the public. They were then transported in coffins to a variety of locations, including a curling rink (now an army surplus store, at 2660 Agricola St.) and **Snow's Funeral Home** (1750 Argyle St.), which is now a seafood restaurant. Some bodies were claimed by families, but most were buried in three local cemeteries. The largest concentration is in a plot donated by the White Star Line within **Fairview Cemetery** (corner of Connaught and Chisholm Aves.). Most of the black headstones simply note the date of the tragedy and a number that relates to the order in which bodies were pulled from the ocean. Others have moving tributes to the bravery of loved ones. John Clarke, a band member famous for continuing to play as the ship was sinking, is buried at **Mount Olivet Cemetery** (Mumford Rd., off Joseph Howe Dr.).

The *Titanic*'s owners, the White Star Line, maintained an office in Halifax at 1682 Hollis Street that still stands. It became a hive of activity when the bodies began arriving, as staff members were an important link between the victims and their families from around the world.

Funerals and services were held at a number of downtown churches, including **St. George's Anglican Church** (222 Brunswick St.), **St. Paul's Anglican Church** (1749 Argyle St.), and **St. Mary's Catholic Church** (corner of Spring Garden Rd. and Barrington St.).

The best place to learn about the tragedy is the **Maritime Museum of the Atlantic** (1675 Lower Water St., 902/424-7490; Mon.-Sat. 9:30am-5:30pm, Sun. 1-5:30pm), which has a dedicated display area with artifacts, such as the only deck chair recovered from the vessel. For archival records, including travel documents, photos, and correspondence related to *Titanic* passengers, visit the **Nova Scotia Archives** (6016 University Ave., 902/424-6060; Mon.-Fri. 8:30am-4:30pm, free).

Halifax was a stockaded settlement backed by the Grand Parade, the town green where the militia drilled. More English settlers arrived in 1750, and by 1807 the city's population topped 60,000. A proper government setting—the sandstone Colonial Building (now Province House)—opened in 1819, followed by a number of noteworthy academic institutions. The harbor front acquired commercial legitimacy when native Haligonian Samuel Cunard, rich from lumbering, whaling, and banking, turned his interests to shipping. By 1838 the Cunard Steamship Company handled the British and North American Royal Mail, and by 1840 Cunard's four ships provided the first regular transport between the two continents. The seaport's incorporation in 1841 ushered in a prosperous mercantile era. Granville Street, with its stylish shops, became, in its day, Atlantic Canada's Fifth Avenue. Less stylish brothels and taverns lined Brunswick, Market, and Barrack Streets, and the military police swept through the area often, breaking up drunken fistfights and reestablishing order.

By the 1960s, Halifax looked like a hoary victim of the centuries, somewhat the worse for wear. Massive federal, provincial, and private investment, however, restored the harbor to its early luster, with its warehouses groomed as the handsome Historic Properties. The city continued to polish its image, as sandblasting renewed the exterior of architectural treasures such as Province House. The Art Gallery of Nova Scotia moved from cramped quarters near the Public Archives and settled within the stunningly renovated former Dominion Building. Municipal guidelines sought to control the city's growth. The unobstructed view on George Street between the harbor and the Citadel was secured with a municipal mandate, and the height of the hillside's high-rise buildings was also restricted to preserve the cityscape. During this time, the waterfront evolved into a bustling tourist precinct, one that is also enjoyed by locals.

ORIENTATION

The layout of Halifax is easy to grasp. **Downtown** lines the western side of **Halifax Harbour.** Lower and Upper Water Streets and Barrington Street run through downtown parallel to the water. This is the core of the city, chock-full of historic attractions, the city's finest accommodations, and a wonderful choice of restaurants. The waterfront itself bustles day and night. From Historic Properties' wharves at the waterfront, sightseeing boats explore the harbor. The splendid Maritime Museum and Art Gallery of Nova Scotia are close by.

A series of short streets rise like ramps

from the waterfront, past the grassy Grand Parade and up **Citadel Hill.** Around the hill, a great swath of green space provides a welcome break from residential and commercial sprawl. Laid out by the city's original surveyor, **Central Common,** on the west side of the hill, marks a meeting of roads. Major thoroughfares merge here (Robie Street running north to south, Bell Road running southeast, and Cogswell Street running east to west). Locals refer to everything south of the commons as the South End, everything to the north the North End, and to the west the West End.

In the South End is the city's **academic area,** site of Dalhousie University, University of King's College, St. Mary's University, and the Atlantic School of Theology. At the southern tip of the downtown peninsula is **Point Pleasant Park,** an oasis of green surrounded by the grays of sprawling loading docks to the north and the surrounding sparkling blue waters of Halifax Harbour.

The **Northwest Arm** of Halifax Harbour nearly cuts the downtown area off from the rest of the city. At the head of this waterway is the **Armdale Rotary,** from where Herring Cove Road spurs south to **Purcells Cove Road,** which passes yacht-filled marinas, Sir Sandford Fleming Park, and York Redoubt National Historic Site.

Across Halifax Harbour from downtown is the city of **Dartmouth.** Linked to downtown by ferry and bridge, this commercial and residential area has a smattering of sights and is also worth visiting for the views back across to Halifax. Beyond the two bridges spanning Halifax Harbour is Bedford Basin, a large body of water surrounded by development. At the head of the basin is the residential area of Bedford and suburbs, including Lower Sackville and Waverly. Traveling down Highway 102 from Truro and **Halifax International Airport** (38 kilometers north of downtown), you'll pass exits for these and other towns.

Sights

Halifax is packed with attractions, all reasonably priced or absolutely free. The biggest concentration is within walking distance of the waterfront precinct and many accommodations. Beyond the downtown core are a number of interesting sights that are easy to miss but easy to reach by public transportation. Whatever your interests—searching out *Titanic*-related sights or exploring coastal parks—you will find plenty to do and see in the capital.

DOWNTOWN

The following sights are within walking distance of each other from the waterfront. You could easily spend a full day exploring this part of the city, taking time out to lunch at an outdoor harbor-front restaurant.

A Long Weekend in Halifax

Halifax is a major destination for conventioneers (modern facilities, well-priced accommodations, centrally located for delegates from both North America and Europe), and in this regard, you may find yourself wanting to hang around for a few days when the last meeting wraps up on Friday. Or, for leisure travelers, many flights to other parts of Atlantic Canada are routed through Halifax, so it will cost little or nothing to have a stopover before continuing to Newfoundland, Prince Edward Island, or elsewhere. This itinerary covers both scenarios, and you don't have to worry about driving.

DAY 1
You've been staying at an upscale downtown Halifax hotel such as Four Points by Sheraton Halifax, and suddenly it's not business anymore. No worries; rates drop dramatically come the weekend, so you won't break the bank by staying another two nights. Join the after-work crowd at the **Seahorse Tavern,** and then plan on dining next door at the **Economy Shoe Shop.**

DAY 2
Visit **Halifax Citadel National Historic Site** to get a feel for the city's colorful history, then walk over to the **Public Gardens.** After lunch, learn about the *Titanic* tragedy at the **Maritime Museum of the Atlantic** before visiting the graves of some of the victims at **Fairview Cemetery.** For a casual seafood dinner with a sublime view, walk along the waterfront to **Salty's.**

DAY 3
The local tour company Ambassatours operates an excellent full-day trip along the South Shore. It hits the highlights—scenic **Peggy's Cove** and the beautiful waterfront **churches of Mahone Bay**—while also allowing time to wander through the historic streets of downtown **Lunenburg,** where there's time for shopping and lunch. You'll be back in Halifax in time for dinner at **Chives Canadian Bistro,** which features lots of fresh seasonal produce.

DAY 4
Check the sailing schedule of the *Bluenose II* and make reservations for a morning cruise if this grand old lady is in port. Otherwise, you could start out with breakfast at the **Coastal Cafe,** followed by shopping at downtown stores as varied as **Nova Scotian Crystal** and **Rum Runners Rum Cake Factory.** Golfers may want to squeeze in a tee time at **Glen Arbour Golf Course,** which is on the way out to the airport.

Downtown Halifax

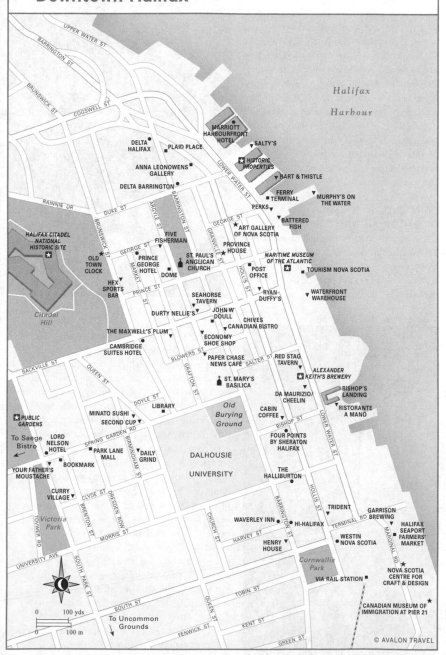

Halifax Harbour

MARRIOTT HARBOURFRONT HOTEL
DELTA HALIFAX
PLAID PLACE
SALTY'S
HISTORIC PROPERTIES
ANNA LEONOWENS GALLERY
HART & THISTLE
DELTA BARRINGTON
FERRY TERMINAL
MURPHY'S ON THE WATER
PERKS
BATTERED FISH
ART GALLERY OF NOVA SCOTIA
HALIFAX CITADEL NATIONAL HISTORIC SITE
FIVE FISHERMAN
PROVINCE HOUSE
OLD TOWN CLOCK
PRINCE GEORGE HOTEL
ST. PAUL'S ANGLICAN CHURCH
MARITIME MUSEUM OF THE ATLANTIC
TOURISM NOVA SCOTIA
HFX SPORTS BAR
DOME
POST OFFICE
WATERFRONT WAREHOUSE
SEAHORSE TAVERN
RYAN DUFFY'S
Citadel Hill
DURTY NELLIE'S
JOHN W DOULL
CHIVES CANADIAN BISTRO
THE MAXWELL'S PLUM
ECONOMY SHOE SHOP
CAMBRIDGE SUITES HOTEL
PAPER CHASE NEWS CAFÉ
RED STAG TAVERN
ST. MARY'S BASILICA
ALEXANDER KEITH'S BREWERY
DA MAURIZIO/ CHEELIN
BISHOP'S LANDING
LIBRARY
Old Burying Ground
CABIN COFFEE
RISTORANTE A MANO
PUBLIC GARDENS
MINATO SUSHI
SECOND CUP
To Saege Bistro
LORD NELSON HOTEL
PARK LANE MALL
DAILY GRIND
FOUR POINTS BY SHERATON HALIFAX
BOOKMARK
DALHOUSIE UNIVERSITY
THE HALLIBURTON
YOUR FATHER'S MOUSTACHE
CURRY VILLAGE
TRIDENT
GARRISON BREWING
Victoria Park
WAVERLEY INN
HI-HALIFAX
HALIFAX SEAPORT FARMERS' MARKET
WESTIN NOVA SCOTIA
HENRY HOUSE
Cornwallis Park
NOVA SCOTIA CENTRE FOR CRAFT & DESIGN
VIA RAIL STATION
CANADIAN MUSEUM OF IMMIGRATION AT PIER 21
To Uncommon Grounds

UPPER WATER ST
BARRINGTON ST
BRUNSWICK ST
COGSWELL ST
LOWER WATER ST
RAINNIE DR
DUKE ST
ARGYLE ST
BARRINGTON ST
GEORGE ST
GRANVILLE ST
HOLLIS ST
GEORGE ST
MARKET ST
PRINCE ST
BLOWERS ST
GRAFTON ST
SALTER ST
SACKVILLE ST
QUEEN ST
DOYLE ST
SPRING GARDEN RD
BIRMINGHAM ST
BISHOP ST
LOWER WATER ST
CLYDE ST
DRESDEN ROW
BRENTON ST
MORRIS ST
TOWER RD
UNIVERSITY AVE
SOUTH PARK ST
CHURCH ST
HARVEY ST
BARRINGTON ST
HOLLIS ST
TERMINAL RD
MARGINAL RD
TOBIN ST
SOUTH ST
QUEEN ST
KENT ST
FENWICK ST
GREEN ST

0   100 yds
0   100 m

© AVALON TRAVEL

★ Historic Properties

Canada's oldest surviving group of waterfront warehouses is also one of the city's main tourist attractions, with excellent shopping and dining spread along a three-block expanse on Upper and Lower Water Streets. The wooden and stone warehouses, chandleries, and buildings once used by shipping interests and privateers have been restored to their early 1800s glory. They now house restaurants, shops, and other sites impressively styled with Victorian and Italianate facades. The history of the precinct is cataloged halfway along the Privateer Wharf building (on the inside) with interpretive panels.

★ Maritime Museum of the Atlantic

The seaport's store of nautical memorabilia lies within the sleek, burnished-red waterfront **Maritime Museum of the Atlantic** (1675 Lower Water St., 902/424-7490, http://maritimemuseum.novascotia.ca; summer

Historic Properties

Maritime Museum of the Atlantic

daily 9:30am-5:30pm, the rest of the year Tues.-Sat. 9:30am-5pm, Sun. 1pm-5pm; adult $9.50, senior $8.50, child $5). The museum is one of the crowning achievements of the city's Waterfront Development Project. Most visitors find the *Titanic* display room most interesting. It contains the world's largest collection of artifacts from the floating palace deemed unsinkable by its owners; you will see the only deck chair recovered at the time of the sinking, a cribbage board, lounge paneling, and more. Also on display is a model of the *Titanic,* the wireless log taken as the vessel foundered, and a variety of information boards that tell the story of the ship's construction. *Titanic 3D,* a National Geographic documentary created from footage taken from the wreck, shows continuously.

Outside, the **CSS *Acadia*** is tied up at the wharf. This sturdy vessel spent its life as Canada's first hydrographic vessel, its crew surveying the east coast using sextants and graphing shoreline features. Admission is $2,

Halifax Harbour

From a maritime standpoint, Halifax Harbour is a jewel, the world's second-largest natural harbor (after Sydney Harbour in Australia). High rocky bluffs notched with coves rim the wide entrance where the harbor meets the frothy Atlantic. McNabs Island is spread across the harbor's mouth and is so large that it almost clogs the entrance. Many an unwary ship has foundered on the island's shallow, treacherous Eastern Passage coastline.

On the western side of McNabs Island, the harbor is split in two by Halifax's peninsula. The Northwest Arm, a fjord-like sliver of sea, cuts off to one side and wraps around the city's back side. Along its banks are the long lawns of parks, estates, yacht clubs, and several university campuses. The main channel continues inland, shouldered by uptown Halifax on one side and its sister city of Dartmouth on the other.

THE TOURIST'S HARBOUR

The harbor puts on its best show directly in front of downtown. White-hulled cruise ships nose into port and dock alongside Halifax's Point Pleasant Park at the peninsula's southern tip. Freighters, tugs, tour boats, and sailboats skim the choppy waters, and ferries cut through the sea traffic, scurrying back and forth between the two cities with their loads of commuters and sightseers.

The scene has a transfixing quality about it. Tourist season unofficially starts and ends when the harbor-front Halifax Sheraton hotel sets tables and chairs for alfresco dining on the waterfront promenade. Stiff summer breezes usually accompany lunch, but the view is worth it. Less hardy diners jostle for tables with a harbor view at Salty's, the nearby restaurant with its enviable wide-windowed dining room overlooking the same scene.

Beyond the tourist's realm and the two cities' harbor fronts, the spacious harbor compresses itself into The Narrows. Two high-flung steel expressways—the MacDonald and MacKay Bridges—cross the Narrows at either end. The MacDonald Bridge permits pedestrians and provides an aerial view of the Maritime Command and Her Majesty's Canadian Dockyard along the Halifax side.

The slender Narrows then opens into 40-square-kilometer Bedford Basin, 16 kilometers long and as capacious as a small inland sea. Sailboats cruise its waters now, but the expanse has seen a parade of ships cross its waters through the years—from the white-sailed British warships of centuries ago to the steel-hulled vessels of the Allies during both world wars.

HALIFAX HARBOUR FROM VARIED ANGLES

Halifax Harbour reveals itself in different views. Its pulse can be probed from one of the ferries or from the harbor front in either city. The approach from the Atlantic can be seen best from the historic fort at York Redoubt on Purcells Cove Road. You'll get a good view of the Northwest Arm's ritzy estate and university scene from Fleming Park's Memorial Tower on the same road. Africville Park beneath the MacKay Bridge overlooks the Narrows where that slender strait meets Bedford Basin.

or free with proof of admission to the maritime museum.

Art Gallery of Nova Scotia

Atlantic Canada's largest and finest art collection is housed in two buildings separated by a cobbled courtyard just up from the harbor at the Art Gallery of Nova Scotia (1723 Hollis St., 902/424-5280, www.

artgalleryofnovascotia.ca; summer Mon.-Sat. 10am-5pm, Sun. noon-5pm, fall-spring Tues.-Sat. 10am-5pm, Sun. noon-5pm; adult $12, senior $10, child $7). The main entrance is within Gallery South (also home to an excellent café). The vast majority of the collection is displayed in Gallery North, the sandstone Dominion Building. Some 2,000 works in oils, watercolors, stone, wood, and other media are exhibited throughout its four floors of spacious galleries. The permanent collections give priority to current and former Nova Scotia residents and include works by Mary Pratt, Arthur Lismer, Carol Fraser, and Alex Colville. The mezzanine-level regional folk-art collection is a particular delight.

Province House

The seat of the provincial government, **Province House** (1726 Hollis St., 902/424-4661; July-Aug. Mon.-Fri. 9am-5pm, Sat.-Sun. 10am-4pm, the rest of the year Mon.-Fri. 9am-4pm; free) was completed in 1819. It's the smallest and oldest provincial legislature building in the country and features a fine Georgian exterior and splendid interior, resembling a rural English mansion more than an official residence. On his visit to modest but dignified Province House in 1842, author Charles Dickens remarked, "It was like looking at Westminster through the wrong end of a telescope…a gem of Georgian architecture."

St. Paul's Anglican Church

The stately white wooden **St. Paul's Anglican Church** (1749 Argyle St., 902/429-2240, www.stpaulshalifax.org; tours Mon.-Sat. 9am-5pm, free) was styled after the Palladian St. Peter's Church on Vere Street in London, England. Dating to 1749, it is the oldest surviving building in Halifax and was the first Anglican church in Canada. The interior is full of memorials to Halifax's early residents. Notice the bit of metal embedded above the door at the back of the north wall—it's a piece of shrapnel hurled from the *Mont Blanc*, two kilometers away, during the Halifax Explosion. The church is between Barrington and Argyle Streets at the edge of the Grand Parade; look for the square belfry topped by an octagonal cupola.

Old Burying Ground

Designated a national historic site in 1991, the **Old Burying Ground cemetery** (June-Sept. daily 9am-5pm, free) sits opposite Government House at Barrington Street and Spring Garden Road. Its history goes back to the city's founding. The first customer, so to speak, was interred just one day after the arrival of the original convoy of English settlers in 1749. Also among the thicket of age-darkened, hand-carved, old-fashioned headstones is the 1754 grave of John Connor, the settlement's first ferry captain. The most recent burial took place more than 160 years ago, in 1844.

St. Mary's Cathedral Basilica

Two popes and hundreds of thousands of parishioners have filed through the doors of the Gothic Revival **St. Mary's Cathedral Basilica** (1508 Barrington St., 902/429-9800, www.halifaxyarmouth.org/cathedral), whose spires cast an afternoon shadow over the Old Burying Ground. It was built in 1860; the title "Basilica" was bestowed during a visit by Pope Pius XII in 1950. The stained-glass windows, replaced after the originals were destroyed by the 1917 Halifax Explosion, are particularly impressive.

★ Alexander Keith's Brewery

At the south end of downtown and one block back from the water, **Alexander Keith's Brewery** (1496 Lower Water St., 902/455-1474, http://keiths.ca; tours June-Oct. Mon.-Sat. noon-8pm, Sun. noon-5pm, Nov.-May Fri. 5pm-8pm, Sat. noon-8pm, Sun. noon-5pm, adult $21, senior $18, child $10) is North America's oldest operating brewery. Keith arrived in Halifax in 1795, bringing with him brewing techniques from his English homeland and finding a ready market among the soldiers and sailors living in the city. Although main brewing operations have been moved to the Oland Brewery, north of downtown, the original brewery, an impressive stone and granite edifice extending along an entire block, produces seasonal brews using traditional techniques. Tours are led by costumed guides, ending with a traditional toast to the "Father of Great Beer."

Alexander Keith's Brewery

ocean to make a new home in Canada. The firsthand accounts begin with the decision to leave home, then go through voyage and arrival to describe onward journeys by rail across Canada. Allow time to view *Oceans of Hope,* a 30-minute film narrated by a fictional immigration officer.

Beside the street-level reception area is the **Research Centre,** which can be used by individuals whose families arrived in Canada through Pier 21. It contains a wide variety of documents, passenger logs, and historic images of passenger vessels.

Nova Scotia Centre for Craft and Design

Provincial crafts development and innovation are nurtured at the **Nova Scotia Centre for Craft and Design** (1061 Marginal Rd., 902/492-2522, www.craft-design.ns.ca; Tues.-Fri. 9am-5pm, Sat.-Sun. 11am-4pm; free), a workshop ensconced in the cruise-ship terminal geared to weaving, woodworking, metal, and multimedia production.

★ Point Pleasant Park

Before dawn on September 29, 2003, Hurricane Juan hit Halifax like no other storm in living memory. Seventy-five-hectare **Point Pleasant Park** (5718 Point Pleasant Dr., www.pointpleasantpark.ca; daily 6am-midnight), at the southern tip of the Halifax peninsula, took the full brunt of the storm. By daybreak the next morning the full extent of the damage was first seen—more than 75,000 of the park's 100,000 trees had been destroyed, and the park's ecology had been changed forever. After the cleanup, a massive rejuvenation project that continues to this day began.

Although much of the forest may be gone, the park is still well worth visiting. To get to the main entrance, take South Park Street south from Sackville Street. South Park becomes Young Avenue, a tree-lined boulevard graced by magnificent mansions; turn left on Point Pleasant Drive. Marginal Road from downtown also terminates at the same waterside entrance. Views from the parking

Canadian Museum of Immigration at Pier 21

As you continue south along Lower Water Street from the brewery (take the Harbourwalk for the full effect), beyond the statue of Samuel Cunard, the waterfront is dominated by Halifax's massive cruise-ship terminal. This 3,900-square-meter structure has a long and colorful history of welcoming foreigners in its original capacity as an "immigration shed," where more than a million immigrants, refugees, and war brides first set foot on Canadian soil between 1928 and 1971. It was also the main departure point for 500,000 Canadians who fought in World War II. Upstairs within the building is the **Canadian Museum of Immigration at Pier 21** (1055 Marginal Rd., 902/425-7770, www.pier21.ca; May-Nov. daily 9:30am-5:30pm, Dec.-Apr. Tues.-Sat. 10am-5pm; adult $12, senior $10, child $6.75). Reopened in 2015 after nearly doubling in size, this immigration museum does a wonderful job of bringing to life the stories of those who traveled across the lot sweep across the harbor, with container terminals on one side and green space on the other. Forty kilometers of trails, many paved, allow for hiking, jogging, and cross-country skiing in winter. Bikes are allowed only Monday-Friday. Most of the main trails have reopened since the storm, allowing access to all corners of the spread, with terns, gulls, and ospreys winging overhead. A bit of real-estate trivia: The park is still rented from the British government, on a 999-year lease, for one shilling per year.

Point Pleasant's military significance is evidenced by the 1796 **Prince of Wales Martello Tower** (July-early Sept. daily 10am-6pm) and Fort Ogilvie, built in 1862, both part of Halifax's defensive system. The former, a thick-walled round tower based on those the British were building at the time to repel Napoleon's forces, was the first of its kind to be built in North America.

CITADEL HILL AND VICINITY

Walk up George Street from the harbor front to reach Citadel Hill. You'll know you're on the right street by the **Old Town Clock,** framed by the buildings of George Street at the base of Citadel Hill. Originally constructed as the official timekeeper for Halifax, the four-faced clock tower was completed in 1803 by order of the compulsively punctual Prince Edward. It is not open to the public but instead stands as a city landmark.

★ Halifax Citadel National Historic Site

Halifax's premier landmark, the **Citadel National Historic Site** (5425 Sackville St., 902/426-5080, www.pc.gc.ca; July-Aug. daily 9am-6pm, Sept.-May daily 9am-5pm; adult $12, senior $10.50, child $6) is also the most visited National Historic Site in Canada. The Citadel crowns the hill at the top of George Street, commanding the strategic high ground above the city and harbor, with magnificent views of the entire area. This star-shaped, dressed-granite fortress, the fourth military works built on the site, was completed in 1856. In its heyday, the Citadel represented the pinnacle of defensive military technology, though its design was never tested by an attack.

In summer, students in period uniforms portray soldiers of the 78th Highlanders and the Royal Artillery, demonstrating military drills, powder magazine operation, changing of the sentries, and piping. At the stroke of noon each day, they load and fire a cannon

the Martello Tower, Point Pleasant Park

Halifax Citadel National Historic Site

with due military precision and ceremony, a shot heard round the city. Most of the fortress is open for exploration; exhibits include a museum, barrack rooms, a powder magazine, and a 50-minute audiovisual presentation on the fort's history. Guided tours are included in the admission price, while within the grounds are a gift shop and café.

The grounds are open year-round, but no services are offered November-April.

Museum of Natural History

The rather plain exterior of the **Museum of Natural History** (1747 Summer St., 902/424-7353, http://naturalhistory.novascotia.ca; mid-May-Oct. daily 9am-5pm, Nov.-mid-May Tues.-Sun. 9am-5pm; adult $6.25, senior $5.50, child $4) belies a treasure trove of exhibits that bring the province's natural world to life. Opposite the ticket desk is a kid-friendly nature center with small critters in enclosures and tanks, and staff on hand to answer any questions. Beyond this point are exhibits that tell the story of Nova Scotia's first human inhabitants, Paleo Indians, who moved into the region 11,000 years ago. The dinosaur displays are a major draw for young and old. You'll also learn about modern-day creatures in a room full of stuffed animals and a large hall dominated by a pilot whale

skeleton. Other highlights include a gem and mineral display and artifacts from Acadian culture. The museum is a five-minute walk from Citadel Hill, but it also has plenty of its own parking.

★ Public Gardens

South across Sackville Street from the Citadel grounds, the **Public Gardens** (www.halifax-publicgardens.ca; May-mid-Oct. daily 8am-dusk) are an irresistibly attractive oasis spread over seven hectares in the heart of the city. Bordered by Spring Garden Road, South Park Street, Summer Street, and Sackville Street, what started in 1753 as a private garden is reminiscent of the handsome parks of Europe and now considered one of the loveliest formal gardens in North America.

Inside the wrought-iron fence (main entrance at the corner of South Park Street and Spring Garden Road), the setting revels in tulips that flower late May through early June, followed by rhododendrons, roses, and perennials through summer. Other highlights are the exotic and native trees, fountains, and lily ponds where ducks and geese make their homes. The ornate bandstand dates from Queen Victoria's Golden Jubilee and is the site of free Sunday afternoon concerts in July and August. Also during the summer, vendors

the Public Gardens

of arts and crafts hawk their wares outside the gardens along Spring Garden Road.

NORTH OF DOWNTOWN

The following sights are north of Cogswell Street. It's a two-kilometer walk from downtown to Fort Needham Memorial Park. Fairview Cemetery is not within walking distance.

St. George's Round Church

Architect William Hughes designed the

Halifax Explosion

On the morning of Thursday, December 6, 1917, Halifax experienced a catastrophic explosion—at the time the largest human-created explosion in history, unrivaled until the detonation of the first atomic bomb. On that fateful morning, Halifax Harbour was busy with warships transporting troops, munitions, and other supplies bound for the war in Europe. A French ship, the *Mont Blanc*, filled to the gunwales with explosives— including 400,000 pounds of TNT— was heading through The Narrows toward the harbor mouth when it was struck by a larger vessel, the *Imo*, which was steaming in the opposite direction, and caught fire. The terrified crew of the *Mont Blanc* took immediately to the lifeboats as the burning ship drifted close to the Halifax shore.

A short time later, at 9:05am, the *Mont Blanc* cargo blew up, instantly killing an estimated 2,000 people, wounding another 10,000, and obliterating about 130 hectares of the North End of downtown Halifax. So colossal was the explosion that windows were shattered 80 kilometers away, and the shock wave rocked Sydney on Cape Breton, 430 kilometers northeast. The barrel of one of the *Mont Blanc's* cannons was hurled 5.5 kilometers, while its half-ton anchor shank landed more than three kilometers away in the opposite direction.

Serving as a memorial to the tragedy is **Fort Needham Memorial Park,** along Gottingen Street north from downtown. Here, a 14-bell carillon is on a high point of land from which the site of the original explosion can be seen. While the harbor-front **Maritime Museum of the Atlantic** has an exhibit dedicated to the explosion, one of the most interesting reminders is up the hill at **St. Paul's Anglican Church** (1749 Argyle St.), where a chunk of metal from the doomed *Mont Blanc* is embedded in the north-facing wall.

unusual and charming timber-frame **St. George's Round Church** (Cornwallis and Brunswick Sts., www.roundchurch.ca), which at once accommodated the overflow of parishioners from the nearby Dutch Church on Brunswick Street and satisfied Prince Edward's penchant for round buildings. The cornerstone was laid in 1800, and the chancel and front porch were added later. A fire in 1994 destroyed the dome, but it has since been replaced. St. George's is a few blocks north of downtown.

Maritime Command Museum

On the grounds of Canadian Forces Base Halifax, the **Maritime Command Museum** (Gottingen St. between North St. and Russell St., 902/721-8250, http://psphalifax.ca/marcommuseum; Mon.-Fri. 9am-3:30pm; free) is ensconced in the 30-room Admiralty House, built in the 1840s as a residence for the base's admiral. Exhibits include presentation swords, memorabilia from the World War II Battle of the Atlantic, a military gun collection, uniforms, ship models, and other artifacts relating to the history of the Canadian Maritime Military Forces.

Fort Needham Memorial Park

Continue north along Gottingen Street from the maritime museum and veer right onto Dartmouth Street to reach the **Fort Needham Memorial Park**, a high point of land with views across the head of Halifax Harbour. The park's most distinctive feature is a 14-bell carillon, a monument to the Halifax Explosion of 1917, at the time the largest human-created explosion the world had ever known. Stand in the break between the memorial's two halves to get views through a clearing to the harbor and the actual site of the explosion.

Africville Park

Halifax's peninsula is bookended by a pair of expansive green spaces. **Africville Park** is at the north end, overlooking Bedford Basin from the foot of the A. Murray McKay Bridge.

This was once the site of Africville, a community of Black Haligonians established in the 1840s but since demolished. The importance of the settlement is reflected in its designation as a National Historic Site. The only physical remainder of its history is a replica of the African United Church. As you head north from downtown along Barrington Street, access is along Service Road. A boat launch provides the only water access.

★ Fairview Cemetery

Take Windsor Street north from Quinpool Road to reach **Fairview Cemetery** (daily dawn-dusk), the final resting place of 121 *Titanic* victims. When the bodies were pulled from the Atlantic Ocean, they were given a number. These numbers, along with the date of the disaster, April 15, 1912 (it is assumed no one could have survived any longer than a day in the frigid ocean), adorn a majority of the simple black headstones paid for by the White Star Line, owners of the *Titanic*. Where identification was possible, a name accompanies the number (such as victim 227, J. Dawson, inspiration for the character Jack Dawson, played by Leonardo DiCaprio, in the movie *Titanic*). Some headstones are engraved with moving tributes, such as that to Everett Edward Elliott, aged 24, which reads, "Each man stood at his port while all the weaker ones went by, and showed once more to all the world how Englishmen should die."

The turn into the cemetery is easy to miss; get in the left lane by Connaught Avenue and turn against oncoming traffic to reach the cemetery's main entrance. The other option is to take Connaught Avenue off Windsor Street and park at the end of Chisholm Avenue. Once you're at the cemetery, the plot is well signposted, with an interpretive board describing the events leading up to identifying victims, even long after they were buried.

Hemlock Ravine Park

The rugged tract of forest known as **Hemlock Ravine Park** lies beside the western side of Bedford Basin between the busy Bedford and Bicentennial highways—but you'd never know urban civilization is so close as you walk along the five interconnecting walking trails. The park's namesake ravine, with its towering hemlocks, takes about 20 minutes to reach from the main parking lot, at the end of Kent Avenue, which branches off the Bedford Highway (Highway 2) one kilometer north of the Kearney Lake Road intersection. Beside the parking lot is a heart-shaped pond designed by Prince Edward, who spent his summers here with his companion Julie St. Laurent.

Uniacke Estate Museum Park

The splendid 930-hectare **Uniacke Estate Museum Park** (758 Main Rd., Mount Uniacke, 902/866-0032, http://uniacke.novascotia.ca; June-early Oct. Mon.-Sat. 9:30am-5:30pm, Sun. 11am-5pm; adult $4, senior and child $2.75) is along Highway 1 beyond city limits, 20 kilometers northwest from the intersection of Highway 102. The easiest way to get there is to take Exit 3 from Highway 101. The home's interior features original furnishings, including four-poster beds and family portraits. The grounds offer seven hiking trails.

Atlantic Canada Aviation Museum

Across the highway from the airport (take Exit 6 from Hwy. 102), the **Atlantic Canada Aviation Museum** (20 Sky Blvd., 902/873-3773, http://atlanticcanadaaviationmuseum.com; May-Oct. daily 9am-5pm; adult $5) is a good place to visit on the way north to Truro or before your flight home. On display are about 30 aircraft—everything from fighter planes to a homemade helicopter—and a couple of simulators.

WEST SIDE OF NORTHWEST ARM

Carefully make your way onto the Armdale Rotary at the west end of Quinpool Road and take the Herring Cove Road exit. A short distance south along this road, Purcells Cove Road veers off to the left. This winding road hugs the Northwest Arm for nine kilometers to the fishing village of Herring Cove. Along the way are two yacht clubs filled with glistening white sailboats.

Sir Sandford Fleming Park

A 38-hectare grassy spread, the delightful **Sir Sandford Fleming Park** (daily 8am-dusk)

Atlantic Canada Aviation Museum

is mostly forested, sloping to a seawall promenade fringing a quiet waterway. The land was donated by the Scottish-born Fleming, best known for establishing time zones. It is said a missed train led the enterprising Fleming to begin formulating a plan that would see the entire world operate on a 24-hour clock with time zones that related to longitude. Fleming, who also designed Canada's first postage stamp, lived in Halifax from the 1880s until his death in 1915.

On a slight rise above the bay is the 10-story **Dingle Tower** (June-Aug. daily 9am-5pm). A stairway winds up the interior of this stone edifice, presenting great views from the top.

The main entrance is off Purcells Cove Road; Dingle Road leads down through the wooded park to the waterfront.

York Redoubt National Historic Site

Set on a bluff high above the harbor entrance, **York Redoubt National Historic Site** (Purcells Cove Rd., 902/426-5080, www.pc.gc. ca; grounds mid-May-Oct. daily 9am-6pm, buildings mid-June-Aug. daily 10am-6pm; free) is six kilometers south of downtown. The setting draws visitors with walking paths that lead down the steep incline to picnic tables and protected coves. Up top are strategic fortifications dating to 1793, when Britain went to war with the French. Most of the fort is from later times, including massive muzzle-loading guns that were designed to fire nine-inch shells capable of piercing armored vessels.

McNABS ISLAND

Whatever your interests, the five-kilometer-long **McNabs Island,** at the entrance to Halifax Harbour, is a wonderful place to spend a day. The island is mostly wooded, its forests filled with birdlife and its shoreline dotted with beaches and tidal pools. Archaeological evidence points to habitation by the Mi'kmaq at least 1,600 years ago, but the most obvious signs of human development are more recent, including two forts and the

remains of a number of residences (including the summer home of Frederick Perrin, of Lea & Perrins Worcestershire sauce fame). Although many of the early residences have disappeared, signs of their formal gardens remain; look for ash, oak, and apple trees.

Recreation

Most visitors come to the island to go hiking. Ferries land at Garrison Pier, from which trails radiate in all directions. The top of Jenkin's Hill, easily reached in 10 minutes, is a good place to get oriented while also enjoying sweeping harbor views. At the 1864 **Fort Ives,** an easy 30-minute walk from the pier, cannons are still in place. **Fort McNab,** a similar distance south of the pier, was built in 1889 and is protected as a National Historic Site. Sandy **Mauger's Beach,** just south of Garrison Pier, is the best and most accessible of many island beaches.

Getting There

Year-round access to the island is provided by **McNabs Island Ferry** (902/465-4563, www. mcnabsisland.com; adult round-trip $20, senior and child round-trip $15), which departs on demand from Fisherman's Cove on the Dartmouth side of the harbor. The crossing takes less than 10 minutes. No services are available on the island, so bring your own food and drink and be prepared for changeable weather by bringing a rain jacket.

DARTMOUTH

Dartmouth is a large residential, commercial, and industrial area across the harbor from Halifax. The two cities are joined by a bridge and Metro Transit's Halifax-Dartmouth ferry from the foot of downtown's George Street to the Alderney Gate Complex in Dartmouth. Ferries operate year-round Monday-Saturday 6:30am-midnight, and daily in summer. The fare is adult $2.50, senior and child $1.75 each way. The ferry arrives within walking distance of Dartmouth Heritage Museum properties and various shops and restaurants.

Dartmouth Heritage Museum

The **Dartmouth Heritage Museum** (www. dartmouthheritagemuseum.ns.ca) comprises two historic homes within walking distance of Alderney Gate. The 1867 **Evergreen House** (26 Newcastle St., 902/464-2300; summer Tues.-Sun. 10am-5pm, the rest of the year Tues.-Sat. 10am-5pm; adult $2.50), filled with period antiques, is the grander of the two. Built by a cooper (barrel maker) in 1785, **Quaker House** (57 Ochterloney St., 902/464-5823; summer Tues.-Sun. 10am-5pm; $2.50) is one of Dartmouth's oldest residences. In addition to period furnishings, exhibits tell the story of the Quakers, who were drawn to Nova Scotia for its abundance of whales.

Bedford Institute of Oceanography

The government-run **Bedford Institute of Oceanography** (Baffin Blvd., 902/426-4306, www.bio.gc.ca; guided tours by appointment only May-Aug. Mon.-Fri. 9am-4pm; free) has a mandate that includes everything from helping maintain Canada's sovereignty to federal fisheries, but it is best known for its work on the sunken *Titanic*. On the guided tour, you'll get to learn about all this work, as well as step aboard a simulated ship's bridge and get up close and personal at the Touch Tank. To get there from downtown Halifax, cross the Narrows and take the Shannon Park exit from the MacKay Bridge (immediately after the toll gates); turn right and then left onto Baffin Boulevard, which crosses under the bridge to the institute.

Shubie Park

In 1858, construction began on an ambitious canal system that linked Halifax Harbour with the Bay of Fundy via a string of lakes and the Shubenacadie River. The canal was abandoned just 12 years later. The canal between Lake Micmac and Lake Charles has been restored, complete with one of nine original locks. **Shubie Park** is laced with hiking and biking trails, but many visitors take to the water in canoes, kayaks, and paddleboards, paddling from the main day-use area to Lake Charles. Access is signposted from Braemar Drive, which branches north from Exit 6 of Highway 111.

Cole Harbour Heritage Farm Museum

Surrounded by a residential subdivision, the outdoor **Cole Harbour Heritage Farm Museum** (471 Poplar Dr., 902/434-0222, http://coleharbourfarmmuseum.ca; mid-May-mid-Oct. Mon.-Sat. 10am-4pm, Sun. noon-4pm; donation) is a great place for children. Buildings include a 200-year-old farmhouse, a blacksmith shop, various barns, and a tearoom, while garden plots represent early crops, with the produce used in the tearoom. Livestock is fenced, but rabbits, geese, and ducks roam free.

EASTERN PASSAGE

The Eastern Passage is a narrow waterway running between the Dartmouth side of Halifax Harbour and McNabs Island. From downtown Dartmouth, take Pleasant Street south to Highway 322. This route passes oil refineries and Canadian Forces Base Shearwater before reaching the delightful Fisherman's Cove. Beyond this point, Highway 322 continues through an oceanfront residential area to Southeast Passage Provincial Park.

Shearwater Aviation Museum

At the entrance to Canadian Forces Base Shearwater, the **Shearwater Aviation Museum** (12 Wing Gate, Pleasant St., 902/720-1083, www.shearwateraviationmuseum.ns.ca; June-Aug. Mon.-Fri. 10am-5pm, Sat.-Sun. noon-4pm, Apr.-May and Sept.-Nov. Tues.-Fri. 10am-5pm, Sat. noon-4pm; free) is home to 10 restored aircraft and an impressive collection of air force memorabilia. The museum is off Pleasant Street (Highway 322); turn left at the first set of lights beyond the Imperial oil refinery.

★ Fisherman's Cove

Fisherman's Cove is no different from the hundreds of picturesque fishing villages that dot the Nova Scotia coastline, with one exception—it's within the city limits of the capital. Lying along the Eastern Passage, two kilometers southeast of Dartmouth along Highway 322, the cove mixes the needs of working fishing vessels with a constant flow of curious visitors. You can drive along Government Wharf Road, which spurs right at the traffic lights in Eastern Passage, onto the main dock area, but it's much more enjoyable to explore the area on foot from the parking lot just beyond the cove's main entrance.

Recreation

WALKING AND HIKING

Even if you're not feeling overly energetic, plan to take a stroll along the downtown waterfront. A **seawall promenade** winds past docks filled with all manner of boats (tall ships, tugboats, and visiting yachts), harborfront restaurants, the Maritime Museum of the Atlantic, Historic Properties, and south to Pier 21. While it's possible to do all your downtown sightseeing on foot, an easier option is to catch a cab to Citadel Hill, from which it's downhill all the way back to the harbor. At Citadel Hill, take the time not only to visit the fort but also to walk around the perimeter, and then cross Sackville Street to the **Public Gardens,** a delightful place for a flower-filled stroll.

McNabs Island is a popular destination for day-tripping hikers.

Point Pleasant Park, 2.5 kilometers south of downtown, off Young Avenue, is laced with hiking and biking trails. The obvious choice is to stick to the water, along a two-kilometer (one-way) trail that hugs the shoreline, passing Point Pleasant itself before winding around to the Northwest Arm. Other trails lead inland to historic fortifications and through the remains of forests devastated by Hurricane Juan in 2003.

Across the Northwest Arm from downtown, **Sir Sandford Fleming Park** flanks the water in an upscale neighborhood. Again, it's the seawall walk that is most popular, but another pleasant trail leads up through the forest to Frog Lake.

Take the Bedford Highway north from downtown and then one kilometer north of the Kearney Lake Road junction and watch for Kent Avenue (to the left), which leads into a dense old-growth forest protected as **Hemlock Ravine Park.** From the pond and picnic area, a world away from surrounding development, five trails branch off into the forest. Some are short and perfect for younger and older walkers, while others, including the trail to the hemlock-filled ravine, are steeper and can be slippery after rain.

BICYCLING

The local municipality, with its many lakes and harbor-side coves, has put considerable effort into making the city as bike-friendly as possible. The Halifax Regional Municipality website (www.halifax.ca) has a PDF bike map, or pick one up at the information center. A centrally located source for rentals and advice is **Ideal Bikes** (1678 Barrington St., 902/444-7433). Standard bikes cost from $25 for two hours or $50 for a full day.

Freewheeling Adventures (902/857-3600 or 800/672-0775, www.freewheeling.ca) is a local tour company that runs recommended guided bike trips along the South Shore, starting from Hubbards, just south of the city. Guests ride for up to six hours per day, stay in cottages or B&Bs, and have all meals included. Rates start at $2,300 per person.

WATER SPORTS
Swimming and Sunbathing

Municipal swimming pools include **Northcliffe Pool** (111 Clayton Park Dr., 902/490-4690) and **Needham Pool** (3372 Devonshire Ave., 902/490-4633).

Crystal Crescent Beach Provincial Park lies a half-hour south of Halifax, off Highway 349, and is the locals' favorite Atlantic beach. Its sand is fine, and the sea is usually cold, but summer crowds heat up the action. Nature lovers will enjoy the 10-kilometer trail to remote Pennant Point, while naturists will want to gravitate to the farthest of the park's three beaches—one of Canada's few official nude beaches.

If you're visiting Fisherman's Cove, head east for eight kilometers along Cow Bay Road to reach **Rainbow Haven Provincial Park.** The park protects wetlands at the mouth of Cole Harbour and an ocean-facing beach. The beach is often windy (it's not uncommon to see people sunbathing back in the dunes), but on calm days it's a delightful place to soak up some rays and maybe, if you're brave, take a dip in the water. At the end of the park access road are changing rooms and a concession selling beachy food (ice cream and hot dogs).

Canoeing and Kayaking

Based on the Northwest Arm, **Saint Mary's Boat Club** (1641 Fairfield Rd., 902/490-4688) rents canoes at no cost on a limited basis through summer. Canoes are available June-September (Sat.-Sun. 11am-7pm).

GOLFING

Halifax and the surrounding area are home to more than a dozen courses, varying from 9-hole public courses to exclusive 18-holers. The **Nova Scotia Golf Association** website (www.nsga.ns.ca) has links to all provincial courses.

The Courses

Host of the 2012 TELUS World Skins, **Glen Arbour Golf Course** (Glen Arbour Way, off Hammonds Plains Rd., 1 km west of Bedford,

902/835-4653) is one of Canada's finest links. Choose from five sets of tees, to a maximum of 6,800 yards. The course has abundant water hazards, 90 bunkers, and fairways lined by hardwood forests. Greens fees top out at $105 in midsummer, dropping as low as $60 for twilight golf in October.

Lost Creek Golf Club (310 Kinsac Rd., 902/865-4653) enjoys the same forested environment as Glen Arbour, but without the valet parking and high greens fees (golfing is just $46). To get there, take Exit 2 from Highway 101 and follow Beaverbank Road north for 10 kilometers; turn right on Kinsac Road and then left on William Nelson Drive.

One of the region's most enjoyable layouts is **Granite Springs** (25 km west of downtown, off Hwy. 333 at 4441 Prospect Rd., Bayside, 902/852-4653). This challenging course winds through 120 hectares of mature forest, with distant ocean views. Greens fees are $58 ($38 twilight).

WINTER SPORTS

In winter, walking paths become **cross-country ski trails** at Point Pleasant Park, Sir Sandford Fleming Park, and Hemlock Ravine. Dartmouth maintains groomed surfaces at Lake Charles, and several lakes in Halifax are great for skating.

Skiing and Snowboarding

The closest downhill skiing and boarding is at **Ski Martock** (902/798-9501, day passes adult $40, child $30), an hour's drive northwest of Halifax off Highway 101 (signposted from Exit 5). It's a popular family hill, with mostly beginner runs accessible by two lifts rising 180 vertical meters. Snowmaking covers the entire resort, while lights keep runs open nightly until 10pm.

Hockey

Through the long winter, when outside activities are curtailed by the weather, there is much interest in ice hockey (known in Canada simply as "hockey"). When they're not watching the National Hockey League on television (the closest teams are in Boston, Montréal, and Toronto), local fans flock to the Halifax Metro Centre to cheer on their own **Halifax Mooseheads** (5284 Duke St., 902/429-3267, www.halifaxmooseheads.ca, tickets $18 and up), who play mid-September to mid-March in the Québec Major Junior Hockey League.

HARBOR CRUISES AND LAND TOURS

If you don't have a lot of time to explore Halifax or just want an introduction to the city, consider one of the many tours available—they'll maximize your time and get you to the highlights with minimum stress.

Bluenose II

The harbor front's premier attraction, the magnificent schooner *Bluenose II* (http://bluenose.novascotia.ca) divides her summer between Halifax, her home port of Lunenburg, and goodwill tours to other Canadian ports. The vessel is an exact replica of the famous *Bluenose,* and after a three-year hiatus ending in 2015 has been returned to her former glory. The schooner is operated by the Lunenburg Marine Museum Society on behalf of the Province of Nova Scotia. When in Halifax, two-hour **harbor tours** (902/634-4794

or 800/763-1963, daily 9:30am and 1pm, adult $45, child $28) are available from the Maritime Museum's wharf. Each sailing has 75 spots—40 spots can be reserved by calling, with the remaining 35 going on sale 90 minutes before departure. Without a reservation, expect to line up for a spot.

Harbour Hopper Tours

Harbour Hopper Tours (902/490-8687, www.mtcw.ca/harbourhopper, adult $30, senior $28, child $17) picks up passengers from the north side of the maritime museum for a quick trip around the historic streets of Halifax. Then the fun really starts, as the company's distinctive green and yellow amphibious vehicles plunge into the water for a cruise around the harbor. The trip lasts around one hour, with up to 20 departures daily May-October (9am-9:30pm). The ticket kiosk is on the waterfront just north of the maritime museum.

Other Harbor Cruises

Many other sightseeing craft also offer harbor tours. **Murphy's on the Water** (Cable Wharf, 1751 Lower Water St., 902/420-1015, www.mtcw.ca) operates several vessels through a sailing season that runs

downtown harborfront

mid-May-late October. The 23-meter wooden sailing ketch *Mar* departs up to six times daily (adult $30, senior $27, child $19). The *Harbour Queen I* is a 200-passenger paddle wheeler offering a narrated harbor cruise (adult $30, senior $26, child $19) and a variety of lunch and dinner cruises ($62 for dinner).

Bus Tours

Ambassatours (902/423-6242 or 800/565-9662) has the local Grayline franchise. The three-hour Deluxe Historic Halifax City Tour includes stops at the Public Gardens, Halifax Citadel National Historic Site, and Fairview Cemetery. The tour also passes all major downtown attractions, working precincts of the harbor, and various university campuses.

This tour departs June-mid-October daily at 9am and 1pm (adult $52, child $30). Another option with Ambassatours is a downtown loop tour aboard an old British double-decker bus (mid-June-mid-Oct.; adult $58, child $29). You can get on and off as you please at any of the 12 stops on the loop, and tickets are valid for two days (a good plan is to ride the entire loop once, and then plan your stops for the second go-round). This same company also has a three-hour trip to Peggy's Cove (departs June-mid-Oct. Tues., Thurs., and Sun. at 1pm; adult $66, senior $58, child $42) and a full-day trip that combines a stop in Mahone Bay with time in Lunenburg (departs June-Oct. Mon., Wed., Fri., and Sat. at 9am; adult $98, senior $89, child $69).

Entertainment and Events

Halifax has a reputation as a party town, partly because of its large population of students. The city has dozens of pubs, many with local brews on tap and Celtic-inspired bands performing to small but raucous crowds. Most pubs close around midnight. The city also has a notable performing arts community. Although most seasons run through the cooler months, many companies put on events especially for summer crowds.

For complete listings of all that's happening around Halifax, pick up the free *Coast* (www.thecoast.ca). Friday and weekend editions of the *Chronicle Herald* (http://thechronicleherald.ca) also offer comprehensive entertainment listings.

PUBS AND BREWERIES

Halifax is renowned for its pubs and its great selection of locally brewed beers. Pubs range from historic homes to waterfront decks, but all are friendly and most also offer a good selection of food.

If you're going to have just one beer in Halifax, quaff it at the **Red Stag Tavern** (1496 Lower Water St., 902/422-0275, www.

redstag.ca; 11:30am-close), part of the Keith's Brewery complex. Best known as North America's oldest working brewery, Keith's still uses traditional British brewing techniques. Its famous India Pale Ale is widely available on draught and in bottles across the country, but it's best enjoyed in the Red Stag, surrounded by a convivial atmosphere and with traditional Maritime music in the background.

Henry House (1222 Barrington St., 902/423-5660; daily from 11am) is ensconced in a historic 1834 stone building a couple of blocks back from Alexander Keith's Brewery. The pub attracts a slightly older crowd of well-dressed locals and has a wide-ranging menu of food and beer, including gluten-free options.

In the harbor-front Historic Properties complex, **Hart & Thistle** (1869 Upper Water St., 902/407-4278) is a big, bright room, with lots of outside waterfront seating. It has its own small brewery and offers a range of other local brews. The food here is also notable, ranging from traditional (lobster rolls) to modern (beet and goat cheese salad). Adjacent to the Hart & Thistle, live music at the **Lower**

Deck (Upper Water St., 902/425-1501; daily from 11:30am) keeps the crowds humming nightly at this waterfront pub within the historic Privateers Warehouse.

The Maxwell's Plum (1600 Grafton St., 902/423-5090) has an excellent selection of imported draft beers (notably Beamish Irish Stout, John Courage, and Newcastle Brown Ale) and single-malt scotches. That alone may be reason enough to visit, but it's also a good venue for straight-ahead jazz, including Sunday afternoon jam sessions.

Best known for its rooftop patio, **Your Father's Moustache** (5686 Spring Garden Rd., 902/423-6766) puts on excellent live, usually local, music most evenings. On Saturday afternoon, it hosts a popular Blues Matinee.

Aside from sidling up to the bar at the above pubs, beer connoisseurs visiting Halifax can buy directly from a number of small breweries scattered around the city. Generally, you can buy regular bottles, "growlers" (one- or two-liter jugs), or kegs up to 50 liters. **Garrison Brewing** (1149 Marginal Rd., 902/453-5343; daily 10am-8pm) is in a touristy location between the farmers market and Pier 21, but that doesn't stop the brewmaster from producing a wonderful range of ales. Garrison also has a large shop and tasting area. Across town, the **Granite Brewery** (6054 Stairs St., 902/422-4954) is tucked away between Robie and Kempt Streets, but it's well worth searching out for its excellent English-style ales.

NIGHTLIFE
Bars

In the basement of the Marquee Ballroom north of downtown is the **Seahorse Tavern** (2037 Gottingen St., 902/423-7200), which has been around since 1948 (although it has moved from its original location). Horsepower Beer, produced by the local Propeller Brewery, is available on tap only at the Seahorse, but most patrons are here for the music. Monday through Thursday are theme nights, such as Mullet Mondays (retro rock and roll) and Indie Wednesdays, while weekends are devoted to live music. Part of the same complex is the **Economy Shoe Shop** (1663 Argyle St.,

Granite Brewery

Economy Shoe Shop

902/423-8845; daily 11am-2am), a drinking and dining venue incorporating three restaurants and the Belgian Bar, with a gaudy but appealing tropical vibe.

HFX Sports Bar (1721 Brunswick St., 902/404-1404) is a cavernous sports bar anchored by a two-story wall of TV screens. It's arguably the best place in the city to go for U.S. sports, but you can also watch British-oriented sports such as cricket and rugby. Food is typical pub fare, but is well priced.

Stayner's Wharf Pub & Grill (5075 George St., 902/492-1800) is in the heart of the tourist district, but since it's a smaller place, the casual visitor often misses this bar, which remains quiet until local jazz and blues bands hit the stage Wednesday through Sunday.

Nightclubs

Around midnight, when the pubs start closing their doors, the crowds move on to nightclubs spread through downtown.

The **Dome** (1726 Argyle St., 902/422-6907; Wed.-Sun. 10pm-3:30am) is a mass of young heaving bodies who dance the night away in sync to one of Canada's most dynamic sound and light systems. It's also a bit of a pickup place. Under the same roof is **Cheers** (902/421-1655), which attracts an older crowd. Another multivenue nightclub is **Pacifico** (corner of Barrington and Salter Sts., 902/422-3633), where **CraveBar** attracts serious dancers and the **Capitol** hosts a martini bar.

Starting out as a gay bar and then making a move to a new location in late 2014, **Reflections** (5187 Salter St., 902/422-2957) now attracts an eclectic mix of locals of all persuasions. Each night has a theme—Tuesday is house and techno, bands play Wednesday, Thursday is an anything-goes talent show—but the biggest crowds are on weekends, when the resident DJ spins tunes until 4am.

HFX Sports Bar (1721 Brunswick St., 902/404-1404) is a cavernous sports bar anchored by a two-story wall of TV screens. It's arguably the best place in the city to go for U.S. sports, but you can also watch British-oriented

sports such as cricket and rugby. Food is typical pub fare, but is well-priced.

Jazz and Blues

The **Seahorse Tavern** (2037 Gottingen St., 902/423-7200) hosts a blues jam every Thursday night. The Belgian Bar, within the **Economy Shoe Shop** (1663 Argyle St., 902/423-8845; daily 11am-2am) features no-charge Monday evening jazz.

The best blues bar in town is **Bearly's House of Blues and Ribs** (1269 Barrington St., 902/423-2526). As the name suggests, ribs ($18 for a full rack) are the dining specialty, but it is the music that draws an enthusiastic crowd. Weekends feature local talent, while weekdays except Monday and Wednesday the stage is turned over to traveling talent. On Saturday afternoons through winter, bluegrass musicians strum their stuff.

PERFORMING ARTS

Haligonians have a sweet and sometimes bittersweet Canadian sense of humor (somewhat like the British), and local theater revels in their brand of fun. A $42 admission will get you into dinner-theater musical productions at **Grafton Street Dinner Theatre** (1741 Grafton St., 902/425-1961), which operates daily except Monday in summer and three times a week through the rest of the year. **Halifax Feast Dinner Theatre** (Maritime Centre, corner of Barrington and Salter Sts., 902/420-1840) costs a few dollars more, but the production often has a historic Halifax angle. A lot of food is served very quickly at both venues, but the quality remains excellent.

At the **Neptune Theatre** (1593 Argyle St., 902/429-7070), private companies such as Legends of Broadway take to the boards during summer with musicals and Gilbert and Sullivan shows.

FESTIVALS AND EVENTS

Halifax hosts a number of well-known events that visitors plan their trips around, as well as many you probably haven't heard of but that are well worth attending if the dates correspond with your own travels. The most popular festivals are held outdoors and in summer, but the cooler months are the season for performing arts. For exact dates of festivals, check the event's website or **Tourism Nova Scotia** (www.novascotia.com).

Spring

The **Scotia Festival of Music** centers on the Music Room (6181 Lady Hammond Rd., 902/429-9467, www.scotiafestival.ns.ca) for two weeks from the last weekend in May. Chamber musicians present piano, cello, and violin recitals in a dignified yet casual atmosphere.

The **Nova Scotia Multicultural Festival** (Halifax Seaport, 945 Marginal Rd., 902/423-6534, www.multifest.ca) fills the waterfront precinct with the sounds, sights, and smells of various cultures the middle weekend of June. You can feast on barbecued Korean short ribs while watching Polish folk dancing or tap your feet to Celtic Highland dancers while juggling a plate of German sausages.

Summer

Nothing reflects Halifax's long military heritage better than the **Royal Nova Scotia International Tattoo** (902/420-1114, www.nstattoo.ca), held annually for 10 days at the beginning of July at the Halifax Metro Centre (5284 Duke St.). A "tattoo" is an outdoor military exercise presented as entertainment. Here it involves competitions, military bands, dancers, gymnasts, and choirs. The event has grown to be regarded as one of the world's greatest indoor events, bringing together thousands of performers from around the world. You can buy tickets (around $32-54) through the Halifax Metro Centre Box Office (902/451-1221).

In mid-July, jazz fans descend on Halifax for the **Halifax Jazz Festival** (902/492-2225, www.halifaxjazzfestival.ca), the largest music festival east of Montréal. In addition to performing in a large tent set up on the waterfront along Lower Water Street at Salter Street, more than 400 musicians from around the world gather at venues as unique as a tugboat and as character-filled as local churches to perform traditional and contemporary jazz.

Halifax and Dartmouth come together to celebrate their birthdays with a civic holiday known as **Natal Day** (www.natalday.org) on the first Monday of every August. Events take place through the entire weekend, including a Saturday parade, talent shows, sporting events, and a grand finale fireworks presentation on the harbor Monday night.

Street performers fill five stages spread along the downtown waterfront for 11 days in early August during the **Halifax International Busker Festival** (www.buskers.ca).

Summer finishes with the **Atlantic Fringe Festival** (902/423-4653, www.atlanticfringe.ca), featuring 200 shows at various downtown venues through the first week of September.

Fall

The mid-September **Atlantic Film Festival** (902/422-3456, www.atlanticfilm.com) has been wowing moviegoers for more than a quarter of a century. It features the very best films from around the world, but the emphasis is on local and Canadian productions. Venues are mostly downtown theaters.

Celebrate **Alexander Keith's birthday** (902/455-1474, www.keiths.ca) on October 5 with hundreds of enthusiastic locals. Or pull up a barstool at any local pub and raise a toast of India Pale Ale to "The Great Man of Beer," who began brewing beer in Halifax in 1820. The brewery (check the website for locations) is the epicenter of celebrations, with plenty of foot-stomping, beer-drinking east coast music.

For four days in early in October, the country comes to the city for the **Maritime Fall Fair** (Exhibition Park, 200 Prospect Rd., 902/876-1811, www.maritimefallfair.com). It has everything a fall fair should—a craft marketplace, agricultural competitions, vegetable judging, a rodeo, and a midway. Exhibition Park is off Highway 333, the main road to Peggy's Cove.

Winter

The middle weekend of November, the

Christmas Craft Village (www.christmas-craftvillage.com) fills Exhibition Park with hundreds of crafty booths selling everything from homemade preserves to self-published books to coastal antiques.

Shopping

Shopping in Halifax—the type visitors to the city will enjoy—centers on the downtown waterfront, with the exception being the boutiques and quirky shops along Spring Garden Road. Expect to find everything from lighthouse Christmas decorations made in China to original oil paintings, and everything in between.

Most shops and all major department stores are generally open Monday-Saturday 9:30am-5:30pm. Stores along the touristy harbor front usually have longer hours and are also open Sunday.

Arts and Crafts

The city's art galleries are superb, and most are located downtown. The newest fine arts trends are on exhibit at Nova Scotia College of Art and Design's **Anna Leonowens Gallery** (1891 Granville St., 902/494-8223; Tues.-Fri. 11am-5pm, Sat. noon-4pm). The gallery displays and sells the work of Nova Scotia College of Art and Design students. This downtown university, one of North America's oldest cultural institutions, was founded by the gallery's namesake, Anna Leonowens, in 1887. Leonowens, a one-time English teacher who was governess to the King of Siam in the 1860s, spent 20 years in Halifax, during which time she established NSCAD.

The capital's definitive crafts source is **Jennifer's of Nova Scotia** (5635 Spring Garden Rd., 902/425-3119; Wed.-Fri. 9am-9pm, Sat.-Tues. 9am-6pm), an outlet for 120 provincial producers of handicrafts such as patchwork quilts, pottery, and soaps.

The **Gallery Shop** at street level of the

Art Gallery of Nova Scotia (1723 Hollis St., 902/424-7542; Mon.-Sat. 10am-5pm, Sun. noon-5pm; adult $12, senior $10, child $7) is an inspiring room filled with the cream of provincial arts and crafts, as well as prints by folk artist Maude Lewis, books, cards, and other assorted arty gifts. Walking west down Hollis Street from the gallery is **Studio 21** (1273 Hollis St., 902/420-1852; Tues.-Fri. 11am-6pm, Sat. 10am-5pm, Sun. noon-5pm), a good source of contemporary paintings by local artists.

For a unique combination of hand-built furniture and porcelain dog dishes, head to **Bellissimo** (2743 Agricola St., 902/423-6014; Mon.-Sat. 10am-5pm).

Crystal

Canada's only traditional glassworks is **Nova Scotian Crystal** (5080 George St., 902/492-0416; Mon.-Fri. 9am-6pm, Sat.-Sun. 10am-6pm), which is ensconced in a waterfront building that contains a showroom and workshop. You can watch master craftspeople at work every day, but Tuesday, Thursday, and Saturday are the days you won't want to miss—this is when the actual glassblowing takes place. Rather than taking a tour, interested folks crowd around open factory doors to watch the goings-on inside. The shop sells pieces such as Christmas ornaments, stemware, toasting flutes, candleholders, and bowls, many with Nova Scotian-inspired designs.

Clothing

Hundreds of clan fabrics and tartans in

kilts, skirts, vests, ties, and other apparel are stocked at **Plaid Place** (1903 Barrington St., 902/429-6872; Mon.-Fri. 9:30-5:30pm, Sat. 10am-5pm). For something a little less traditional, stop by **Island Beach Co.** (1655 Lower Water St., 902/422-4060), where you'll find casual clothing in a bright, subtly nautical-themed setting. Starting out by selling shirts from a log church, this local company has grown into a 30-store chain with outlets across Atlantic Canada. The downtown Halifax store is along the harbor; another is at Halifax International Airport.

Markets

Halifax Seaport Farmers' Market happens Tuesday to Sunday 8am-4pm at Pier 20 (1209 Marginal Rd., 902/492-4043). North America's oldest such market (although the location is new) fills a massive waterfront building with local produce and handmade arts and crafts that make the perfect memento of your time in Nova Scotia.

In the same vicinity, **Pavilion 22** (May-Oct. when cruise ships have docked) is designed as a market-style shopping experience for cruise-ship visitors, but is also worth stopping by if you are at this end of town.

Local Delicacies

You'll no doubt eat a lot of seafood while in Nova Scotia, but it can also make a great souvenir to take home for friends and family. Or plan a get-together upon your return and impress everyone with a Nova Scotian feast.

Clearwater (757 Bedford Hwy., 902/443-0333; daily 9am-7pm) is a high-profile supplier with a huge shopfront along the Bedford Highway waterfront. The outlet is anchored by a massive lobster tank divided into sections that make choosing the right-size lobster easy (from $10 per pound). You can also pick up cooked crab legs to go, attend cooking demonstrations, and buy all manner of seafood cookbooks. Better still for those departing Halifax International Airport, Clearwater has an airport location (902/873-4509; daily 5am-8pm) with a lobster tank. For an additional fee, live lobsters can be packaged for air travel. Clearwater also sells crabs, scallops, clams, and shrimp.

The days of Prohibition, when smuggling rum into the United States was a way to make a living for seafaring Nova Scotians, may be a distant memory, but at the **Rum Runners Rum Cake Factory** (Bishop's Landing, 1479 Lower Water St., 902/421-6079; mid-April-late

Halifax Seaport Farmers' Market

Dec. daily 8am-dusk), you can buy rum cakes from a rum-running family's recipe. The cakes are deliciously rich and sweet, and they travel well.

Outdoor and Camping Gear

Halifax's largest outdoor equipment store is **Mountain Equipment Co-op** (1550 Granville St., 902/421-2667; Mon.-Wed. 10am-7pm, Thurs.-Fri. 10am-9pm, Sat. 10am-6pm). This is a cooperative owned by its members; to make a purchase, you must be a member (a one-time $5 charge). The store holds a massive selection of clothing, climbing and mountaineering equipment, tents, backpacks, sleeping bags, books, and other accessories. To obtain a copy of the mail-order catalog, call 800/663-2667 or go online to www.mec.ca.

The Trail Shop (6210 Quinpool Rd., 902/423-8736, www.trailshop.com; Mon.-Sat. 9am-6pm) has been a Halifax staple in the outfitting business since 1967. The selection of camping equipment, footwear, and field guides is particularly strong.

Accommodations and Camping

Accommodations in Halifax vary from a hostel and budget-priced roadside motels to luxurious B&Bs. Downtown is home to a number of full-service hotels catering to top-end travelers and business conventions. In general, these properties offer drastically reduced rates on weekends—Friday and Saturday nights might be half the regular room rate. No matter when you plan to visit, arriving in Halifax without a reservation is unwise, but it's especially so in the summer, when gaggles of tourists compete for a relative paucity of rooms.

All rates quoted are for a double room in summer.

DOWNTOWN
Under $50

Also known as the Halifax Heritage House Hostel, **HI-Halifax** (1253 Barrington St., 902/422-3863, www.hihostels.ca) has 75 beds two blocks from the harbor and a 15-minute walk to attractions such as the maritime museum and Citadel Hill. Facilities include a communal kitchen, a laundry room, television in the common room, and a storeroom for bikes. Beds in four- to eight-bed dorms are $32 per night ($37 for nonmembers), while those in private rooms are $59-64 s or d ($65-70 for nonmembers).

$150-200

Oscar Wilde and P. T. Barnum both slept (not together) at the **Waverley Inn** (1266 Barrington St., 902/423-9346 or 800/565-9346, www.waverleyinn.com; $135-235 s, $175-235 d), which, at its completion in 1866, was one of the city's grandest residences. Rates for the 34 rooms include a cooked breakfast and wireless Internet, and tea, coffee, and snacks are offered all day and evening in the hospitality suite. Rooms are furnished with Victorian-era antiques, and deluxe rooms contain whirlpool tubs and feather beds. The least expensive single rooms are very small, while the deluxe twins are spacious and extravagantly luxurious.

★ **Cambridge Suites Hotel** (1583 Brunswick St., 902/420-0555 or 800/565-1263, www.cambridgesuiteshalifax.com; $175-225 s or d) is a modern, centrally located, all-suite hotel with 200 rooms. Even the smallest suites have separate bedrooms, and continental breakfast is included in the rates. Rooms are packed with amenities, including wireless Internet, beautiful bathrooms, lounge and work areas, and basic cooking facilities. The rooftop patio, a fitness center, and a bistro-style restaurant are pluses. Ask about rates that include free parking, full breakfast, and extras for traveling families.

★ **The Halliburton** (5184 Morris St., 902/420-0658 or 888/512-3344, www.thehalliburton.com; from $185 s or d) is a beautiful heritage property transformed into a boutique hotel. The 29 rooms come with super-comfortable beds topped with goose-down duvets and luxurious en suite bathrooms. Rates include continental breakfast, and wireless Internet is available throughout the building. The intimate in-house dining room, Stories, is open nightly (except Monday) for dinner.

Halifax is home to two Delta properties. In both cases, click on the "Special Offers" link at www.deltahotels.com for the best rates. **Delta Barrington** (1875 Barrington St., 902/429-7410 or 888/890-3222; from $195 s or d) shares space with Barrington Place Mall in the historic area and has 200 comfortable rooms. Amenities include a fitness room, an indoor pool, a business center, a street-side café (with a summer seafood menu), and a lounge bar. Rack rates are around $190 s or d midweek and $160 on weekends. Nearby, the **Delta Halifax** (1990 Barrington St., 902/425-6700 or 888/890-3222; $195 s or d) was one of the city's first grande dame hotels, and the old girl's still a handsome dowager. A highlight is the lavish indoor pool complex, complete with whirlpools and a sauna as well as an adjacent fitness room.

$200-250

In any other Canadian capital, you'd pay a lot more for a room of similar standard as those at the full-service **Prince George Hotel** (1725 Market St., 902/425-1986 or 800/565-1567, www.princegeorgehotel.com; from $245 s or d), one block below the Halifax Citadel and seven blocks uphill from the harbor. The rooms feature contemporary furnishings and amenities include a midsize indoor pool, a business center with Internet access, a restaurant, a lounge, and quiet public areas off the main lobby. Although rack rates start at over $200, check the website for weekend specials or upgrade to the Crown Service rooms for an extra $40.

Part of the Casino Nova Scotia complex, **Marriott Harbourfront Hotel** (1919 Upper Water St., 902/421-1700 or 800/943-6760, www.marriott.com; $245 s or d) is a modern edifice designed to resemble the garrison that once occupied the waterfront. Although many guests are from Atlantic Canada and are

Waverley Inn

A big draw at the Prince George Hotel is the indoor pool.

staying especially to play the tables, the hotel is also a convenient choice for leisure travelers. In addition to the casino, there is an upscale restaurant with harbor views, a stylish English pub, and live entertainment. Almost no one pays rack rates; check the website for a world of options starting at $149 s or d.

Over $250

If you're after modern accommodations, consider **Four Points by Sheraton Halifax** (1496 Hollis St., 902/423-4444, www.starwoodhotels.com; from $255 s or d), one block back from the harbor. The 177 guest rooms are filled with modern conveniences (free wireless Internet, 27-inch TVs, multiple phones, and well-designed work areas), while other facilities include an indoor pool and fitness room. Disregard the rack rates and book online, and you'll pay as little as $160 s or d, even in midsummer.

Opened in 1930 to coincide with the arrival of the first passenger trains to Halifax, the station's adjacent **Westin Nova Scotian** (1181 Hollis St., 902/421-1000 or 877/993-7846, www.thewestinnovascotian.com; from $275 s or d) was extensively renovated in 2008.

Linked to the railway station—many guests are still rail passengers—it oozes old-world charm throughout public areas (poke your head into the Atlantic Ballroom) and the 300 guest rooms. Amenities include a fine-dining restaurant featuring contemporary cooking, a fitness room, an indoor pool, spa services, and a shuttle to the central business district (one kilometer away).

CITADEL HILL AND VICINITY

The following accommodations are in the vicinity of Citadel Hill, from which it's downhill all the way to the harbor. Even the fittest visitors may not feel like tramping back up to the Citadel Hill area after a full day of sightseeing or a big meal at a downtown restaurant. No worries; a cab will cost around $7.

$50-100

A rambling old house directly opposite North Common has been renovated as **Fountain View Guest House** (2138 Robie St., between Williams St. and Compton Ave., 902/422-4169 or 800/565-4877; $35 s, $50 d). The seven rooms share bathrooms, there is no kitchen or laundry, and parking is limited to what you can find on the street.

$100-150

Across North Common from Citadel Hill is the **Commons Inn** (5780 West St., 902/484-3466 or 877/797-7999, www.commonsinn.ca; $100-150 s or d), an older three-story building with 40 basic guest rooms. The rooms are on the small side, but they are smartly outfitted with comfortable beds, en suite bathrooms, free local calls, and cable TV. The spacious suite, complete with a separate sitting area and jetted tub, is an excellent value. Other pluses are free parking, a rooftop patio, and a continental breakfast.

$200-250

The grandiose ★ **Lord Nelson Hotel** (1515 S. Park St., 902/423-6331 or 800/565-2020, www.lordnelsonhotel.com; from $215 s or d) presides over a busy Spring Garden Road intersection and overlooks the famous Public Gardens. Originally opened in 1928, the Lord Nelson underwent a transformation in the late 1990s, reopening as one of the city's finest hotels. It is probably a little too far for some to walk to from downtown, but location aside, it is one of Halifax's best and best-value accommodations. Beyond the extravagant marble-floored lobby are 260 elegantly furnished rooms, each with a large bathroom, wireless Internet access, a coffeemaker, and an iron. Other amenities include a fitness room, restaurant, English-style pub, and room service. Parking is $16 per night. Check the website for specials.

BEDFORD HIGHWAY

Running along the western edge of the Bedford Basin, the Bedford Highway (Highway 2) is the original route north from downtown to the airport and beyond. A few motels from pre-bypass days exist, providing inexpensive accommodations a 10-minute (or quicker) drive from the city center. If you make this part of the city your base, you'll need a vehicle, or be prepared to ride transit buses. To get there from the north, take Exit 3 from Highway 102 and follow the signs toward downtown.

$50-100

Nestled in wooded grounds on the harbor side of the Bedford Highway is the **Travelers Motel** (773 Bedford Hwy., 902/835-3367 or 800/565-3367, www.travelersmotel.ca, $60-95). It is a classic 1950s park-at-the-door roadside motel, where rates start at $89 for smallish rooms with dated decor, cable TVs, and phones. Summer-only cabins with TV but no phones are $60-95 s or d. This place is surprisingly busy, so you'll need reservations in summer.

$100-150

Over the rise toward the city, opposite a busy diner of the same name, is the **Esquire Motel** (771 Bedford Hwy., 902/835-3367 or 800/565-3367, www.esquiremotel.ca; $95-155 s or d). Amenities are similar to its neighbor, the cheaper Travelers Motel, with the only real difference being a small outdoor pool and free local calls. Outside of summer, rates drop as low as $75.

NEAR THE AIRPORT

From the airport, it's only 40 minutes to downtown on the Airporter. Here are a few options just in case you must stay in the vicinity.

$100-150

Across the highway from the airport and linked by free shuttle is the **Quality Inn Halifax Airport Hotel** (60 Sky Blvd., 902/873-3000 or 800/667-3333, www.airporthotelhalifax.com; $130 s or d), which has regularly revamped rooms, indoor and outdoor pools, wireless Internet, a fitness room, and a restaurant where guests enjoy complimentary breakfast.

★ **ALT Hotel** (40 Silver Dart Dr., 902/334-0136 or 855/258-5775, www.althotels.ca; $139 s or d) is a no-frills hotel located right at the airport. The rooms are simply decorated in a modern chic theme, while downstairs is a café filled with "grab and go" meals, and a pool. There's no room service or valet parking; in return there are no seasonal price adjustments.

$150-200

Four kilometers south of the airport, **Hilton Garden Inn** (200 Pratt & Whitney Dr., Enfield, 902/873-1400, www.hilton.com; from $189 s or d) offers 24-hour shuttle service for guests. It's a newer property with a high standard of guest rooms, as well as a restaurant and fitness room.

About halfway between the airport and downtown is **Inn on the Lake** (3009 Hwy. 2, Fall River, 902/861-3480 or 800/463-6465, www.innonthelake.com; from $179 s or d), which is a full-blown resort, complete with multiple dining rooms, recreational opportunities spread over two hectares of landscaped lakefront, and even a sandy beach.

FISHERMAN'S COVE

If you don't need to be right downtown, consider the following oceanfront accommodation—it's both an excellent value and a world away from the bustle of the city.

$100-150

Overlooking the historic fishing village, the ★ **Inn at Fisherman's Cove** (1531 Shore Rd., Eastern Passage, 902/465-3455 or 866/725-3455, www.theinnatfishermanscove.com; $115-165 s or d) is a modern three-story building with its own private dock on the "crick" that has been chock-full of fishing boats for more than 200 years. Each room has an en suite bathroom and TV, while downstairs is a breakfast room that opens to the dock. Four of the eight guest rooms face the water and have private balconies. Rates include a light breakfast.

CAMPGROUNDS

A few commercial campgrounds lie within a 30-minute drive of downtown. Farther out are two provincial parks that offer camping without hookups.

The ALT Hotel is right at the airport.

Dartmouth

The closest camping to downtown is at ★ **Shubie Park Campground** (Jaybee Dr., Dartmouth, 902/435-8328, www.shubiecampground.com; mid-May-mid-Oct.; tents $29, hookups $34-43). Facilities such as the washrooms have been recently renovated, while public Internet access and landscaping have been added. The adjacent beach on Lake Charles comes with supervised swimming, and the campground is linked to walking trails along the Shubenacadie Canal. On the downside, sites offer little privacy.

West

Woodhaven RV Park (1757 Hammonds Plains Rd., 902/835-2271, www.woodhavenrvpark.com; May-mid-Oct.; $30-35) is 18 kilometers from downtown and handy for an early-morning start out to the South Shore. Facilities include coin-operated showers, two launderettes, a swimming pool, a playground, a games room, and wireless Internet access.

Halifax West KOA (3070 Hwy. 1, Upper Sackville, 902/865-4342, www.koa.com;

mid-May-mid-Oct.; $34-55, cabins with shared bathrooms $68) is northwest of the city, farther out than Woodhaven and a 45-minute drive from downtown.

North

Laurie Provincial Park (coming from the north, take Exit 7 south to Highway 2) lies on the southern shore of Grand Lake. Here, 71 sites are spread around a tree-lined loop. Each site has a picnic table and fire pit, while park amenities include toilets, a short walking trail, and a day-use area, but no showers or hookups. The campground is open mid-June to early September and sites are $26 per night.

Dollar Lake Provincial Park (mid-June-mid-Oct.; $26) is farther from the city than Laurie Provincial Park, but it has showers and a concession, as well as a nicer beach, with swimming, boating, walking trails, and a playground. Sites are spread around three loops, with Loop A closest to the water.

Food

Halifax may not have a reputation as a gastronomical wonderland, but the dining scene has improved greatly during the last decade. Not only is the standard of food high in many of the better restaurants, but prices are generally reasonable, with mains in even the very best restaurants rarely more than $35.

Naturally, seafood dominates many menus—especially lobster, crab, mussels, scallops, shrimp, halibut, and salmon, all of which are harvested in Nova Scotia. Some of the best seafood is found in the touristy waterfront precinct. You can also buy it fresh from trawlers at Fisherman's Cove and even pick up live lobsters packed for flying out at the airport.

DOWNTOWN

Cafés

You can get a caffeine hit at outlets of Second Cup and Tim Hortons spread throughout the city, but the absence of coffeehouse chains in downtown Halifax is refreshing.

Perks (1781 Lower Water St., 902/429-9386; daily 6:30am-11:30pm, lunches $6-10) is always busy. Sure, the coffee is good, food such as chicken Caesar salad is well priced, there's wireless Internet, and the service is efficient, but it's its location—at a busy waterfront intersection where ferries from Dartmouth unload—that ensures a constant lineup.

Step inside **Cabin Coffee** (1554 Hollis St., 902/422-8130; Mon.-Fri. 6:30am-6pm, Sat. 7:30am-5pm, Sun. 8:30am-5pm; lunches $6-9) and you'll be surprised by the relaxed and friendly ambience of this smaller café in the heart of downtown. In addition to top-notch coffee, the wraps, sandwiches, and muffins are all tasty and well priced.

Head down Bishop Street from Cabin Coffee to Bishop's Landing and you'll find **Smiling Goat** (1475 Lower Water St., 902/446-3366; Mon.-Sat. 7am-7pm, Sun. 8am-6pm; lunches $6-9), a stylish espresso bar with outdoor seating in a paved courtyard.

At ★ **Paper Chase News Café** (5228 Blowers St., 902/423-0750; Mon.-Thurs. 8am-8pm, Fri.-Sat. 8am-9pm, Sun. 9am-8pm; lunches $5-8), a narrow stairway leads upstairs to a funky space where windows roll up garage door-style and seating spreads from one side of the building to the other, with a split level and slightly arty decor in between. The food is remarkably inexpensive. The café also has wireless Internet access.

On the south side of downtown, **Trident** (1256 Hollis St., 902/423-7100; Mon.-Fri. 8am-5pm, Sat. 8:30am-5pm, Sun. 10am-5pm; lunches $6-10) is a secondhand bookstore on one side and an old-fashioned café with leather-backed chairs on the other—the perfect place to relax with a newly bought literary treasure, or to take advantage of the free wireless Internet.

Booths and Burgers

Beyond the white linens and perfectly presented seafood of Halifax's finer restaurants are a smattering of old-style diners. The following are my favorites—one downtown, another overlooking the city's most notorious intersection, and another handy for those traveling into downtown from the north.

In the heart of the central business district, the venerable **Bluenose II** (1824 Hollis St., 902/425-5092; daily from 7am) is named for the famous schooner that calls Halifax home on a part-time basis. The booths fill with an eclectic crowd of locals for breakfast, but the space is bright and welcoming, and many regulars are families. Eggs Benedict is $7.50, steak and eggs $8.50, while the rest-of-the-day choices vary from a lobster sandwich ($10) to Greek specialties ($9-14).

Overlooking the confusing-even-for-the-locals Armdale Rotary is **Armview Restaurant** (7156 Chebucto Rd., 902/455-4395; Mon.-Wed. 11am-10pm, Thurs.-Sun. 8:30am-10pm; $8-21), one of Halifax's oldest restaurants. Although it's undergone renovations and the menu has been expanded to include options like mango halibut salad, you can still order no-frills breakfasts and burgers for around $10.

On Monday, Tuesday, and Wednesday, coupon-clipping retirees fill **Esquire Restaurant** (772 Bedford Hwy., 902/835-9033; daily 7am-9pm; $7-15) for specials such as home-style pork dinners for $8. The restaurant is across from the Bedford Basin, and there's plenty of parking, or, if you're staying across the road at the Esquire Motel, you need only to negotiate traffic zooming along the busy Bedford Highway.

Seafood Along the Waterfront

The least expensive way to enjoy seafood along the waterfront is by ordering fish and chips from **Battered Fish** (1751 Lower Water St., 902/491-3474; May-Oct. daily 11am-dusk; $9-14), where the haddock is fresh and the quality very good. The deep fried clams and scallops are also worth trying.

In the Historic Properties, **Salty's** (1869 Lower Water St., 902/423-6818; daily 11:30am-10pm; $17-27) mixes seafood with succulent meat dishes in a sublime setting. Kick back with a margarita and watch the boats in the harbor. Sit indoors or out to enjoy some of the city's best food in a casual atmosphere, and don't miss the scrumptious desserts. The upstairs dining room is slightly more formal, with a menu and prices to match. Here, mains such as scallops roasted in red Thai curry and butter-poached halibut are in the $27-36 range.

Diners at **Murphy's on the Water** (1751 Lower Water St., 902/420-1015; daily 9am-10pm; $19-34) also enjoy panoramic harbor views. This restaurant fills a converted warehouse, with outside tables at the end of the pier. The emphasis is on seafood, like the lobster sandwich.

Waterfront Warehouse (1549 Lower Water St., 902/425-7610; May-Oct. daily 11:30am-10pm; $23-35) is exactly that—a converted waterfront warehouse where tugboats were once repaired. The setting, with white linens, nautical-themed furnishings, and an oversized fireplace. The seafood chowder is a hearty starter, while seafood-oriented mains include bouillabaisse served in an iron pot and the signature dish—maple-glazed salmon grilled on a cedar plank.

Other Seafood Restaurants

★ **Five Fishermen** (1740 Argyle St., 902/422-4421, daily lunch and dinner; $24-40) occupies one of Halifax's oldest buildings—it was built in 1816 and once used by famed governess Anna Leonowens (of *Anna and the King* fame) for her Victorian School of Art and Design. The restaurant is popular with seafood-loving Haligonians for its large dish menu, which includes shellfish linguini, pan-seared halibut, PEI oysters, and lobster-stuffed Digby scallops, as well as Alberta beef.

Henry House

from throughout Nova Scotia. Add immaculate presentation to fresh and healthy cooking styles, and you have a meal to remember. Mains such as shepherd's pie (cooked with lamb) are all delicious and well presented. Save room for the lemon tart.

A Halifax Original

The stretch of Argyle Street between Sackville and Blowers Streets has emerged as a dining hot spot, with the utterly original ★ **Economy Shoe Shop** (1663 Argyle St., 902/423-8845; daily 11:30am-2am; $11-23) anchoring the strip. The unusual name originated when one of the owners was starting out in the restaurant business; with little cash to spare, he found an old neon sign bearing the name and hung it out front. The original space has grown to encompass three very different restaurants and a bar—one a bohemian-themed space, another a glass-roofed room enclosing a rainforest that adds a tropical vibe even in the dead of winter. On offer is everything from run-of-the-mill hamburgers to baked halibut and scallops Mornay. Throw entertaining servers into the mix and you get a unique dining experience without spending a fortune.

Pub Dining

Durty Nelly's (1660 Argyle St., 902/406-7640; daily from 10:30am; $9-16) is Irish in more than name. All furnishings in the traditionally stylish room were actually built in Ireland and transported across the Atlantic. The menu includes traditional treats such as lamb shank braised in Guinness, cottage pie, and corned beef with boiled potatoes, as well as local seafood.

It's a little away from the tourist precinct, but ★ **Henry House** (1222 Barrington St., 902/423-5660; daily 11:30am-12:30am; $17-29) offers excellent food. Melt-in-your-mouth baby back ribs are a house specialty, or choose healthy options such as salmon baked in crushed cashews.

Steakhouses

For carnivorous cravings, prepare to splurge at **Ryan Duffy's** (1650 Bedford Row, 902/421-1116; Mon.-Fri. 6:30am-11pm, Sat.-Sun. 7am-11pm; $20-55). Some cuts, such as the signature strip loin, are wheeled to your table by a waitperson, who asks how much of the loin you'd like before carving the cut and telling you the price. Back in the kitchen, it is cooked exactly the way you ordered it over charcoal coals. You'll be charged extra for accompanying vegetables.

Bistros

Chives Canadian Bistro (1537 Barrington St., 902/420-9626; daily 5-9:30pm; $23-28) is well worth searching out, and even though it's away from the touristy waterfront, you'll need a reservation. The menu revolves around seasonal ingredients and produce sourced

Italian

A truly traditional Italian restaurant in downtown Halifax is ★ **Ristorante a Mano** (Bishop's Landing, 1477 Lower Water St., 1496 Lower Water St., 902/423-0859; Mon.-Sat. 11:30am-10pm; $16-22), a bustling space with typical Italian trattoria food at very reasonable prices. The menu changes regularly, but one staple is pasta and pizza handmade daily.

In the vicinity of Ristorante a Mano but more upscale, **Da Maurizio** (1496 Lower Water St., 902/423-0859; Mon.-Sat. 5pm-10pm; $29-35) is a character-filled room within the historic brewery building. Decorated in mellow hues, its walls are lined with Italian art, the wine rack filled with thoughtfully selected bottles from around the world, and the linen-draped tables highlighted by vases of fresh flowers. The menu represents the best of northern Italian cooking, with mains such as veal delicately sautéed with lobster in a brandy and cream sauce.

Asian

Throughout downtown you'll find a smattering of good Asian restaurants. One of the best is **Cheelin** (1496 Lower Water St., 902/422-2252; Mon.-Sat. 11:30am-2:30pm and 5pm-10pm, Sun. 5pm-10pm; $15-24), within the Alexander Keith's Brewery complex. The atmosphere is informal, with chefs in an open kitchen churning out flavorful Chinese favorites. The seafood-stuffed eggplant is a unique treat.

Hamachi Steakhouse (Bishop's Landing, 1477 Lower Water St., 902/422-1600; Mon.-Sat. 11:30am-10pm, Sun. 4pm-10pm; $23-45) is a contemporary Japanese restaurant specializing in *teppan* cooking. In the center of communal tables are grills; chefs slice, dice, and then grill your choice of beef, chicken, or seafood main as you sample starters such as *niku balu* (tenderloin meatballs with pineapple-chili dipping sauce). For dessert, the Mount Fuji (a combination of brownie, ice cream, cream, and chocolate sauce) is an easy choice.

SPRING GARDEN ROAD AND VICINITY

This restaurant-lined thoroughfare begins at Barrington Street and heads uphill past the main library and the Sexton Campus of

Spring Garden Road

Dalhousie University to the Public Gardens. Downstairs in **Spring Garden Place** is one of the city's better food courts.

Cafés

Serious coffee-lovers gravitate to a restored Victorian-era home that houses **Just Us!** (5876 Spring Garden Rd., 902/423-0856; Mon.-Fri. 7am-7pm, Sat. 8am-5pm, Sun. 10am-4pm, lunches $7-10), which does an admirable job of sourcing fair-trade coffee from throughout Central America.

Just off the busy strip is **Daily Grind** (1479 Birmingham St., 902/429-6397; Mon.-Fri. 7am-10pm, Sat.-Sun. 8am-10pm; lunches $7-9), a longtime favorite with locals looking to avoid the chains. Cooked breakfasts are small, but sandwiches, hot dishes such as lasagna, and muffins are all delicious and inexpensive.

South of Spring Garden Road a few blocks, **Uncommon Grounds** (1030 South Park St., 902/404-3124; daily 7am-10pm; lunches $6-10)

at reasonable prices, consider a meal at **Minato Sushi** (1520 Queen St., 902/420-0331; Mon.-Sat. 11:30am-9pm; $12-20). Dishes such as sautéed scallops and mushrooms in butter sauce are all under $20, and *bulkokee* (sweet beef teriyaki), a Korean dish, is $17.

Bistros

Further from downtown than these previous recommendations is ★ **Saege Bistro** (5883 Spring Garden Rd., 902/429-1882; Mon.-Fri. 11:30am-2:30pm, Tues.-Fri. 4:30pm-9pm, Sat. 9:30am-10pm, Sun. 9:30am-8pm; $15-28) has a distinctly Scandinavian look and a globally inspired menu that includes lime-marinated shrimp, lobster ravioli, and a burger topped with guacamole and tomato. On weekends, brunch items such as smoked salmon eggs Benedict are served until 3pm.

Head to Uncommon Grounds for great coffee.

is very popular spot—both for its excellent coffee and university district vibe.

Casual Dining

Your Father's Moustache (5686 Spring Garden Rd., 902/423-6766; daily 10am-midnight; $14-22) is a casual favorite with a reasonably priced menu of seafood, steaks, and pasta. It's open year-round daily for lunch and dinner, and a popular brunch is served Sunday 11am-3pm.

Indian

My favorite Indian restaurant in Halifax is **Curry Village** (1569 Dresden Row, 902/429-5010; daily 10am-9:30pm; $15-22), on the north side of Spring Garden Road, toward the Citadel. This place prepares chicken tandoori, *biryanis,* lamb *vindaloo,* and other Indian dishes to order.

Asian

For no-frills Japanese and Korean cooking

Saege Bistro

NORTH OF DOWNTOWN

Cafés

A few blocks northwest of the Citadel, **Java Blend** (6027 North St., 902/423-6144; Mon.-Fri. 6:30am-6pm, Sat. 7:30am-5pm, Sun. 9am-4:30pm) has been in business as a coffee roaster since 1938. Today, they roast over 30 blends of coffee—and many locals will tell you it's the best in town.

Delis

Well worth searching out, ★ **Italian Market** (6061 Young St., 902/455-6124; Mon.-Sat. 8am-7pm, Sun. 10am-6pm; lunches $7-11) is an absolute delight. Along one side is a deli counter with premade dishes, while another side is home to desserts and drinks. The shelves are lined with goodies imported from around the world. Choose from cabbage rolls, quiche, meatloaf meatballs, sun-dried tomato-crusted chicken breasts, smoked salmon pâté, and more. Prices are reasonable, and there are a few tables at which to eat.

DARTMOUTH AND VICINITY

Ask a local where to go for the best fish and chips, and many will send you to **John's Lunch** (352 Pleasant St., 902/469-3074; daily 10am-9pm; $10-14), a simple diner within walking distance of the ferry terminal that has been dishing up popular seafood dishes since 1969. Not much has changed in the last quarter-century—seating choices include stools at the counter, vinyl booths, or picnic tables out front. Haddock is the fish of choice and is sourced daily at the market, but the deep-fried clams are also tasty.

From **Wooden Monkey** (88 Alderney Dr., 902/466-3100; Mon.-Fri. 11:30am-9pm, Sat. 11:30am-10pm; $22-26), views extend back across Halifax Harbour to downtown, a real treat when the nighttime lights of downtown are sparkling across the water. The menu is dominated by simple yet stylish dishes that will please all tastes, including vegetarians and vegans, all reasonably priced and well presented. The bacon-wrapped scallops are a good starter to share, while seafood chowder is a tasty yet inexpensive main. Wooden Monkey is on the upper floor of the Alderney Gate complex, where ferries from Halifax terminate. With ferries running until midnight, there's plenty of time to enjoy a meal before returning to your downtown accommodation.

Fisherman's Cove

At this historic fishing village, two kilometers southeast of Dartmouth alongside the Eastern Passage, it's no surprise that seafood dominates local menus. The most obvious place to eat is **Boondocks** (200 Government Wharf Rd., 902/465-3474; daily 11am-9pm; $14-24), a big, red-roofed building with a pleasant oceanfront patio. The menu offers the usual collection of seafood, including an excellent seafood chowder filled with Digby scallops, pan-seared halibut and chips, and a decadently rich lobster stew.

For a more authentic atmosphere, visit smaller places such as **Fish Basket** (100 Government Wharf Rd., 902/465-5902; Mon.-Fri. 9am-6pm, Sat. 11am-6pm; $9-14), which is primarily in business selling fresh seafood but also sells lobster sandwiches for $9.50.

Information and Services

For information on Halifax, contact **Destination Halifax** (902/422-9334 or 877/422-9334, www.destinationhalifax.com). The **Halifax Regional Municipality** website (www.halifax.ca) has general information about the city, such as festivals and events, transportation, and park programs.

TOURIST INFORMATION

Downtown

Tourism Nova Scotia (1655 Lower Water St., 902/424-4248; daily 8:30am-6pm) operates an information center along the downtown waterfront at Sackville Landing. Its shelves are filled with province-wide information, so this is the place to get help planning your travels beyond the capital.

Airport

After retrieving your bags from the luggage carousels, you'll pass right by the **Airport Visitor Information Centre** (902/873-1223; daily 9am-9pm), which is a provincially operated facility. Most questions thrown its way relate to Halifax, but the center represents the entire province.

EMERGENCY SERVICES

The city's hospital services are coordinated under the auspices of the **Queen Elizabeth II Hospital** (1796 Summer St., 902/473-3383).

Municipal **police** are assigned to Halifax and Dartmouth; in emergencies, dial 911, and for nonemergency business, call 902/490-5026. The **RCMP** can be reached by calling 911 or 902/426-1323.

ACCESS FOR TRAVELERS WITH DISABILITIES

The good news about Halifax is that its major attractions, as well as a small percentage of rooms in most major hotels, are wheelchair-accessible. Theaters and performing arts venues are also usually wheelchair-accessible. Halifax's public transit system, Metro Transit, has low-floor buses along all major routes as well as the **Access-A-Bus** program, providing wheelchair-accessible transportation on a door-to-door basis. Register at 902/490-6681.

BANKS

As Nova Scotia's capital, Halifax has banks by the dozens. **Scotiabank** (Mon.-Fri. 10am-5pm) has branches throughout the city and does not charge to convert foreign currency to Canadian dollars. The fee for cashing travelers checks is $2, so it pays to convert several checks at one time.

Hotel desks also exchange currency, but rates are more favorable at the banks.

Getting There

CAR

From Truro, it's 100 kilometers (a one-hour drive) south to Halifax along wide, divided Highway 102. From Digby, the 230-kilometer drive takes under three hours along Highway 101, which enters Halifax from the northwest.

From other Canadian provinces, you will enter Nova Scotia along the TransCanada Highway east of Sackville. From Sackville, it's around 200 kilometers (two hours) into downtown Halifax via Truro. From Charlottetown, on Prince Edward Island, allow four hours for the 330-kilometer drive to Halifax via the Confederation Bridge ($49 toll).

It's 260 kilometers (three hours) to Halifax from Moncton along Highway 104 then 102. It's 430 kilometers (4.5 hours) from Fredericton on Highway 2, 104, and 102. It's 1,230 kilometers (12 hours) from Montreal on the TransCanada Highway. It's 1,800 kilometers (18 hours) from Toronto on the TransCanada Highway.

From the United States, you can either travel up I-95 through Bangor, Maine, to New Brunswick via Moncton (480 kilometers, 4.5 hours), or catch the ferry from Portland, Maine, to Yarmouth (11 hours sailing time; adult $139, vehicle $119, children free), from where it's 310 kilometers (four-hour drive) to Halifax along Highway 103.

AIR

Halifax International Airport (YHZ, www.flyhalifax.com) is beside Highway 102, 38 kilometers north of Halifax. It is Atlantic Canada's busiest airport, handling more than 3.4 million passengers annually.

Beyond the baggage carousels are the car rental desks and an information counter specifically for helping out with airport transportation. The arrivals area is linked to the rest of the terminal by a short concourse. In between is the main concentration of food and retail shops, including a currency exchange (daily 7am-9pm); **Clearwater Seafood,** which plucks live lobsters from a tank and packs them for air travel; a bookstore; and a variety of locally themed souvenir shops. There are also a play area and wireless Internet hotspots.

The airport's website has lots of information about the airport itself, as well as general travel-planning information and a nifty virtual flight map that tracks flights in real time as they arrive and depart from Halifax.

Airport Transportation

The **Halifax Airport Express** (902/429-2029, www.halifaxairportexpress.com) runs between the airport and major downtown hotels ($22 one-way, $40 return) at least once every hour between 5am and 1am. You need reservations only when returning to the airport from your hotel.

Taxi and limousine services are available curbside in the domestic arrivals area for all arriving flights. A one-way trip to Halifax city center is $58 by taxi or limousine.

Airport Car Rental

Once you've picked up your bags from the baggage carousels, you'll find a row of check-in desks for major car rental companies immediately behind you. Airport phone numbers are **Avis** (902/429-0963), **Budget** (902/492-7553), **Enterprise** (902/873-4700), **Hertz** (902/873-2273),

National/Alamo (902/873-3505), and **Thrifty** (902/873-3527).

Along the airport access road is **Petro Canada,** so you can avoid outrageous charges for not returning the vehicle with a full tank of gas.

Parking

Short-term covered airport parking within walking distance of the terminal costs $4 per hour, to a maximum of $20 per day and $100 per week. For long-term parking, nearby **Park 'N Fly** (668 Barnes Dr., 902/873-4574, www.parknfly.ca) charges $15 per day and $75 per week, inclusive of a free ride to and from the airport. (Check the Park'N Fly website for a discount coupon.)

RAIL

Halifax is served by **VIA Rail** (416/366-8411 or 888/842-7245, www.viarail.ca) passenger trains from Montréal (22-24 hours; $160 pp). Trains run up to three times a week.

The **VIA Rail Station** is one kilometer south of downtown at the corner of Barrington and Cornwallis Streets. It's a classic old terminal with a colonnaded facade, high ceiling, and tiled floors, but it is only ever busy when a train rolls in. **Hertz** has a desk at the terminal, and a concourse links the terminal to the grand Westin hotel.

BUS

Long-distance bus services arrive and depart from the **VIA Rail Station** (corner of Barrington and Cornwallis Sts.), one kilometer south of downtown and within walking distance of HI-Halifax. The main carrier is **Maritime Bus** (902-429-2029, www.maritimebus.com), which has departures from Halifax to points throughout the province and beyond, including daily service to Wolfville (1.5 hours, $20), Moncton (4 hours, $49), and Sydney (7 hours, $70). Maritime runs as far as Quebec, from where connections can be made to Greyhound buses.

Getting Around

PUBLIC TRANSPORTATION

Metro Transit (902/490-4000, www.halifax.ca/metrotransit) buses saturate city streets; charge adult $2.50, senior and child $1.75 (exact change only) with free transfers; and operate daily 6am-midnight. Main bus stops are on Water, Barrington, Cornwallis, Cogswell, and Duke Streets, Spring Garden Road, and Gottingen Street, with service to Quinpool Road and Bayers Street. If you're at a stop waiting for a bus, dial 465 followed by the four-digit route number (marked in red at every stop) for real-time information on when the next bus will be arriving.

Ferries

Metro Transit runs the **Halifax-Dartmouth ferry** from the foot of George Street (beside Historic Properties) to Alderney Drive in Dartmouth. It is the oldest saltwater passenger service in North America, having transported its first passengers by rowboat more than 200 years ago. Today, three modern vessels ply the route in just 12 minutes. The service runs year-round, Monday-Saturday 6:30am-midnight, and June-September also on Sunday, same hours. The one-way fare is the same as by bus—adult $2.50, senior and child $1.75.

Taxi

Cabs are easiest to flag outside major hotels or transportation hubs, such as the VIA Rail Station. All rides start at $3.50, with an additional $2.65 charged for each kilometer plus $0.60 for each additional person. Taxi fares within downtown usually run around $10, while the trip between the airport and downtown is set at $53. The two main companies are **Casino Taxi** (902/429-6666) and **Yellow Cab** (902/420-0000).

DRIVING

Getting into the city is made easy by a number of major arteries that spill right into downtown. Once in the commercial core, Haligonians are painstakingly careful and slow drivers—a wise way to go, as hillside streets are steep and many roads are posted for one-way traffic. Pedestrians have the right-of-way on crosswalks. Two **bridges** link Halifax and Dartmouth, the A. Murray MacKay and the Angus L. MacDonald; the toll is $1 one-way for vehicles, free for bicyclists and pedestrians.

Downtown Parking

Metered parking costs $1.50-2 per hour but is difficult to find during business hours. Most major hotels have underground public parking, and a few multistory parking lots are scattered throughout the city core. The most convenient parking lots are along Lower Water Street, at the foot of Prince and Salter Streets, but these are also the most costly ($5 per hour). If you're staying at a downtown hotel, expect to pay up to $24 per day for parking (ask about free parking for weekend reservations).

Car Rental

Each of the major car rental companies is represented at the airport and downtown. As always, book as far in advance as possible, and use the Internet to find the best deals. Vehicles rented from downtown are generally the same price as out at the airport, but the final bill comes with fewer taxes.

South Shore

Halifax to Mahone Bay 68

Mahone Bay 72

Lunenburg 77

Lunenburg to Shelburne 86

Shelburne and Vicinity 91

Yarmouth 94

Nova Scotians must have had this region in mind when they coined the province's motto, "So Much to Sea." The crashing Atlantic lays itself out in foaming breakers along the deeply scored Atlantic coastline that extends from Lunenburg to Yarmouth. It's a three-hour drive between these two towns, but you'll want at least two days and preferably more to explore the hidden corners of this quintessential corner of Nova Scotia. The seaports and towns follow one another, like a series of glossy, life-size picture postcards. There are those that outsiders will know by name—Peggy's Cove, Mahone Bay, and Lunenburg—but one of the joys of touring the South Shore is discovering your own Peggy's Cove.

The South Shore ends at Yarmouth, where the Atlantic meets the Bay of Fundy. Locals say the Vikings came ashore a thousand years ago and inscribed the boulder that now sits at the Yarmouth County Museum's front door. Yarmouth's ragged coastline impressed early explorer Samuel de Champlain, who named the seaport's outermost peninsula Cap Forchu ("Forked Cape"). Like the Vikings, Champlain arrived and departed, as do thousands of visitors driving around the South Shore.

PLANNING YOUR TIME

It is possible to visit the best-known towns along this stretch of coast in a day and return to Halifax, but don't. More realistically, plan a day in each place that interests you. As elsewhere in Nova Scotia, dining at its best is superb, and the region's specialty is its abundance of top-notch country inns with public dining rooms. Many lodgings are in historic houses and mansions converted to country inns and in categories best described as better, best, and beautiful. But it is the towns themselves that are this region's highlight. Even with just one week to explore the entire province, plan to spend at least one night in **Mahone Bay** or **Lunenburg,** the former recognized for its three waterfront churches and the latter a UNESCO World Heritage

---

Previous: Summerville Beach; Peggy's Cove. **Above:** Fisheries Museum of the Atlantic.

Look for ★ to find recommended
sights, activities, dining, and lodging.

Highlights

© AVALON TRAVEL

★ **Peggy's Cove:** Nova Scotia's most famous village is a photogenic gem you won't want to miss (page 68).

★ **Mahone Bay Churches:** Lining up along the waterfront, three historic churches reflect across the waters of charming Mahone Bay (page 73).

★ **Pirate Festival:** In early August, Mahone Bay fills with "pirates" to celebrate the town's link to the treasures of nearby Oak Island (page 74).

★ **Historic Downtown Lunenburg:** Designated a World Heritage Site by UNESCO, Lunenburg is as interesting as it is charming (page 79).

★ **Blue Rocks:** A world away from the crowds of Peggy's Cove, this picture-perfect fishing village clings to the shore of a rocky harbor (page 80).

★ *Bluenose II:* Lunenburg is a wooden-ships kind of town, and what better way to tour the harbor than aboard one (page 81)?

★ **Crescent Beach:** Just a short detour from the busy South Shore highway, this is my favorite beach among many choices south of Halifax (page 87).

★ **Shelburne Historic District:** A wonderful collection of 200-year-old wooden buildings brings the shipbuilding era to life (page 91).

South Shore

Ferry to Portland, Maine

Yarmouth
Hebron
CAPE FORCHU LIGHT STATION
Port Maitland
Cape St. Mary's
Mavillette
Meteghan
Weymouth
Westport
Tiverton
Church Point
Gilbert's Cove
St. Mary's Bay
Mink Cove
Sandy Cove
Centreville
Digby
Smith Cove
Annapolis
Upper Clements
South Milford
Maitland Bridge
Kejimkujik National Park
Lake Rossignol
Ellenwood Lake Provincial Park
Cape Sable Island
Barrington
Ingomar
Sand Hills Beach Provincial Park
The Islands Provincial Park
Shelburne
SHELBURNE HISTORIC DISTRICT
Jordan Bay
Port Joli
White Point
Liverpool
Summerville Beach Provincial Park
Kejimkujik National Park Seaside Adjunct
Mersey Harbour
Risser's Beach Provincial Park
LaHave Islands
CRESCENT BEACH
Ovens Natural Park
BLUE ROCKS
Lunenburg
BLUENOSE II
Mahone Bay
MAHONE BAY CHURCHES
PIRATE FESTIVAL
HISTORIC DOWNTOWN
Bridgewater
LaHave River
Big Tancook Island
Mahone Bay
Chester
East Chester
Hubbards
Black Point
Head of St. Margaret's Bay
St. Margaret's Bay
PEGGY'S COVE
Prospect
HALIFAX

ATLANTIC OCEAN

0 15 mi
0 15 km

© AVALON TRAVEL

1, 101, 217, 334, 335, 3, 309, 103, 203, 340, 8, 208, 210, 10, 331, 332, 12, 14, 329, 333

Site. While the detour to **Peggy's Cove** is almost de rigueur, you should work into your itinerary less publicized villages, such as **Blue Rocks,** near Lunenburg. Taking part in two highlights of the South Shore involves some planning—Mahone Bay's **Pirate Festival** requires a visit in early August, while a sailing trip on the *Bluenose II* calls for reservations.

Travelers on a tight schedule make Lunenburg a turnaround point, but the rest of the South Shore is well worth exploring and sets you up for exploring the Fundy Coast. This stretch of coast is dotted with coastal provincial parks and hideaways such as **Crescent Beach,** which is a long stretch of white sand. The major historic attraction between Lunenburg and Yarmouth is the **Shelburne Historic District.** If you are planning to circumnavigate southwestern Nova Scotia, Shelburne is an ideal location for an overnight stay. Couple that with a night in Lunenburg or Mahone Bay to give yourself three days for the South Shore—not enough time to see everything, but a chance to spend quality time visiting each of the highlights.

Halifax to Mahone Bay

From downtown Halifax, it's 105 kilometers (1.5 hours) along Highway 103 to Lunenburg, but for the most scenic views and interesting insights, forget the expressway and drive the secondary coastal routes. The best-known village in all of Nova Scotia is Peggy's Cove, a 40-minute drive south from downtown Halifax along Highway 333. Meanwhile, Highway 103 takes a direct route across to St. Margaret's Bay, from where secondary Highway 3 passes the charming towns set around Mahone Bay and its islands. One of these, Oak Island, looms large in the world of treasure-hunting legends—pirates are believed to have buried incalculable booty on it in the 1500s.

★ PEGGY'S COVE

Atlantic Canada's most photographed site is a 40-minute drive southwest from Halifax, and the place is everything its fans say it is. With the houses of the tiny fishing village clinging like mussels to weathered granite boulders at the edge of St. Margaret's Bay, the Atlantic lathering against the boulder-bound coast, the fishing boats moored in the small cove, and the white octagonal lighthouse overlooking it all, the scene is the quintessence of the Nova Scotia coast.

Sightseers clog the village during the daytime (to miss the worst of the crowds, get there before 9am or after 5pm), wandering along the wharves and around the weathered granite boulders surrounding the photogenic lighthouse. Peggy's Cove has a population of just 60 souls, so don't come expecting the

the lighthouse at Peggy's Cove

Halifax to Mahone Bay

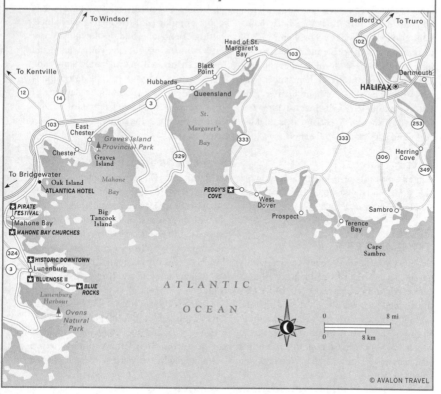

© AVALON TRAVEL

services of a tourist town. The village has just one B&B, a restaurant, and the **deGarthe Gallery** (902/823-2256; mid-May-mid-Oct. daily 9am-5pm; free). The latter, along the main road through town, displays the work of Finnish-born artist William deGarthe, whose stunning nautically themed oil paintings grace galleries the world over. Behind the gallery, deGarthe sculpted a 30-meter-long frieze on a granite outcropping. It depicts 32 of the seaside village's fishermen and families.

The town received worldwide attention in September 1998, when a Swissair MD-11 jetliner bound from New York City to Geneva crashed in shallow waters off the coast here, killing all 229 people aboard. A small memorial overlooks the ocean along Highway 333, two kilometers west of the village.

Accommodations

The only accommodation has just five guest rooms, so book well ahead if you'd like to stay overnight in this delightful village. At the head of the actual cove, ★ **Peggy's Cove Bed and Breakfast** (17 Church Rd., 902/823-2265 or 877/725-8732, www.peggyscovebb.com; $145 s or d including breakfast) has well-furnished guest rooms with wireless Internet, a living area, a dining room, and a deck promising magnificent views across the cove. It's open year-round; rates are discounted to $95-115 in winter.

Food

The road through the village ends at the **Sou'wester Restaurant** (178 Peggy's Point Rd., 902/823-2561; June-Aug. daily 8am-8:30pm, Sept.-May daily 9am-8pm; $9-20), a cavernous room with a menu designed to appeal to the tourist crowd. And as the only place in town to eat, attract them it does—try to plan your meal before 10am or after 5pm. The menu does have a distinct maritime flavor, with dishes such as fish cakes, pickled beets, and eggs offered in the morning.

Getting There

Peggy's Cove is about 45 kilometers southwest of Halifax, on Highway 333. The drive takes about 40 minutes.

PEGGY'S COVE TO CHESTER

Highway 333 beyond Peggy's Cove winds north past a string of small fishing villages before reaching Highway 3 (Highway 103, the divided highway along the South Shore, takes an inland route, so turn at the older Highway 3). Rather than promising places at which you simply must stop, this route that lazily rounds St. Margaret's Bay is simply an enjoyable drive.

Continue west to **Hubbards,** where the ★ **Trellis Café** (22 Main St., 902/857-1188; daily 8am-9pm; $16-25) is a casual restaurant with colorful decor and occasional live entertainment on weekends. The namesake trellised deck is a good spot for lunch on warmer days. Most mains are less than $20, but you can spend less by ordering a combination of starters, such as seafood chowder and Caesar salad.

Beyond Hubbards, **Queensland Beach** is a popular stretch of sand with safe but chilly swimming and a freshwater lagoon that attracts lots of birdlife.

CHESTER AND VICINITY

The bayside town of Chester, first settled by New Englanders in 1759, lies at the northern head of Mahone Bay. Its first hotel was built in 1827, and the town, with its ideal sailing conditions and many vacation homes, has been a popular summer retreat ever since. Getting oriented beyond the downtown core can be confusing, so start your visit at the **Tourist Information Centre** (20 Smith Rd., 902/275-4616; May-early Oct. daily 10am-5pm), which is on the Mahone Bay side of town (coming into town from Halifax, continue up the hill to the right of the downtown turnoff).

Sights and Recreation

Most visitors to Chester are content to browse through downtown shops and wander lazily along the Front Harbour waterfront.

An easy excursion is to **Big Tancook Island** (adult $5.50, cash only) via ferries departing regularly from Front Harbour. Big Tancook is mostly residential, but it's a pleasant trip across, and walking parks lace the island.

Dating to 1914, **Chester Golf Club** (Golf Course Rd., Prescott Point, 902/275-4543) is an old-style golf course that opens up along the oceanfront to offer sweeping views on holes lapped by the water. Greens fees are a good value at $63.

Chester Playhouse (22 Pleasant St., 902/275-3933 or 800/363-7529, www.chesterplayhouse.ca) hosts some form of live entertainment weekly between March and December. Its Summer Theatre Festival draws professional talents in July and August. Past seasons have included musicals, Broadway-style revues, comedy improv, puppet shows, and children's programs.

Accommodations and Camping

The most noteworthy of Chester's inns is ★ **Mecklenburgh Inn** (78 Queen St., 902/275-4638, www.mecklenburghinn. ca; May-Dec.; $105-165 s, $125-165 d), a 120-year-old sea captain's home that has been given a bohemian-chic look. Guests tend

Chester

SOUTH SHORE

HALIFAX TO MAHONE BAY

Map labels: To Mahone Bay and Highway 103, HADDON HILL RD, TOURIST INFORMATION CENTRE, Stanford Lake, CHESTER COMMONS RD, To Graves Island Provincial Park, Halifax, and Hubbards, NORTH ST, Chester Connection Trail, WALKER RD, MAIN ST, VALLEY RD, DUKE ST, To Chester Golf Club, Back Harbour, TREMONT ST, GRANITE ST, VICTORIA ST, PRINCE ST, CENTRAL ST, KING ST, QUEEN ST, REGENT ST, BRUNSWICK ST, PIG LOOP RD, CHANDLER RD, MECKLENBURGH INN, POST OFFICE, UNION ST, Front Harbour, NAUSS POINT RD, JULIEN'S BAKERY, CHESTER PLAYHOUSE, WATER ST, PLEASANT ST, KIWI CAFÉ, FERRY TERMINAL, Mahone Bay, SOUTH ST, Ferry to Big Tancook Island, PENINSULA RD, 0 200 yds, 0 200 m, © AVALON TRAVEL

to gather on the wide veranda to watch the world of Chester go by, and then, after dinner at a local restaurant, gravitate to the comfortable couches set around two fireplaces in the living room. Three of the four rooms have en suite bathrooms with claw-foot tubs, while the fourth has a private bathroom down the hall. A big breakfast of pancakes or smoked salmon eggs Benedict will set you up for a day of sightseeing.

Signposted from Highway 3, three kilometers northeast of Chester, **Graves Island Provincial Park** (mid-May-mid-Sept.; $26) covers a small island connected to the mainland by a causeway. An open area at a high point of the island allows for pull-through RVs, while tent sites are scattered around the surrounding forest. If you're just visiting for the day, plan on a picnic at the waterfront day-use area just across the causeway.

Food

In downtown Chester, the **Kiwi Café** (19 Pleasant St., 902/275-1492; daily 8am-5pm; $8-25) offers simple and healthy breakfasts and lunches along with a wide range of hot drinks, including chai tea and creamy hot chocolate. It's painted a cheery blue and kiwifruit green,

The bright and cheery Kiwi Café is a great place for a light meal in Chester.

with outside tables down one side. Around the corner and up the hill, **Julien's Bakery** (43 Queen St., 902/275-2324; Tues.-Sat. 8am-5pm, Sun. 8am-4pm; $7-11) serves delectable fresh breads, pastries, and desserts, as well as more substantial healthy cooking.

Getting There

Chester is just off Highway 103 (take Exit 8), about 70 kilometers (45 minutes) from Halifax. It's around 70 kilometers from Peggy's Cove via Highway 333 and Highway 103.

Mahone Bay

The town of Mahone Bay (pop. 1,000), on the island-speckled bay of the same name, is one of the most charming in all of Nova Scotia. The town's prosperous past is mirrored in its architecture, with Gothic Revival, Classic Revival, and Italianate styles in evidence. Many of these buildings have been converted to restaurants specializing in seafood and shops selling the work of local artisans. The distinctive bayside trio of 19th-century churches reflected in the still water here has become one of the most photographed scenes in Nova Scotia.

SIGHTS AND EVENTS

Most visitors to Mahone Bay are quite happy to spend their time admiring the architecture, browsing through the shops, and enjoying lunch at one of the many cafés. If you are interested in the town's architectural highlights, ask for the three walking-tour brochures at the museum.

Mahone Bay Settler's Museum

Inside a 150-year-old wooden house, the **Mahone Bay Settler's Museum** (578 Main St., 902/624-6263; June-early Sept. Tues.-Sun. 10am-4pm; donation) describes the town's 250-year history. One room is dedicated to settlement of the area in the mid-1700s by German, French, and Swiss Protestants and the story of how they were enticed by the British government's offer of free land, farm equipment, and a year's "victuals." You'll also learn about the importance of shipbuilding to the area, which thrived in a dozen shipyards from the 1850s to the early part of the 20th century, and you can admire historic arts and crafts.

Mahone Bay

*Map labels:*
KEDY'S INLET CAFÉ
3 To Chester and Halifax
VISITOR INFORMATION CENTRE
OAKLAND RD
CLEARWAY ST
TRINITY UNITED CHURCH
MAHONE BAY CHURCHES
EDGEWATER ST
FISHERMAN'S DAUGHTER B&B
ST. JOHN'S LUTHERAN CHURCH
ST. JAMES ANGLICAN CHURCH
To Bridgewater
Mahone
W MAIN ST
MEDICAL CENTRE
PARISH ST
ORCHARD ST
BISCUIT EATER
JO ANN'S DELI
Bay
SUTTLES & SEAWINDS
CALVARY TEMPLE PENTECOSTAL
BANDSTAND
TEA BREWERY
AMOS PEWTER
CLAIRMONT ST
POST OFFICE
MAHONE BAY TRADING COMPANY
SETTLER'S MUSEUM
MAIN ST
PIRATE FESTIVAL
PLEASANT ST
FAIRMONT HOUSE B&B
Town Wharf
UNITED BAPTIST CHURCH
3
To Kip & Kaboodle and Lunenburg
FAIRMONT ST
FAUXBURG RD
0 200 yds
0 200 m
© AVALON TRAVEL

★ Mahone Bay Churches

From the flower-bedecked bandstand on Main Street, three churches can be seen shoulder to shoulder across the water. The oldest (and farthest from this viewpoint) is the **Trinity United Church** (Edgewater St., 902-624-9287), which dates to 1861 and was dragged by oxen to its current site in 1885. **St. John's Lutheran** (Edgewater St., 902/624-9660) is a symmetrical wooden structure standing in the middle of the three. Right on the corner is the Gothic Revival **St. James Anglican Church** (Edgewater St., 902/624-8614). This is the only one of the three open for tours (July-Aug. Thurs.-Sat. 11am-3pm).

Music at the Three Churches is a series of classical music concerts hosted by the churches on select Friday nights through summer. The cost is adult $15, child free. Visit www.threechurches.com or check with the information center for a schedule and pay at the door.

If you walk along the waterfront beyond the information center, you'll see a different angle on the churches, as well as two others. Completed in 1875, the white spire you see rising above the trees is the **United Baptist Church** (56 Maple St., 902/624-9124), open for services Sunday at 11am. The **Calvary Temple Pentecostal** (at the traffic circle where Main and Edgewater Sts. meet, 902/624-8420) opens its doors Sunday at 7pm for hymn singing.

★ Pirate Festival

Mahone Bay's annual **Pirate Festival** (902/624-0348, http://mahonebayregatta. wordpress.com) centers on the Town Wharf the weekend closest to August 1. This annual event draws thousands of spectators, who gather to celebrate the days that the bay was a favorite pirate haunt. Visitors take part in workshops, marvel over boatbuilding demonstrations, listen to tales from the sea, and cheer on competitors in boat-race series that vary from classic old yachts to floating contraptions constructed in less than four hours. A parade of pirates, live entertainment, and the re-creation of a boat-launching using oxen are other highlights. Best of all, everything is free.

SHOPPING

Many artists are attracted to Mahone Bay for its scenic setting, and the main street has developed into a hub for shoppers. Most shops are open from late spring to Christmas.

At **Amos Pewter** (589 Main St., 902/624-9547), you can watch artists at work as they

The Mystery of Oak Island

In 1795, on Oak Island, a small island in Mahone Bay, a young man came upon an area where the forest had been cut away. Besides the stumps, he found a large forked limb with an old tackle block and a "treenail," and the ground nearby was sunken in a pit. His first thought would have been buried treasure, as the bay was a known haunt for pirates such as "Captain" William Kidd, Sir Henry Morgan, and Edward "Blackbeard" Teach 100 years previously.

After hours of digging, Daniel McGinnis and two farmer friends reached a depth of 10 feet and hit wood. It turned out, however, not to be the rotted lid of a treasure chest but rather a platform of logs. So the men pressed on, convinced that the treasure lay just below. At a depth of 25 feet, digging became difficult, and they abandoned the effort.

The first organized dig occurred in 1804, when a boat loaded with equipment arrived. Another log platform was uncovered at the 30-foot level, and others 40 and then 50 feet from the surface. At 60 feet, the men uncovered a layer of coconut fiber, which hinted at cargo from warmer climes. At the 90-foot level, a large slab of granite (which was later verified as being from Europe) was uncovered. The next morning, the men returned to the pit to find it had filled with water. They had no success pumping the water out, so the search was halted until the following spring.

In 1805 a second shaft was dug, and at the 100-foot mark a horizontal tunnel was dug in the hope of reaching the treasure, but this search too was abandoned. It would be another 40 years before the next serious attempt was made to retrieve whatever lay deep below Oak Island. While the secondary shafts filled with water only when linked to the original pit, it was noted that the level of water in all three shafts rose and fell with that of the tide. This deepened the mystery even further, but what the men found next amazed everyone present. Along the adjacent bay, just below the low-tide mark, were five drains that, it was later found, converged on a single tunnel. While it was understood that this simple manmade flooding system had been put in place after the treasure pit had been dug, this didn't help solve the mystery. Nor did it help the next round of investors, who spent the summer of 1863 in a futile attempt to reach below the 100-foot level, or the numerous other treasure seekers who attempted to get to the bottom of the pit during the next 140 years.

The saga has cost six lives, left many investors broke, and created numerous feuds between island property owners. Two treasure hunters, Dan Blankenship and Fred Nolan, spent a combined 100 years trying to outsmart those who designed the "Money Pit" many centuries ago. In 2005, Blankenship, who had sole road access to the island via a causeway, sold his share of the island to the government of Nova Scotia in the hopes that it would be opened to tourism. Incredibly, one of the world's great mysteries and longest treasure hunts continues to this day.

Mahone Bay's photogenic churches

cast, spin, and finish pewter pieces. Tea connoisseurs will be in their element at the **Tea Brewery** (525 Main St., 902/624-0566), while up the hill from the Tea Brewery, **Suttles and Seawinds** (466 Main St., 902/624-8375) sells stylish but colorful clothing.

ACCOMMODATIONS

Through summer, especially on weekends, demand is high for a limited number of rooms, so plan accordingly and book as far in advance as possible.

$50-100

Mahone Bay is home to one of Nova Scotia's only privately operated backpacker lodges, ★ **Kip and Kaboodle** (9466 Hwy. 3, Mader's Cove, 902/531-5494 or 866/549-4522, www.kiwikaboodle.com; dorms $30, $69 s or d), which is three kilometers from the center

Mahone Bay Pirate Festival

one of the many shops along Mahone Bay's main street

of town toward Lunenburg. It's small, with facilities to match, but everything is well maintained, including a communal kitchen, living area, and outdoor pool. Other amenities include a barbecue and wireless Internet access. Rates include linen and a light breakfast.

Opposite the Town Wharf, you can sit on the veranda of **Fairmont House B&B** (654 Main St., 902/624-8089, www.fairmonthouse. com; $95-165 s or d) and watch the world of Mahone Bay go by. A local shipbuilder built this Gothic Revival home in 1857, and it was converted to a B&B in 1991. In the ensuing years, its exterior has been given a coat of stately blue paint, and three guest rooms have been outfitted in stylish colored themes. All rooms have en suite bathrooms, air-conditioning, and niceties such as hair dryers and irons. Downstairs is a library with board games and a TV. Rates include a continental breakfast.

$100-200

Nestled amid the famous three churches is ★ **Fisherman's Daughter B&B** (97 Edgewater St., 902/624-0660, www.fishermans-daughter.com; $110-135 s or d). Built in 1840 by a local shipbuilder, the home is understated but shows a restrained Gothic Revival

style. A couple of the four guest rooms have funky layouts (such as beds nestled under the eaves), but this adds to the charm. Throw in a host of modern amenities and a full breakfast to make this place an excellent choice.

A few kilometers north of Mahone Bay back toward Chester, **Atlantica Oak Island Resort** (off Hwy. 103 at 36 Treasure Dr., 800/565-5075, www.atlanticaoakisland.com; $179-350 s or d) is one of the province's only full-service resorts. Located right on the water and overlooking mystery-filled Oak Island, it offers indoor and outdoor pools, kayak rentals, boat tours, tennis courts, mini-golf, a children's program (summer only), and a restaurant with tables that spill out onto a huge ocean-facing deck. The main building holds standard guest rooms (some with balconies and ocean views), modern condos overlook the marina, and down a gravel road are two-bedroom cottages. The latter are right on the ocean, and each has a fire pit and picnic table out front.

FOOD

Mahone Bay's main street has a smattering of cafés, but most close in the late afternoon.

With a bag of carrots serving as a counterweight on the front door, ★ **Jo Ann's**

Atlantica Oak Island Resort

Deli (9 Edgewater St., 902/624-6305; late May-Oct. daily 9am-7pm) is a welcoming food shop filled with goodies. Locals come for organic produce, but everyone comes out with something—gourmet sandwiches, filled bagels, oatmeal cakes, brownies, homemade jams and preserves, and more. If you're planning a picnic, this is the place to get everything together.

More of a restaurant than a café, ★ **Kedy's Inlet Cafe** (249 Edgewater St., 902/531-3030; Mon.-Thurs. 11:30am-4pm, Fri.-Sun. 11:30am-8pm; $17-27) sits at the head of the bay, a 10-minute waterfront walk from downtown and with a classic view of all five Mahone Bay churches and tables on a stone patio perfect for warmer weather. Most mains are under $20, including almond-crusted salmon and a wide range of pastas. Leave room for a slice of the delicious mud cake.

INFORMATION AND SERVICES

The **Visitor Information Centre** (165 Edgewater St., 902/624-6151; summer Mon.-Sat. 9am-5pm, Sun. 11am-5pm) is in a small building just before you reach the first church.

GETTING THERE

Mahone Bay is about 30 kilometers (20 minutes) from Chester. You can get there via Highway 103 or Highway 3. From Halifax, follow Highway 103 to Exit 10. From there, Mahone Bay is a short drive south. Allow just over an hour for this 80-kilometer trip.

Lunenburg

Lunenburg (pop. 2,300) lies about equidistant between Halifax and Shelburne off Highway 103. Sited on a hilly peninsula between two harbors, this is one of the most attractive towns in Nova Scotia, with a wealth of beautiful homes painted in a crayon box of bold primary colors. In 1991 Lunenburg's Old Town was designated a national historic district, and in December 1995 the town received the ultimate honor when UNESCO designated it a World Heritage Site—one of only two cities in North America to enjoy

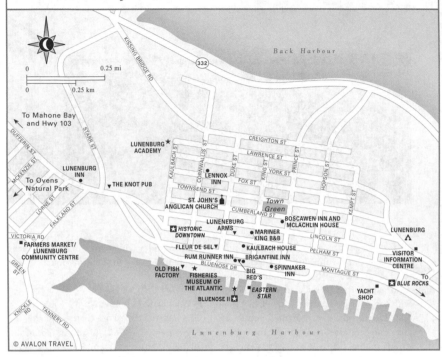

Lunenburg

Back Harbour

0   0.25 mi

0   0.25 km

To Mahone Bay
and Hwy 103

DUFFERIN ST

STARR ST

KISSING BRIDGE RD

332

LUNENBURG
ACADEMY

CREIGHTON ST

LAWRENCE ST

KAULBACH ST

CORNWALLIS ST

DUKE ST

KING ST

YORK ST

PRINCE ST

HOPSON ST

MCKENZIE ST

LUNENBURG
INN

To Ovens
Natural Park

THE KNOT PUB

LENNOX
INN

FOX ST

TOWNSEND ST

LORNE ST

FALKLAND ST

KAULBACH ST

ST. JOHN'S
ANGLICAN CHURCH

CUMBERLAND ST

Town
Green

KEMPT ST

VICTORIA RD

HISTORIC
DOWNTOWN

LUNENEBURG
ARMS

BOSCAWEN INN AND
MCLACHLIN HOUSE

LINCOLN ST

LUNENBURG

FARMERS MARKET/
LUNENBURG
COMMUNITY CENTRE

GREEN ST

FLEUR DE SEL

RUM RUNNER INN

MARINER
KING B&B

KAULBACH HOUSE

PELHAM ST

BRIGANTINE INN

VISITOR
INFORMATION
CENTRE

OLD FISH
FACTORY

BLUENOSE DR

FISHERIES
MUSEUM OF
THE ATLANTIC

BIG
RED'S

SPINNAKER
INN

MONTAGUE ST

To

BLUE ROCKS

BLUENOSE II

EASTERN
STAR

YACHT
SHOP

KNICKLE RD

TANNERY RD

Lunenburg Harbour

© AVALON TRAVEL

that status (the other is Québec City). More recently, in 2005, the provincial government stepped in and bought a chunk of waterfront buildings and wharves, saving them from development that would have taken away from the town's well-preserved history.

History

To understand what the fuss is all about, you have to go back in time a couple of centuries. Protestant German, Swiss, and French immigrants, recruited by the British to help stabilize their new dominion, settled the town in 1753; their influence is still apparent in the town's architectural details. With its excellent harbor—a protected inner arm of the Atlantic embraced by two long, curving peninsulas— Lunenburg became one of Nova Scotia's premier fishing ports and shipbuilding centers in the 19th century. In 1921, the famous schooner *Bluenose* was built here. The 49-meter fishing vessel won the International Fisherman's Trophy race that same year, and for the next 18 years it remained the undefeated champion of the Atlantic fleets. The ship has become the proud symbol of the province, and its image is embossed on the back of the Canadian dime.

Today, the fishing industry that fostered the town's growth and boatbuilding reputation is comatose, and the Atlantic fisheries are mere shadows of their former selves. But here in Lunenburg, the townspeople carry on the shipbuilding and shipfitting skills of their ancestors. The port is still known as a tall ship mecca, and big multimasted sailing ships, old and new alike from around the world, continue to put in here for repairs, shipfitting, or provisions—whatever excuse the owners can come up with. Underneath the tourist glitz, the community pride in this tradition runs strong and deep, and the town's international reputation among mariners remains formidable. Strike up a conversation with a local about sailing ships and see what happens.

★ HISTORIC DOWNTOWN

The port's oldest part is set on the hillside overlooking the harbor. The nine blocks of **Old Town,** designated a World Heritage Site by UNESCO, rise steeply from the water, and the village green spreads across the center. Bluenose Drive, the narrow lane along the harbor, and Montague Street, a block uphill, define the main sightseeing area. A mesh of one-way streets connects Old Town with the newer area built with shipbuilding profits. One of the pleasures of Lunenburg is strolling the residential and commercial streets, admiring the town's many meticulously preserved architectural gems. At the northern end of the harbor is the **Scotia Trawler Shipyard,** where the *Bluenose* was built. This shipyard, 16 other properties, and most of the wharves are off-limits, but the long-term plan is that the holdings will be opened to the public.

Fisheries Museum of the Atlantic

The spacious bright-red **Fisheries Museum of the Atlantic** (68 Bluenose Dr., 902/634-4794; mid-May-mid-Oct. daily 9:30am-5:30pm, adult $10, senior $7, child $3) boasts a trove of artifacts and exhibits on shipbuilding, seafaring, rum-running, and marine biology. This thoroughly fascinating museum engages the visitor with demonstrations of fish filleting, lobster-trap construction, dory building, net mending, and other maritime arts. Inside are aquariums, tanks of touchable marine life, a gallery of ship models, full-size fishing vessels from around Atlantic Canada, a theater, a restaurant, and a gift shop. Tied up at the wharf outside are the fishing schooner *Theresa E. Connor,* built in Lunenburg in 1938; the steel-hulled trawler *Cape Sable,* an example of the sort of vessel that made the former obsolete; the *Royal Wave,* a Digby scallop dragger; and, when it's in its home port, the *Bluenose II.* All the vessels can be boarded and explored.

St. John's Anglican Church

St. John's Anglican Church (Cumberland and Cornwallis Sts., 902/634-4994; early

Lunenburg's Old Town is a UNESCO World Heritage Site.

St. John's Anglican Church

June-Sept. daily 11am-7pm; free) stood for almost 250 years. In 2001, at the time the second-oldest church in Canada, it was destroyed by fire. It has now been rebuilt and can be visited on volunteer-led tours.

Lunenburg Academy

High above the port and surrounded by parkland, the imposing **Lunenburg Academy** (97 Kaulbach St.) is easily spotted from afar. Dating to 1885, this black-and-white wooden building, with its mansard roof and worn wooden stairways, was originally a prestigious high school. Today, it is the local elementary school, but it remains one of the oldest academies in Canada.

OTHER SIGHTS
★ Blue Rocks

Follow any of Lunenburg's downtown streets eastbound to link with a road that leads eight kilometers to **Blue Rocks,** toward the end of the peninsula. This tiny fishing village is set along a jagged coastline wrapped with blue-gray slate and sandstone, and the combination of color and texture will inspire photographers. Blue Rocks has no official attractions or services. Instead, drive to the end of the road, from where you need to explore on foot to get the full effect of a part of Nova Scotia far removed from touristy Lunenburg and Peggy's Cove. The shoreline is littered with boats and fishing gear, such as nets and traps in various states of repair, while simple but colorful homes cling to the rocky foreshore.

Ovens Natural Park

A 15-minute drive south of Lunenburg on Highway 332, spectacular sea caves have been scooped out of the coastal cliffs. Early prospectors discovered veins of gold embedded in the slate and white quartz cliffs, sparking a small gold rush in 1861. During the following several decades, the cliffs surrendered 15,500 grams of the precious metal, while the Cunard family, of shipping fame, had the beach sand transported to England to retrieve the gold. Today, **Ovens Natural Park** (902/766-4621, adult $8, senior and child $4) is privately owned, combining camping, cabins, hiking trails, and a restaurant on a 75-hectare site. Below the main parking lot, visitors can try their hand at panning for gold along Cunard's Beach. A trail leads along the sea cliffs and into one of the "ovens," and you can jump aboard an inflatable boat to get a sea-level view of the caves.

Blue Rocks

RECREATION
★ Bluenose II

To immerse yourself fully in the Lunenburg experience, set sail aboard the *Bluenose II* (902/634-8483 or 877/441-0347, www.bluenose.novascotia.ca), an exact replica of the famous sailing ship. She underwent multi-year restorations from 2010 through to 2014 to return her to her former glory.

When not in Halifax or visiting other Canadian ports, the *Bluenose II* can be found here at her home berth, outside the Fisheries Museum. Rather than separating you from the maritime experience with cushy reclining seats, acrylic windows, and a cocktail lounge, the *Bluenose II* takes you to sea as a sailor. Cruising out of the harbor under a fresh breeze—the sails snapping taut and the hull slicing through the chilly waters—you'll begin to understand and actually feel the history and lifeblood of Lunenburg.

When in Lunenburg, she departs twice daily (9:30am and 1pm; adult $45, child $25) for a two-hour harbor cruise. A total of 75 spots are offered on each sailing. Of these, 40 can be reserved through the phone numbers or website. The remaining 35 are offered on a first-come, first-served basis from the booth at the entrance to the Fisheries Museum, 90 minutes before departure. Tickets are always in high demand, so making a reservation well in advance is essential.

Other Boat Tours

The *Bluenose II* isn't always in port, and when she is, tickets sell fast. An excellent alternative is the *Eastern Star,* operated by **Star Charters** (waterfront, 902/634-3535, www.novascotiasailing.com; adult $26-30, child $12-16). The *Eastern Star* is a character-imbued 48-foot wooden ketch tended by an amiable and knowledgeable crew intent on perpetuating the seafaring tradition that put Lunenburg on the map. The *Eastern Star* makes four 90-minute cruises a day June-October, with a two-hour sunset cruise added in July and August.

Lunenburg Whale Watching Tours (902/527-7175; adult $53, child $32) depart Government Wharf May-October four times daily. While whales are definitely the highlight, regular sightings are also made of sunfish, turtles, dolphins, seals, and puffins.

ENTERTAINMENT AND EVENTS
Nightlife

The seaport is usually quiet evenings and Sundays. Locals frequent **The Knot Pub** (4

The Famous *Bluenose*

Featured on Nova Scotian license plates and the back of the Canadian dime, the original *Bluenose* was launched from Lunenburg in 1921. Built as a fishing schooner, she was designed specifically for competing in the International Fishermen's Trophy, a racing series that pitted working ships from Canada and the United States against one another. Much to the joy of Canadians, the *Bluenose* won every racing competition she entered, while also serving as a working fishing boat. But by 1942, the era of the sail-powered fishing industry was giving way to that of modern steel-hulled trawlers, and the great *Bluenose* was sold to carry freight in the West Indies. Four years later, she foundered and was lost on a Haitian reef.

The ship herself was black. The name is thought to have originated from local fishermen, who, when conditions were cold and wet, would wipe their noses with their blue mittens, causing the dye to run.

In July 1963, the *Bluenose II* was re-created from the plans of the original and launched at Lunenburg. Some of the same craftspeople who had built the first *Bluenose* even participated in her construction.

Dufferin St., 902/634-3334; daily noon-11pm), a comfortable and lively place where you can get "knotwurst" and kraut with your draught beer. Up from the harbor, the **Lunenburg Arms** (94 Pelham St., 902/640-4040, daily 11am-close) has a lounge bar with tables that spill out onto a quiet patio.

Performing Arts

Drama, dance, puppet shows, children's theater, and music performances regularly take place at **Pearl Theatre** (37 Hall St., 902/634-1987). **Lunenburg Opera House** (290 Lincoln St., 902/640-6500) hosts gigs by musicians from throughout Atlantic Canada. Cover charges are up to $20.

Lunenburg Folk Harbour Festival

For four days from the second Thursday in August, a roster of traditional, roots, and contemporary folk musicians come together for the **Lunenburg Folk Harbour Festival**

(902/634-3180, www.folkharbour.com). They perform under a tent atop Blockhouse Hill, at the Opera House, in the downtown bandstand, and out on the wharf. Many performances are free, with big-name acts under the big tent costing $20.

SHOPPING

The **farmers market** at Lunenburg Community Centre (corner of Victoria Rd. and Green St.; July-Oct. Thurs. 8am-noon) lures crowds for fresh produce, smoked meats, and crafts at the former railroad depot grounds; wares are high quality and priced accordingly.

Nautical gifts are available at the **Yacht Shop** (280 Montague St., 902/634-4331), which is also a full-service marine-supply center, and at the nonprofit *Bluenose II* **Company Store** (121 Bluenose Dr., 902/634-8483), which sells all manner of *Bluenose* clothing, gifts, and art to support preservation of the vessel.

ACCOMMODATIONS AND CAMPING

Whatever Mahone Bay may lack in accommodation is more than made up for in Lunenburg, where more than 60 B&Bs—more than Halifax, which has more than 100 times the population—clog the historic streets. You should still try to make reservations ahead of time in summer, but be prepared for an answering machine in winter, when many lodgings are closed.

$50-100

Many of the B&Bs in the $100-150 range have rooms under $100 outside of summer, but in July and August, your choices are limited. One of the best is the ★ **Lennox Inn** (69 Fox St., 902/521-0214 or 888/379-7605, www.lennoxinn.com; March-Nov.; $95-120 s or d), which dates to 1791, making it Canada's oldest inn. The present owners breathed life into the building through a meticulous restoration using the original plans. Two guest rooms share a single bathroom, and the other two are en suite. Breakfast in what was originally the tavern is included in the rates.

Right downtown, above Grand Banker Restaurant, the tidy **Brigantine Inn and Suites** (82 Montague St., 902/634-3300 or 800/360-1181, www.brigantineinn.com; $95-180 s or d) provides excellent value. It offers seven nautically themed rooms, each with a private bathroom and named for a famous sailing ship. The smallest of the rooms is the brightly decorated Cutty Sark room, while the much larger Brigantine Romance room features a jetted tub on a glass-enclosed balcony overlooking the harbor. Part of the inn is a complex of seven suites one block from the main building. These have separate bedrooms, as well as sitting areas, coffeemakers, microwaves, and fridges.

Incorporating two (circa 1888 and 1905) buildings, the **Boscawen Inn and McLachlan House** (150 Cumberland St., 902/634-3325 or 800/354-5009, www.boscawen.ca; $95-225 s or d) also has a couple of rooms under $100, but most are higher-priced. This European-style hotel occupies a scenic perch above the harbor and is surrounded by gardens. The five guest rooms in McLachlan House are less expensive than those across the road at what was originally known as the Boscawen Manor, but all guests enjoy a light breakfast included in the rates. Other amenities include a formal dining room and sun-soaked terrace, both open to the public for meals.

$100-150

Kaulbach House (75 Pelham St., 902/634-8818 or 800/568-8818, www.kaulbachhouse.com; $129-169 s or d) is one of Lunenburg's many historic treasures (circa 1880) converted to an inn, complete with the unique "Lunenburg bump," an enlarged dormer that extends past a building's eaves. Two blocks up from the harbor but with partial water views, the six antique-filled rooms have en suite or private bathrooms, flat-screen TVs, air-conditioning, and wireless Internet. A full breakfast is included in the rates.

With rooms and suites spread through three buildings on King Street, the ornately detailed **Mariner King B&B** (15 King St., 902/634-8509 or 800/565-8509, www.marinerking.com; $115-225 s or d) is also right downtown. Its cheaper rooms are a little more threadbare than those at Kaulbach House, but the character-filled Attic Suite is a gem. It even has its own rooftop patio.

Rum Runner Inn (66 Montague St., 902/634-9200 or 888/778-6786, www.rumrunnerinn.com; $109-169 s or d) is right along the busy restaurant strip opposite the waterfront. It's a historic building, but the 13 rooms are thoroughly modernized and look no different from a regular motel. Each has a coffeemaker, a fridge, air-conditioning, and Internet connections. The most expensive rooms have a king bed and glassed-in veranda. A light breakfast is included.

If you're looking to stay in a historic building with a modern feel, consider the centrally situated ★ **Spinnaker Inn** (126 Montague St., 902/634-4543 or 888/634-8973, www.spinnakerinn.com; $115-170 s or d). Overlooking the harbor, all four guest rooms have polished hardwood floors and antique-style beds. Two are split-level with jetted tubs in the en suite bathrooms and harbor views.

The **Lunenburg Inn** (26 Dufferin St., 902/634-9419 or 800/565-3963, www.lunenburginn.com; Apr.-Oct.; $149-189 s or d) is an elaborate Victorian home that has been taking in guests since 1924. It underwent serious renovations in the mid-1990s and now provides some of the nicest rooms in town, with rates including a full breakfast. If I had a choice, I'd stay in one of the two suites, which each have a sitting area with a TV, a jetted tub in the en suite bathroom, and a private entrance from the veranda. Guests enjoy a sitting room with a fireplace, a private bar, and wireless Internet.

Campgrounds

The **Lunenburg Campground** (Blockhouse Hill Rd., 902/634-8100; May-late Oct.; $26-38) sits on Blockhouse Hill, high above downtown and beside the information center. It's on the small side (55 sites), but the facilities are adequate (showers, views, Internet access).

A lot more than a campground, ★ **Ovens Natural Park** (off Hwy. 332, 902/766-4621, www.ovenspark.com; mid-May-mid-Oct.) has campsites (tents $28, hookups $43-60)

and cabins varying from those with shared bathrooms ($60 s or d) to self-contained two-bedroom chalets ($190). Amenities include lawn games, a playground, evening bonfires, a restaurant, and a gift shop. Stephen Chapin, younger brother of Harry Chapin (of "Cat's in the Cradle" fame) owns and operates the property with his family, making the evening sing-alongs a real treat. The middle weekend of August, the entire Chapin family comes together as a tribute to the singer, with everyone welcome to join in the fun.

FOOD

Lunenburg has a great number of restaurants, nearly all serving seafood in a casual setting. Local specialties appearing on some menus include Solomon Gundy (pickled herring, usually served with sour cream), Lunenburg pudding (pork sausage), and fish cakes topped with rhubarb relish.

Seafood

In the big red building down on the water, the **Old Fish Factory** (68 Bluenose Dr., 902/634-3333; mid-May-mid-Oct. 11am-9pm; $13-28) is a large restaurant in a converted fish storehouse. Specialties include creamy seafood chowder, beer-battered haddock, and

Lunenburg Inn

fish baked on a cedar plank. After Solomon Gundy, a sour-tasting local specialty, you'll be ready for Blueberry Grunt, sweet dumplings floating in a blueberry compote and topped with whipped cream. Non-seafood dishes with a Canadian twist are also offered, such as maple-glazed chicken. Lunch features similar offerings, but with lower prices.

One block back from the harbor, several restaurants line Montague Street. All have decks or floor-to-ceiling windows facing the water. **Big Red's** (80 Montague St., 902/634-3554; daily 9am-9pm, until 10pm on weekends; $14-28) is exactly that—a cavernous family-friendly restaurant with a standard seafood menu and lots of pizza choices. Portions are generous and prices reasonable.

Grand Banker Bar & Grill (82 Montague St., 902/634-3300; daily 11am-9:30pm; $14-26) offers similarly great views from an enclosed dining room and serves a wide-ranging menu of seafood, salads, pastas, and sandwiches. The food is well prepared and the atmosphere pleasant and relaxed. Mains include crab cakes, Acadian seafood stew, and maple-pecan glazed salmon. A half dozen good beers and a couple of Nova Scotia wines are available. The Grand Banker puts on a fine brunch (weekends 11am-2:30pm) that includes lobster eggs Benedict.

French

Although it's more expensive than the touristy restaurants facing the harbor, my favorite Lunenburg restaurant is ★ **Fleur de Sel** (53 Montague St., 902/640-2121; late May-early Oct. daily 5pm-10pm; $26-36). Located in a beautifully restored home, the dining areas are bright and airy, and made more so with original art. The menu highlights simple French bistro-style cooking while making the most of local seafood and produce. The admirable wine list includes many choices from Nova Scotia.

INFORMATION AND SERVICES

Lunenburg Visitor Information Centre (Blockhouse Hill Rd., 902/634-8100, www. lunenburgns.com; May-June and Sept.-Oct.

daily 9am-6pm, July-Aug. daily 9am-8pm) stocks locally written, informative literature about the port's historic architecture. Staff will help those without reservations find accommodation. The office can be a little hard to find. As you enter town, stay on Lincoln Street as it passes the signs for the waterfront, and you'll soon find yourself on Blockhouse Hill.

Fishermen's Memorial Hospital (14 High St., 902/634-8801) is between Dufferin and Green Streets. For the **RCMP,** call 902/634-8674.

GETTING THERE AND AROUND

Along divided Highway 103, it takes a little more than one hour to reach Lunenburg from Halifax (100 kilometers), taking Exit 10 via Mahone Bay for the final stretch.

If you're in Halifax without a vehicle, consider a six-hour tour with **Ambassatours** (902/423-6242 or 800/565-7173). These depart June-October Wednesday, Friday, and Saturday at 8:30am.

Fleur de Sel is one of Lunenburg's best restaurants.

Lunenburg to Shelburne

Beyond Lunenburg, the divided highway continues south to Bridgewater, but the crowds thin out quickly. This is one of the best reasons to continue south—the rugged coastline is dotted with Peggy's Cove-like villages steeped in history but unaffected by tourism, and parks with designated hiking trails and sandy beaches beckon.

The 140-kilometer drive between Lunenburg and Shelburne takes less than two hours nonstop. As accommodations are limited along this stretch of coast, a sensible schedule is to plan to leave Lunenburg after breakfast, spend the day exploring the following parks and towns, and have a room booked in Shelburne for the night.

BRIDGEWATER

Situated on the LaHave River, west of Lunenburg, Bridgewater (pop. 8,200) is the main service town of the South Shore. Industry revolves around a Michelin tire plant, and if you're traveling south, this is the last place to fill up on fast food and do your mall shopping.

Sights

The 1860 **Wile Carding Mill** (242 Victoria Rd., 902/543-8233; June-mid-Sept. Mon.-Sat. 9:30am-5:30pm, Sun. 1pm-5:30pm; adult $3.50, senior $2.25, child $2) was once a wool-processing mill. The wool was carded for spinning and weaving or made into batts for quilts. The original machinery is still in operation, powered by a waterwheel, and now demonstrates old carding methods. It's on the south side of the river (take Exit 13 from Highway 103).

Surrounded by parkland on the south side of downtown off King Street, **DesBrisay Museum** (130 Jubilee Rd., 902/543-4033; June-Aug. Tues.-Sat. 9am-5pm, Sun. 1pm-5pm, Sept.-May Wed.-Sun. 1pm-5pm; adult $3.50, senior $2.50, child $2) looks unappealing from the outside, but inside displays tell the story of Bridgewater's first European settlers and the importance of local industries. Highlights include Mi'kmaq quilting and a wooden plough dating to 1800.

Bridgewater and the LaHave River

Accommodations and Food

Nova Scotia's oldest accommodation is Bridgewater's **Fairview Inn** (25 Queen St., 902/543-2233 or 800/725-8732, www.thefairviewinn.ca; $105-155 s or d), a gracious three-story wooden building that dates to 1863. It has been beautifully restored, now with 24 stylish guest rooms that vary from simple but comfortable to a nautically themed suite. In-room niceties include plush linens, bathrobes, and room service, while other amenities include an outdoor pool and hot tub, a restaurant, a lounge, wireless Internet, and even room service. To get there from Highway 103, take Exit 13 and follow Victoria Road to Queen Street.

About six kilometers east of town along Highway 331 on the south side of the LaHave River is the **Lighthouse Motel** (1101 Hwy. 331, Conquerall Bank, 902/543-8151, www.lighthousemotel.ca; May-Oct.; $75-100 s or d). It occupies a prime riverside location, and guests have access to a private beach, a picnic area, and a playground.

Cranberry's (Fairview Inn, 25 Queen St., 902/543-2233; daily 7am-9pm; $17-30) is an inviting space with a creative menu to match. It's very popular in the morning ($8 for a full cooked breakfast with coffee or $12 for eggs Benedict with smoked salmon), but it is lunch and dinner that set this restaurant apart. You could start with hot crab dip, and then choose a main as traditional as beef Wellington or as rich as pan-seared scallops smothered in a rum and raisin sauce. Just make sure to save room for the divinely rich chocolate mousse.

Getting There

Bridgewater is about 20 kilometers west of Lunenburg via Highway 3. It's 110 kilometers (1.5 hours) southwest of Halifax.

HIGHWAY 331 TO LIVERPOOL

Highway 331, which begins in downtown Bridgewater as King Street, follows the LaHave River to its mouth and then winds along the coast to Exit 17 of Highway 103. It adds just 30 minutes to the trip between Bridgewater and Liverpool, but you'll want to allow longer—it's a beautiful introduction to the untouristy South Shore beyond Lunenburg.

★ Crescent Beach

Around 20 minutes southeast of Bridgewater is **Crescent Beach,** a beautiful two-kilometer stretch of finely ground quartz sand that links

Crescent Beach

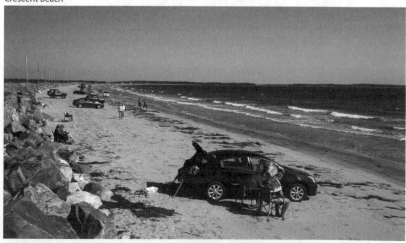

the mainland to the LaHave Islands. Like the rest of Nova Scotia, the water is cool, but on a hot summer's day, many people dive in for a swim. But it is the beach itself that is the draw, with sand dunes up to two meters high separating the beach from a shallow bay popular with kite surfers.

Crescent Beach is day-use only, but adjacent **Rissers Beach Provincial Park** boasts the same white sand and an area of pristine salt marsh laced with boardwalks. The park campground (902/688-2034; mid-May-mid-Oct.; $26) fills every weekend through summer, but midweek even sites close to the sandy beach remain empty. The park is just south of the turn-off to Crescent Beach.

GETTING THERE
Crescent Beach is about 30 kilometers (30 minutes) southeast of Bridgewater via Highway 331. It's 140 kilometers south of Halifax on Highways 103 and 331 (just under two hours).

LaHave Islands
The causeway along Crescent Beach crosses to **Bush Island,** from where quirky old iron bridges provide access to **Bell Island** and **LaHave Island.** Just three of dozens of islands in the group, they are dotted with old fishing cottages inhabited by those who have escaped the rat race. On Bell Island, a museum filled with local history is in the church, while Bush Island Provincial Park is little more than a boat launch, but the rugged scenery and funky fishing cottages make the drive to the end of the road a delightful detour from the main South Shore tourist route.

LIVERPOOL
This historic town, at the mouth of the Mersey River, about 50 kilometers south of Bridgewater, doesn't get as much attention as it deserves. Throughout the compact downtown core are a number of interesting attractions, while Privateer Days (early July) provide a lively glimpse of the town's colorful past.

Sights and Events
THE PORT OF PRIVATEERS
Privateers were government-sanctioned pirates who had permission to capture enemy vessels. American privateers found their way to Nova Scotia during the American Revolution, but the British responded by attacking American boats. Privateers were required by law to take captured vessels to Halifax's Privateers Wharf, where the boats and cargo were auctioned off, a portion of which was handed back to the privateer and his crew. Liverpool local Simeon Perkins had a share in a privateering boat, along with dozens of others who used Liverpool as their home port. The most prolific of the privateer vessels was the *Liverpool Packet* captained by Joseph Barss, which captured an estimated 200 vessels during its lifetime. With plundered goods from a single vessel selling for up to $1 million at auction, Liverpool became a wealthy town, and many of the grand homes still standing were financed by privateering.

OTHER SIGHTS
Well-known Canadian photographer Sherman Hines injected his own resources into developing the **Rossignol Cultural Centre** (205 Church St., 902/354-3067; mid-May-mid-Oct. Mon.-Sat. 10am-5:30pm and July-Aug. also Sun. noon-5:30pm; adult $4, child $3) in a school building once slated for demolition. One block south of Main Street along Old Bridge Street, it encompasses multiple small museums, including one devoted to outhouses (Hines is known for his outhouse photography), and others to folk art, the Mi'kmaq, and wildlife.

Built by infamous privateer Simeon Perkins, **Perkins House** (105 Main St., 902/354-4058; June-mid-Oct. Mon.-Sat. 9:30am-5:30pm, Sun. 1-5:30pm; adult $4) is a classic example of a New England planter's adaptation to Nova Scotia. Built in 1766, it is furnished with antiques and displays that tell the story of Perkins's colorful life on the high seas.

Country music legend Hank Snow, who sold 70 million records, was born in nearby

Brooklyn. Between Highway 103 and downtown, a railway station has been converted to the **Hank Snow Home Town Museum** (148 Bristol St., 902/354-4675; mid-May-mid-Oct. Mon.-Sat. 9am-5pm, and July-Aug. also Sun. noon-5:30pm; adult $5, senior $4, children free) in his memory. Displays catalog his life, from the earliest performances in Halifax through details of his seven number-one hits from 120 albums, to his Grand Ole Opry performances, his role in introducing Elvis Presley to the entertainment world, and, finally, the huge collection of awards accumulated through six decades of performing.

PRIVATEER DAYS

There's no better place to immerse yourself in the colorful history of Nova Scotia's privateers than **Privateer Days** (902/354-4500, www.privateerdays.com), a Liverpool tradition held annually in late June. Walking tours led by locals in period dress and a re-creation of when two American privateer boats once invaded the town are highlights, but events go on all week, culminating with a bang during the final night's fireworks.

Accommodations and Food

Once home to a privateer, **Lane's Privateer Inn** (27 Bristol Ave., 902/354-3456 or 800/794-3332, www.lanesprivateerinn.com; $105-125 s, $115-145 d) has everything you need for an overnight stay under one roof. The 27 rooms all have en suite bathrooms and air-conditioning, while some have king beds and balconies overlooking the Mersey River. Downstairs is an excellent restaurant. Breakfast includes all the usual options, with Nova Scotian specialties such as smoked salmon sausage as a substitute for bacon. The lunch and dinner includes haddock cakes served with baked beans for $14 and local scallops for $22.

Getting There

Liverpool is about 50 kilometers south of Bridgewater via Highway 103. It's 160 kilometers (two hours) south of Halifax, also via Highway 103.

LIVERPOOL TO PORT JOLI

If you've left Highway 103 to explore Liverpool, continue south through town along the older Highway 3 to reach White Point before rejoining the main route south at Summerville.

White Point

Activities at **White Point Beach Resort** (White Point Beach, 902/354-2711 or 800/565-5068, www.whitepoint.com) make this lodging a destination in itself. Stretching along a wide swath of white sand, it has indoor and outdoor pools, swimming in a freshwater lake, surfboard and kayak rentals, tennis courts, a nine-hole golf course, a games room, two restaurants, and nightly entertainment in the lounge. Most guests are families, many returning annually for summer vacation. Comfortable motel-like rooms are $165-190 s or d depending on the view, and cottages are $295-335.

Continuing along Highway 3 from White Point to Hunts Point, you'll come to **Hunts Point Beach Cottages** (Hwy. 3, 902/683-2077, www.huntspointbeach.com; mid-May-mid-Oct.), a much quieter spot, where guests laze their time away on the grassy grounds, which extend to the beach. The newly renovated cottages have one or two bedrooms ($130 s, $140 d), kitchens, covered decks, and living rooms with TVs.

GETTING THERE

White Point is less than 10 kilometers (10 minutes) south of Liverpool via Highway 3. It's 170 kilometers (two hours) south of Halifax via Highways 103 and 3.

Summerville Beach Provincial Park

Just before Highway 3 rejoins Highway 103, a short gravel road leads along the back of the small **Summerville Beach Provincial Park,** which protects a spit of sand jutting across Port Mouton. It's a day-use park with picnic tables and plenty of room to spread your towel on the beach.

White Point Beach

Kejimkujik National Park Seaside Adjunct

About 25 kilometers southwest of Liverpool is one of the largest remaining undisturbed areas of Nova Scotian coastline. Affiliated with the inland Kejimkujik National Park (along Highway 8 between Liverpool and Annapolis Royal), the **Kejimkujik National Park Seaside Adjunct** encompasses unspoiled beaches and offshore isles. The park is accessible only on foot. The main access is along an easy three-kilometer trail beginning at the parking lot on St. Catherine's Road (turn off in Port Joli) and ending at the southwest end of St. Catherine's River Beach. Some sections of this beach close late April-late July to protect piping plover nesting sites. The Seaside Adjunct has no visitor facilities, and camping is not permitted.

PORT JOLI

Port Joli is a picturesque coastal village with a seaside park that gets busy only on the hottest of summer weekends.

Thomas Raddall Provincial Park

This gem known as **Thomas Raddall Provincial Park** protects rock formations that suggest it was the point where the Gondwana and North American continents collided many millions of years ago. But for most, the beaches are the main draw. Left behind by the retreating ice cap at the end of the last ice age, banks of sand have washed ashore, forming beautiful stretches of beach now protected by the park.

The park has an 11-kilometer trail system, half of which is paved and set aside for both cyclists and walkers. The most popular destination is Sandy Bay, a short beach bookended by rocky headlands. If you can pull yourself away from the beach, follow the **Sandy Bay Trail** over the northern headland to the **Herring Rock Trail,** where the remains of a 1700s fishing station can be seen. Take both these trails and you'll be back on your beach towel within an hour. In the north of the park, beaches are lapped by the protected waters of Port Joli Harbour. Starting from the top end of the campground, the **Port Joli Trail** (one kilometer each way) winds south past interpretive panels to Scotch Point Beach. To the north, a string of beaches spread out well beyond the park boundary.

The park campground (902/683-2664; mid-May-mid-Oct.; $26) has 82 large sites, including a few designated for tents. Each site has a picnic table and fire pit, while other amenities include washrooms with showers, a playground, and firewood sales.

To get to the park, continue along Highway 103 south from Port Joli and turn south on East Port L'Herbert Road; it's three kilometers from the highway.

Getting There

Port Joli is 25 kilometers (15 minutes) south of Liverpool, along Highway 103. It's 185 kilometers (over two hours) south of Halifax via Highway 103.

Shelburne and Vicinity

Like Lunenburg, 140 kilometers to the northeast, Shelburne (pop. 2,300) sits at the innermost end of a long harbor formed between two peninsulas. The seaport was established in 1783 when Loyalists fleeing the newly independent American colonies settled here by the thousands, establishing shipbuilding and fish processing businesses. But eventually the seaport began to show its age. Then Hollywood came to town. In 1992, the motley collection of historic buildings along the waterfront was used as a setting for Fairfield, Connecticut, circa 1780 in the American Revolution movie *Mary Silliman's War.* In 1995, Shelburne again hit the big screen as the setting for 1600s Boston in *The Scarlet Letter,* an adaptation of Nathaniel Hawthorne's novel. Demi Moore and Robert Duvall may be long gone, but the two movies created an impetus for preservation. While some "historic" buildings were added to the mix, many original buildings were spruced up, power lines were buried, and generally the town came together to promote its past.

★ SHELBURNE HISTORIC DISTRICT

Dock Street is dotted with some of Canada's oldest wooden buildings. The local historical society has done a wonderful job of breathing life into the **Shelburne Historic District,** while businesses such as a cooperage and boatbuilder help bring its history to life. In between are grassy areas, a waterfront pathway, and kayak rentals. Admission to each of the buildings is $3, or buy a ticket for $8 to visit all four.

Shelburne County Museum

The **Shelburne County Museum** (8 Maiden Ln., 902/875-3219; June-mid-Oct. daily 9:30am-5:30pm, mid-Oct.-May Tues.-Sat. 2pm-5pm) is the best place to make your first stop. It contains exhibits covering Shelburne's Loyalist heritage and shipbuilding history. One highlight is the 250-year-old fire engine, believed to be the oldest in Canada.

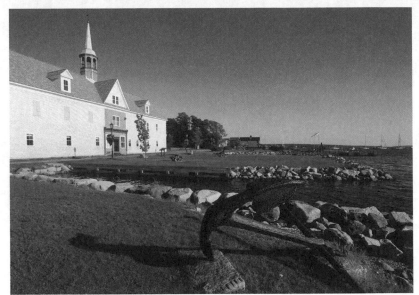

Shelburne Historic District

Dory Shop Museum

First used in the mid-1800s, dories were small, skifflike wooden boats that were essential to the success of fishing the Grand Banks. Rather than fishing from the mother vessel, a dozen or more dories would be transported to the fishing grounds, allowing hundreds of hooks to be laid out at once. Adding to their usability, they were inexpensive to make and stackable. On the waterfront across from the county museum, the **Dory Shop Museum** (11 Dock St., June-mid-Oct. daily 9:30am-5:30pm) is the last of seven once-thriving boat factories in town. The seven shops turned out thousands of handcrafted wooden fishing dories between 1880 and 1970. The shop now houses interpretive displays and gives demonstrations of the dying art.

Ross-Thomson House and Store Museum

The **Ross-Thomson House and Store Museum** (9 Charlotte Ln., 902/875-3141; June-mid-Oct. daily 9:30am-5:30pm) was built in 1785 as a Loyalist store. The last example of its kind today in Nova Scotia, it depicts the period setting with sample wares such as lumber and salted codfish, which were traded for tobacco, molasses, and dry goods. Upstairs is a military display, and outside the garden has been planted as it would have been in the late 1700s.

Muir-Cox Shipyard

At the far south end of Dock Street, the small **Muir-Cox Shipyard** was closed at the time of publication. If it reopens in the near future, expect to see local men building traditional boats. It operated continuously between the 1820s and 1980s, launching square-rigged barques in its earliest days and wooden racing yachts in more modern times.

ACCOMMODATIONS AND CAMPING
$50-100

The centrally located **Loyalist Inn** (160 Water St., 902/875-3333, www.theloyalistinn.com; $70-105 s or d) is a late-1800s wooden hotel with 11 smartly decorated guest rooms on the top two floors and a downstairs bar and restaurant.

Better value is **Shelburne Harbourside Cottages** (10 George St., 902/875-4555, www.shelburneharboursidecottages.com; $95 s or d). Each of two modern cottages enjoys harbor views and has cooking facilities, a separate bedroom, a TV, and a deck. Extras include bike rentals ($18 per day) and kayak rentals ($25 per day).

$100-150

Cooper's Inn (36 Dock St., 902/875-4656 or 800/688-2011, www.thecoopersinn.com; Apr.-Oct.; $110-185 s or d) is a two-story colonial beauty overlooking the harbor and next to the tourist bureau and museum. Built in 1784 by a merchant and restored and opened in 1988, the lodging has six rooms, all with private baths ($110-150), and a large top-floor suite with water views ($185). Rates include a full breakfast in a cheery dining room.

★ **Whispering Waves Cottages** (Black Point Rd., Ingomar, 902/637-3535 or 866/470-9283, www.novascotiacottages.info; $149-165 s or d) may be out of town, but an overnight stay at this welcoming waterfront property is as enjoyable as one could imagine. The modern cottages are stylishly furnished in wilderness, nautical, or romance themes, and each has a separate bedroom, kitchen, lounge room with a fireplace, and a deck with ocean views. A lobster dinner, delivered to your cottage door, is a delicious extra.

Campgrounds

Rustic and pretty, **The Islands Provincial Park** (off Hwy. 3, 5 km west of Shelburne, 902/875-4304; mid-May-early Sept.; $26) faces the town across the upper harbor. It offers 64 unserviced sites with table shelters and grills, pit toilets, running water, and a spacious modern shower room.

FOOD

The bright and cheery ★ **Charlotte Lane Café** (13 Charlotte Ln., 902/875-3314; Tues.-Sat. 11:30am-2:30pm and 5pm-8pm; $18-33), between Water and Dock Streets, has an established reputation for fine dining. Its Swiss owner-chef, Roland Glauser, specializes in local seafood prepared with cooking techniques from around the world. The seafood chowder is one of the best I've tasted.

The dining room at the **Loyalist Inn** (160 Water St., 902/875-3333; $12-19) on Water Street is usually jammed with bus-tour diners. A table is easiest to get before noon, during midafternoon, or after 8pm. The specialty is seafood prepared any way you like it.

INFORMATION AND SERVICES

While Dock Street is the historic heart of Shelburne, Water Street, running parallel one block to the west, is lined with all the services of a small town, including banks and the post office. **Whirligig Book Shop** (135 Water St., 902/875-1117; Wed.-Fri. 10am-4pm, Sat. 10am-1pm) stocks a good selection of local and Nova Scotian literature.

GETTING THERE

Shelburne is 140 kilometers from Lunenburg along Highway 103. The drive takes less than two hours nonstop. It's 220 kilometers (almost three hours) from Halifax via Highway 103.

SHELBURNE TO YARMOUTH
Barrington and Vicinity

Highway 103 takes a mainly inland route between Shelburne and Yarmouth. One place it does come in contact with the ocean is near Barrington, just off the main highway along Highway 3, where coastal views are exquisite. In Barrington itself, the **Old Meeting House Museum** (2408 Hwy. 3, 902/637-2185; June-Sept. Mon.-Sat. 9:30am-5:30pm, Sun. 1-5:30pm; donation) is a variation on planter life. Built by 50 Cape Cod families in 1765, the New England-style church is Canada's oldest nonconformist house of worship.

Beyond Barrington, at Villagedale, is **Sand Hills Beach Provincial Park,** so named for a complex dune system where wide tidal flats extend into the ocean. Time your arrival for high tide, and the water is warm enough for swimming—in summer only, of course.

GETTING THERE

Barrington is about 35 kilometers (25 minutes) southwest of Shelburne, on Highway 103. It's 255 kilometers (under three hours) from Halifax via Highway 103.

Cape Sable Island

At Barrington West, Cape Sable Island is well worth the detour. Connected to the mainland by a causeway, the island forms the southernmost point in Nova Scotia. Feared by early sailors because of its jagged shores, the island was settled by brick-making Acadians during the 17th century. The island also served as a summer base for fishermen from New England, and fishing prevails today as the community's main industry, with tourism a close second.

The island's four main beaches offer surfing, clam digging, swimming, fishing, and bird-watching. At **Hawk Beach,** on the eastern side (turn at Lower Clark's Harbour at Hawk Road and go left), you can see the **Cape Lighthouse** on a small nearby sandbar. The original tower, built in 1861, was Canada's first eight-sided structure; the present lighthouse, a protected heritage building, was constructed in 1923. At low tide on Hawk Beach you can also see the remains of a 1,500-year-old forest.

Causeway Beach (turn right at the Corbett Heights subdivision) is a prime sunbathing and fishing (mackerel) spot. **Stoney Island Beach,** as the name implies, is not as popular with sunbathers as it is with seals, which like to sun themselves on the rocks. **South Side Beach** (turn on Daniel's Head Road in South Side) is also popular as a seal-watching and beachcombing locale.

Services and accommodations are limited. **Cape Sable Cottages** (37 Long Point Rd., Newellton, 902/745-0168, www.capesablecottages.com; $170-190 s or d) are my favorite. These five spacious and modern cottages sit on a private peninsula jutting into Barrington Passage. Each cottage has water views, a separate bedroom, a living area, a kitchen, a wide deck supplied with a barbecue and outdoor furniture, and its own fire pit. The property is open year-round, with cottages dropping to $130 in winter.

GETTING THERE

Cape Sable Island is about 50 kilometers southwest of Shelburne along Highway 103, continuing on Highway 3 through Barrington. Allow 40 minutes. From Halifax, allow three hours for the 270-kilometer drive down Highway 103 and 3.

Yarmouth

Yarmouth (pop. 6,800) was the center of a shipbuilding empire during Canada's Great Age of Sail, when it ranked as the world's fourth-largest port of registry. Still the region's largest seaport, the town is a prosperous and orderly place supported by shipping—primarily lumber products, Irish moss, and Christmas trees—and fishing. Yarmouth's herring fleet is a major contributor to the local economy. The fleet sails at night and anchors with all its lights blazing farther up the Fundy coast, creating a sight known as "herring city."

SIGHTS

If historic architecture interests you, take a leisurely walk along Main Street, where the commercial buildings demonstrate late-19th-century Classic Revival, Queen Anne Revival, Georgian, and Italianate styles. At the tourist information center on Forest Street, pick up the *Walking Tour of Yarmouth* brochure, which details about two dozen points of architectural and historical interest on a self-guided four-kilometer walk.

Yarmouth

Lake Milo

To Churchill Mansion
Country Inn,
and Digby

To Ellenwood Lake
Provincial Park

MAIN SHORE RD

PROSPECT ST

MAIN ST

HIBERNIA ST

1

VANCOUVER ST

GROVE RD

LAKELAWN MOTEL

REGIONAL
HEALTH
CARE

To Cape Forchu

CHESTNUT ST

101

0   0.25 mi

0   0.25 km

103

To Shelburne

WATER ST

HUNTINGTON ST

PLEASANT ST

BRUNSWICK ST

MAIN ST

STARR'S RD

HARDSCATCH RD

FIREFIGHTERS'
MUSEUM

PORTER ST

Broad Brook

HALEY RD

RUDDER'S

PUBLIC LIBRARY

COLLINS ST

YARMOUTH
COUNTY
MUSEUM

WATER ST

Yarmouth
Harbour

CLEMENTS AVE

PARADE ST

3

To Camper's
Haven and
Shelburne

CLIFF ST

CUMBERLAND ST

FERRY
TERMINAL

NOVA SCOTIA VISITOR
INFORMATION CENTRE

FOREST ST

ALBERT ST

© AVALON TRAVEL

Firefighters' Museum

The **Firefighters' Museum of Nova Scotia** (451 Main St., 902/742-5525; June-Sept. Mon.-Sat. 9am-5pm, July-Aug. Mon.-Sat. 9am-9pm and Sun. 10am-5pm; adult $4, senior $3, child $2) is a museum dedicated solely to firefighting equipment. Among the extensive vintage collection is an 1819 Hopwood and Tilley hand pump and other sparkling tools.

Yarmouth County Museum

An enjoyable walk from downtown through a tree-lined residential area east of Main Street leads to **Yarmouth County Museum**

(22 Collins St., 902/742-5539; June-mid-Oct. Mon.-Sat. 9am-5pm, mid-Oct.-May Tues.-Sat. 2pm-5pm; adult $3, senior $2.50, child $1). It showcases Canada's largest ship-portrait collection and exhibits a trove of seafaring lore, musical instruments, ship models, furniture, and more. The research library and archives store extensive records and genealogical materials.

Scenic Drive to Cape Forchu

The region's most scenic drive is to Cape Forchu, where the red-and-white **Cape Forchu Light Station** guides ships into the harbor. Follow Main Street north and turn left at Vancouver Street. Just past the hospital complex, turn left on Grove Road. The Faith Memorial Baptist Church marks the site where the famous Yarmouth runic stone, believed to have been inscribed by Leif Eriksson's men, was found. Next you come to the lighthouse (July-Aug. daily 11:30am-7pm) perched on a stone promontory. The actual lighthouse is open to climb, and you get good views from the top. Below the lighthouse, a paved walking trail leads from the parking lot down to **Leif Ericson Picnic Park,** overlooking the rocky coast.

ACCOMMODATIONS AND CAMPING
$50-100
North of downtown, where Vancouver Street crosses the head of Yarmouth Harbour, is the **Lakelawn Motel** (641 Main St., 902/742-3588 or 877/664-0664, www.lakelawnmotel. com; from $99 s or d). The centerpiece of this lodging is a grand 1864 mansion that holds a breakfast room and four upstairs B&B rooms. Spread around its perimeter is a U-shaped wing of 27 motel rooms that are a little worn but still a good value.

$100-150
Churchill Mansion Country Inn (44 Old Post Rd., Darlings Lake, 902/649-2818 or 888/453-5565, www.churchillmansion.com; May-mid-Nov.; $170-235 s or d) was the hilltop summer home of Aaron Flint Churchill, who made his fortune in the shipping trade after establishing the Churchill Line out of Savannah, Georgia. Overlooking a lake and with distant ocean views, the house was converted to an inn in the 1980s. All the beautifully restored rooms are super spacious. The most expensive is Churchill's master bedroom, with a balcony overlooking the lake. A gourmet breakfast and evening snacks are included in the rates, while dinner is available for an extra charge in the restaurant. The town of Darlings Lake is 15 kilometers north of Yarmouth.

Cape Forchu Light Station

Campgrounds
The closest campground to Yarmouth is **Campers' Haven** (5 km east of Yarmouth, off Hwy. 3 in Arcadia, 902/742-4848, www. campershavencampground.com; mid-May-mid-Oct.; $25-45). The lakeside campground offers more than 200 sites, as well as canoe rentals, a pool, a camp store, a launderette, and a recreation hall with a fireplace.

For a wilderness experience, travel a little farther out to **Ellenwood Lake Provincial Park** (mid-June-mid-Oct.; $26), which has a beach with swimming, a short hiking trail through a mixed forest typical of the southwest region, showers, and a playground. To get there, drive 19 kilometers north of Yarmouth on Highway 101, take Exit 34, and follow the signs along Highway 340 for seven kilometers.

FOOD
Rudder's (96 Water St., 902/742-7311; daily 11am-10pm; $15-28) is a large brewpub set right on the water. It's a big room that manages to maintain a warm atmosphere, with

even more tables spread across a veranda facing the harbor. The menu blends traditional pub food with Nova Scotian specialties. Think maple-glazed salmon baked on a cedar plank ($22), lobster and scallop crepes, and steak and lobster. The lobster dinner is a major draw.

INFORMATION AND SERVICES

Greeting visitors as they arrive in town is the cavernous **Nova Scotia Visitor Information Centre** (228 Main at Forest St., 902/742-5033; May-Oct. daily 8am-5pm, until 7pm July-Aug.), where you'll find literature and information on just about everything imaginable in the city and the province. In advance of your visit, visit www.yarmouthandacadianshores.com.

The **Regional Health Centre** is at 50 Vancouver Street (902/742-1540). For the **RCMP,** call 902/742-8777.

GETTING THERE

Yarmouth is 310 kilometers from Halifax via the South Shore (Highway 103) and 330 kilometers via the Annapolis Valley (Highway 101); allow at least four hours for either route.

Ferries from Portland, Maine, dock downtown in Yarmouth. **Nova Star Cruises** (866/864-6295, www.novastarcruises.com) operates this service between May and October, charging adult $139, $139 vehicle, and kids ride free. Cabins are $79 to $199. The crossing takes 11 hours, with departures from Portland leaving in the evening and from Yarmouth in the morning.

Fundy Coast

La Côte Acadienne............. 102
Digby and Vicinity............. 105
Annapolis Royal 111

Kejimkujik National Park 116
Annapolis Valley............... 118
Wolfville and Vicinity 121

The natural beauty of Nova Scotia's Fundy coast is sublime. Sea breezes bathe the shore in crisp salt air, and the sun illuminates the seascape colors with a clarity that defies a painter's palette. Wildflowers bloom with abandon, nourished

by the moist coastal air. And fog, thick as cotton, sometimes envelops the region during the summer. This is the Fundy Coast, which stretches from Yarmouth in the west to the farthest reaches of the Bay of Fundy in the east. Quietly and relentlessly, twice a day, a tidal surge that has its beginnings far away pours into the bay, creating the highest tides on the planet. Fishing boats are lifted from the muddy sea floor, and whales in pursuit of silvery herring hurry along the summertime currents, their mammoth bulks buoyed by the 100 billion tons of seawater that gush into the long bay between Nova Scotia and New Brunswick. The cycle from low to high tide takes a mere six hours. The tide peaks, in places high enough to swamp a four-story building, and then begins to retreat. As the sea level drops, coastal peninsulas and rocky islets emerge from the froth, veiled in seaweed. The sea floor reappears, shiny as shellac and littered with sea urchins, periwinkles,

and shells. Where no one walked just hours ago, local children run and skip on the beaches, pausing to retrieve tidal treasures. Locals take the Fundy tides for granted. For visitors, it's an astounding show.

To a great extent, the history of the province's Fundy Coast is the story of all of Nova Scotia, and this is reflected in the region's wealth of historic and cultural wonders. France's colonial ambitions began at Port-Royal and clashed head-on with England's quest for New World dominance, and multiple national historic sites along the coast lie in testament to these troubled times. The trim Acadian villages of La Côte Acadienne, the historic streetscape of Annapolis Royal, and the gracious towns of Wolfville and Windsor add to the appeal.

PLANNING YOUR TIME

You can drive between Yarmouth and Halifax in a single day, but you should allow a

Previous: Annapolis Royal; whale-watching, Brier Island. **Above:** Grand Pré National Historic Site.

Look for ★ to find recommended
sights, activities, dining, and lodging.

Highlights

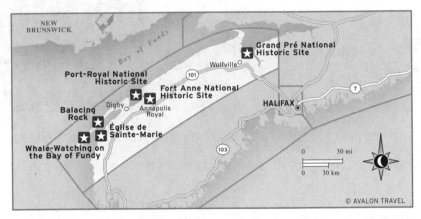

© AVALON TRAVEL

★ **Église de Sainte-Marie:** A pocket of Acadian villages along the Fundy Coast allows visitors to immerse themselves in this uniquely French culture by trying Acadian cooking at Rapure Acadienne, visiting the local museums, and straining their necks to view Église de Sainte-Marie, the tallest wooden church in North America (page 104).

★ **Balancing Rock:** Out on Digby Neck, a short trail suddenly emerges at the Bay of Fundy—and this stunning pillar balanced precariously over the water (page 109).

★ **Whale-Watching on the Bay of Fundy:** Use Digby Neck and the adjacent islands as a base for whale-watching trips into the Bay of Fundy (page 110).

★ **Fort Anne National Historic Site:** After centuries of changing hands between the British and the French, this site of numerous fortifications and the onetime capital of Nova Scotia is now managed by the government as a tourist attraction (page 112).

★ **Port-Royal National Historic Site:** The oldest European settlement north of St. Augustine, Florida, has been re-created at this important site (page 113).

★ **Grand Pré National Historic Site:** This outdoor museum brings the Henry Wadsworth Longfellow story of Evangeline, a young girl caught up in the Acadian deportation, to life (page 125).

Fundy Coast

Bay of Fundy

WHALE-WATCHING ON THE BAY OF FUNDY ✚

BALANCING ROCK ✚

POINTE DE L'EGLISE (CHURCH POINT) ✚

Yarmouth
Port Maitland
Hebron
Salmon River
Mavillette
Cape St. Mary's
Smuggler's Cove Provincial Park
Brier Island
Westport
Meteghan River
Meteghan
Comeauville
Saulnierville
St. Bernard
Grosses Coques
Church Point
Weymouth
Tiverton
East Ferry
Long Island
Mink Cove
Sandy Cove
Centreville

La Côte Acadienne

Ellenwood Lake Provincial Park

Digby Neck

St. Mary's Bay

Gilbert's Cove

Smith Cove
Bear River
South Milford
Maitland Bridge

Digby

Annapolis Basin

Digby Gut

PORT-ROYAL NATIONAL HISTORIC SITE ✚

Upper Clements

Granville Ferry
Delops Cove
Parker's Cove

Ferry to Saint John, NB

Annapolis Royal

FORT ANNE NATIONAL HISTORIC SITE ✚

Valleyview Provincial Park

North Mountain

Bridgetown

Middleton

Margaretsville

Kejimkujik National Park

Lake Rossignol

Kejimkujik National Park Seaside Adjunct

White Point
Liverpool

Bridgewater
Lunenburg
Mahone Bay
Chester

Ovens Natural Park

Mahone Bay

New Albany

Annapolis Valley

Morristown
Greenwood
Kingston
Berwick
South Alton
Kentville
Port Williams
Canning
Star's Point
Wolfville
Hantsport
Windsor

South Mountain Park

Cape Split
Blomidon Peninsula
Scots Bay
Blomidon Provincial Park

Minas Channel

GRAND PRÉ NATIONAL HISTORIC SITE ✚

FORT EDWARD NATIONAL HISTORIC SITE ✚

Kingsport

Minas Basin

HALIFAX

© AVALON TRAVEL

0
0
30 km
30 mi

minimum of two days, which lets you reserve a room at one of Annapolis Royal's many historic inns. This small town is definitely the historic heart of the Fundy Coast, with sights such as **Fort Anne National Historic Site** and **Port-Royal National Historic Site** easily filling out a full day of sightseeing. For this reason, two days and two nights should be allotted for exploring the Fundy Coast. At the western end, the detour through La Côte Acadienne and stops at Acadian icons such as **Église de Sainte-Marie** add only slightly to the length of the drive. The most impressive Acadian attraction, **Grand Pré National Historic Site,** is farther east, and it deserves at least three hours of your time. At some point during your travels through the region you'll want to focus on the Bay of Fundy (digging into a plate of plump Digby scallops doesn't count). Taking the above into consideration, if you have two nights planned for the Fundy Coast, and you are traveling east from Yarmouth, spend the first morning meandering along La Côte Acadienne, order scallops for lunch in Digby, and continue to Annapolis Royal. Spend the rest of the afternoon and the first part of the next morning exploring the town before moving on to Wolfville. Spend the night, rise early for a short hike through Blomidon Provincial Park, and then move on to Grand Pré National Historic Site. You'll be back in the capital by late afternoon. With an extra day and night, plan on driving along Digby Neck and combining a hike to **Balancing Rock** with whale-watching.

La Côte Acadienne

Those who zoom along Highway 101 between Yarmouth and Digby will miss the charming La Côte Acadienne (Acadian Coast), also known as the Municipality of Clare, a 50-kilometer coastal stretch populated by descendants of the French who resettled here after the Acadian expulsion of 1755. The place-names, the soaring Catholic churches, and the proud Acadian flags (a French tricolor with a single yellow star) announce that you're in the largest Francophone enclave in Nova Scotia.

MAVILLETTE AND VICINITY

For a look at the dynamic Fundy, check out **Mavillette Beach Provincial Park,** on the south side of Cap Sainte-Marie (Cape St. Mary's). The sign for Cape View Restaurant signals the turn from Highway 1; the road peels down to the sea and runs alongside high dunes. Boardwalks cross the dunes to the 1.5-kilometer-long beach, where sandbars trap water in warm pools at low tide. On sunny days, beachcombers walk the expanse and hunt for unusual seashells. Though this is one of the finest beaches in all Nova Scotia, crowds are nonexistent.

Accommodations and Food

Along the beach access road you'll find **Cape View Motel and Cottages** (124 John Doucette Rd., 902/645-2258, www.capeviewmotel.ca; May-Oct.). The motel's 10 basic rooms ($80-145 s or d) and five cottages ($100-130) overlook sand dunes and the provincial park.

Across the road from the Cape View Motel and with wonderful views of the beach and its stunning sunsets is **Cape View Restaurant** (157 John Doucette Rd., 902/645-2519; mid-May-Oct. daily for breakfast and dinner; $14-23), which dishes up breakfasts such as scrambled eggs with lobster ($13.50) and seafood with an Acadian twist the rest of the day.

Smuggler's Cove Provincial Park

From Mavillette Beach, it's 16 kilometers north to **Smuggler's Cove Provincial Park.** Walkways here lead to great bluff-top views of the coast and down steep tree-lined steps to the rocky shoreline. The coastal cliffs in this area are notched with caves, which were used by Prohibition-era rum runners. Some of the caves can be explored at low tide. The park also holds numerous picnic tables (making it an ideal lunch stop), but no campsites.

Getting There

Mavillette is just over 30 kilometers (25 minutes) north of Yarmouth via Highway 1. From Halifax, the quickest way to reach Mavillette is via Highway 101 along the Bay of Fundy (300 kilometers, 3.5 hours).

METEGHAN AND VICINITY

Settled in 1785, the seaport of Meteghan, 15 kilometers north of Mavillette, is the district's commercial hub, although the population still numbers fewer than 1,000. The main wharf is a hive of activity throughout the day, but the official attraction is **La Vieille Maison** (Old House Museum, 902/645-2389; July-Aug. daily 9am-7pm, June and Sept. daily 10am-6pm; donation) on Highway 1. In the Robicheau family's former homestead, this museum features 18th-century furnishings and exhibits explaining the area's history, with help from bilingual guides in traditional Acadian costume. Part of the museum is operated as the **Meteghan Visitor Centre.**

Accommodations and Food

For a place to overnight, the tidy **Bluefin Motel** (7765 Hwy. 1, 902/645-2251 or 888/446-3466, www.bluefinmotel.com; $79-139 s or d) is a good choice. Situated on the south side of town, the rooms don't take full advantage of its cliff-top setting, but a few outdoor chairs can be found on a deck behind the restaurant. The view, the lobster traps strung across the adjacent lot, and scallop trawlers making their way slowly across the bay all add to the appeal. The motel restaurant is open daily from 8am for breakfast, lunch, and dinner.

A seafood cornucopia is brought in daily by the seaport's scallop draggers, herring seiners, and lobster boats. **Seashore Restaurant** (Hwy. 1 near the museum, 902/645-3453; daily for lunch and dinner; $11-19) is a good place for seafood dining.

Getting There

Meteghan is 45 kilometers (35 minutes) north of Yarmouth along Highway 1. It's 280 kilometers (3.5 hours) west of Halifax along Highway 101.

North from Meteghan

The village of **Meteghan River,** about two kilometers north of Meteghan, is Nova Scotia's largest wooden ship-building center. One of the nicest lodgings along La Côte Acadienne is **Au Havre du Capitaine** (9118 Hwy. 1, 902/769-2001, www.havreducapitaine.ca, $95-120 s or d), a country-style inn with hardwood floors and a sitting area set around a large stone fireplace. Choose from rooms with private baths and TVs or larger suites with whirlpool tubs. The inn's licensed dining room is open daily for breakfast, lunch, and dinner.

Also in Meteghan River, lobster lovers should stop in at **Nova Lobster** (Hwy. 1, 902/645-3919; Mon.-Fri. 9am-5pm), where you can buy live lobsters kept in flow-through crates at the large warehouse—perfect if you're camping or if your accommodation has cooking facilities.

Comeauville

The village of Comeauville, around eight kilometers north of Meteghan River, is notable for **La Galerie Comeau** (761 Hwy. 1, 902/769-2650; call for hours), where artist Denise Comeau displays and sells her watercolors that reflect the region and its Acadian roots.

POINTE DE L'ÉGLISE (CHURCH POINT)

This aptly named community is the last major Acadian community for northbound travelers, but it's also the most interesting.

★ Église de Sainte-Marie

Built between 1903 and 1905, the enormous **Église de Sainte-Marie** (St. Mary's Church), the largest and tallest wooden church in North America, dominates this village of 490 inhabitants. The building is laid out in the shape of a cross, and its soaring 56-meter steeple has been ballasted with 40 tons of rock to withstand the winter wind. Inside, **Le Musée Sainte-Marie** (902/769-2808; June-mid-Oct. daily 9am-5pm; adult $2, child free) exhibits religious artifacts and historical documents and photos. Mass takes place Sunday at 10:30am.

Camping

Campers can head to the full-service **Belle Baie Park** (Hwy. 1, 902/769-3160, www.bellebaiepark.ca; May-late Sept.; tents $23, hookups $28-38), an oceanfront campground with its own beach, an outdoor pool, a playground, Internet access, and a launderette.

Food

Through town to the south is ★ **Rapure Acadienne** (1443 Hwy. 1, 902/769-2172; Mon.-Sat. 8am-5:30pm), the most authentic place in all of Nova Scotia to try rappie pie, a traditional Acadian chicken dish with a rather

Église de Sainte-Marie is the architectural highlight of La Côte Acadienne.

unusually textured potato filling. The pies are massive (and also come with beef and clam fillings) and cost $8, including a side of butter or molasses. Order at the inside window (where you can peek through at the big ovens)

Rapure Acadienne serves rappie pie, an Acadian delicacy.

and eat at the one indoor table or the picnic tables outside.

Getting There
Pointe de l'Église is just over 60 kilometers north of Yarmouth, on Highway 1.

NORTH TO DIGBY
Grosses Coques
The last of the Acadian communities is **Grosses Coques,** a small village immediately north of Pointe de l'Église that takes its name from the huge bar clams harvested here on the tidal flats, an important food source for early settlers.

Grosses Coques is almost 65 kilometers north of Yarmouth via Highway 1.

Gilbert's Cove
A short unpaved road leads from Highway 101 to **Gilbert's Cove Lighthouse** (Hwy. 101, www.gilbertscovelighthouse.com, mid-June-mid-Sept. Mon.-Sat. 10am-4pm, Sun. noon-4pm). Built in 1904 to help vessels navigate the upper reaches of St. Mary's Bay, it has been restored and is open to the public in July and August.

Gilbert's Cove is on Highway 101. It's about 85 kilometers north of Yarmouth, via Highway 101. Allow about 70 minutes.

Digby and Vicinity

The port of Digby (pop. 2,100), 105 kilometers northeast of Yarmouth and 235 kilometers west of Halifax, is the terminus for the ferry from Saint John (New Brunswick) and home for the world's largest scallop fleet. The Mi'kmaq name for the area is Te'Wapskik, meaning "flowing between high rocks," a reference to Digby Gut, a narrow opening in the Annapolis Basin to the north of town. Digby derived its English name from Admiral Robert Digby, who sailed up the Fundy in 1793 and settled the place with 1,500 Loyalists from New England. The scallop fleet ties up off Fishermen's Wharf off Water Street; be there at sunset when the pastel-painted draggers lie at anchor in a semicircle, backlit by the intense setting sun.

SIGHTS AND RECREATION
A couple of worthwhile attractions are scattered through town, but the highlights are farther afield—Digby Neck and Kejimkujik National Park, both covered in this section.

Admiral Digby Museum
Digby's place in history is on display at the harbor front **Admiral Digby Museum** (95

Montague Row, 902/245-6322; mid-June-Aug. Mon.-Sat. 9am-5pm, the rest of the year Wed. and Fri. 9:30am-4:30pm; donation), housed in a trim two-story Georgian-era residence with exhibits of old photographs, interesting maps, and maritime artifacts.

Bear River
Calling itself the "Switzerland of Nova Scotia" may be a stretch, but the small village of **Bear River,** straddling the waterway of the same name, eight kilometers south of Digby, is nestled in a delightful little valley, where the trees turn glorious colors in late September. Along the main street are a motley collection of wooden buildings in various states of repair, many built on stilts above the river far below. Those that have been restored now hold craft shops.

ENTERTAINMENT AND EVENTS
Montague Row to Water Street is the place for people-watching, especially at sunset. **Club 98 Lounge** (28 Water St., 902/245-4950) in the Fundy Restaurant has a band (cover charge) or disc jockey Friday-Saturday. The lounge at the **Pines Resort** (103 Shore Rd.,

Digby

To Nova Scotia Visitor
Information Centre, Ferry
Terminal, Admiral Digby
Inn, and Pines Resort

SHORE RD

MT PLEASANT

RACQUETTE RD

Annapolis

Basin

CARLETON ST

BIRCH ST

MAIDEN LN

CAPTAIN'S
CABIN

ROYAL FUNDY
FISH MARKET

PRINCE WILLIAM ST

KING ST

2ND AVE

QUEEN ST

1ST AVE

WATER ST

FUNDY RESTAURANT
CLUB 98 LOUNGE
DOCKSIDE SUITES

PUBLIC
LIBRARY

SYDNEY ST

WEST ST

3RD AVE

DIGBY VISITOR
INFORMATION CENTRE

BREAKERS B&B

CHURCH ST

To Digby Neck

MOUNT ST

SHREVE ST

ADMIRAL DIGBY ★
MUSEUM

MOUNT ST

2ND AVE

SIESTA
MOTEL

VICTORIA ST

SUMMER'S
COUNTRY INN

MONTAGUE ROW

WARWICK ST

0   250 yds
0   250 m

303

To Hwy 101
and Bear River

ST MARY'S ST

© AVALON TRAVEL

902/245-2511; Mon.-Sat.) is known for tamer pursuits, low lighting, a comfortable ambience, and finely tuned mixed drinks.

The port's famed scallops attract appropriate fanfare the second week of every August during **Digby Scallop Days** (www. digbyscallopdays.com), with a parade, scallop-shucking competitions, street vendors, the crowning of the Scallop Queen and Princesses, music, fireworks, and a parade of the scallop fleet.

ACCOMMODATIONS AND CAMPING
$50-100

Digby has a few motel rooms under $100, including the **Siesta Motel** (81 Montague Row, 902/245-2568, www.siestamotel.org; $75-90 s or d), but there are no real bargains in town.

Two blocks from the waterfront, **Summer's Country Inn** (16 Warwick St., 902/245-2250, www.summerscountryinn.ca; May-Oct.; $90-110 s or d) has 11 guest rooms in an 1830s home. Each room has a private bath and comfortable bed, although the decorations in some are a little flowery for my taste.

$100-150

The **Admiral Digby Inn** (441 Shore Rd., 902/245-2531 or 800/465-6262, www.digbyns.com; early Apr.-Oct.; $119-249 s or d) is across the road from the Annapolis Basin, halfway between town and the ferry terminal. Better-than-average motel rooms start at $121 s or d, and for $160 you get a balcony with water views. Cottages with one and two bedrooms are $179 and $249 respectively. All rates include a light breakfast. Amenities include a restaurant, a lounge, an indoor pool, and a laundry.

Breakers Bed and Breakfast (5 Water St., 902/245-4643 or 866/333-5773, www.thebreakersbb.com; May-Oct.; $145 s or d, including full breakfast) is an 1853 two-story home across from the waterfront. The three guest rooms are extra-large and furnished

Digging into Digby Scallops

Digby is home to the world's largest fleet of scallop trawlers.

Digby is known for its scallops, so there is no better place to try them than this small Fundy Coast port. Unlike other bivalves (such as clams), scallops do not bury themselves in the sand. Instead, they live on the bottom of the Bay of Fundy and "swim" by quickly opening and closing their shells. The fishermen of Digby harvest scallops by dragging large wire baskets over the sea floor. They are shucked (opened) immediately and put on ice until reaching the shore.

The water temperature in the Bay of Fundy varies only slightly through the year, which, combined with the tides' creating lots of nutrient movement, creates ideal conditions for the scallops. The result is the plumpest yet most delicate and succulent meat you could imagine. As a bonus, scallops are low in fat and full of protein.

Across Nova Scotia and beyond, Digby scallops appear on menus by name. In better dining rooms they are sautéed in butter with light spices or combined in seafood casseroles or dishes such as bouillabaisse. Local eateries such as the **Fundy Restaurant** (34 Water St., 902/245-4950; 8am-10pm), which has views of the fishing fleet, get creative with scallop omelets, scallop chowder, and scallop fettuccine. At the wharfside **Royal Fundy Fish Market** (Prince William St., 902/245-6528; Mon.-Fri. 9am-5:30pm, Sat. 10am-5pm), you can buy them fresh from the trawler and prepare them as you please back at your kitchen-equipped accommodation.

in keeping with a heritage theme. A covered front porch with water views and the book-filled sitting room add to the charm.

Dockside Suites (26 Water St., 902/245-4950, www.fundyrestaurant.com; $129-159 s or d) is part of the Fundy Restaurant complex. Each of the seven units is air-conditioned and has a balcony with harbor views and a separate bedroom. Other in-room amenities include a TV/DVD combo and wireless Internet.

Over $200

Appealing to visitors looking for an old-fashioned resort experience, the baronial **Pines Resort** (103 Shore Rd., 902/245-2511 or 800/667-4637, www.digbypines.ca; mid-May-mid-Oct.; from $239 s or d) peers down over the port from the brow of a hill on the town's outskirts. The French-Norman manor of stucco and stone was built in 1903 and served as a Canadian Pacific Railway hotel until the province bought it in 1965. The accommodations include more than 80 rooms in the manor and 30 cottages shaded by spruce, fir, and pine. The hotel offers a dining room of provincial renown, an 18-hole golf course (greens fee $73), an outdoor pool, a fitness center, a day spa, tennis courts, hiking trails, and afternoon tea. Most guests stay as part of a package.

Campgrounds

Close to town is **Digby Campground** (Smith's Cove, 230 Victoria St., 902/245-1985; mid-May-mid-Oct.; $24-40). To get there, take Exit 26 from Highway 101 and follow the signs toward the ferry for three kilometers. Within walking distance of downtown, it has an outdoor pool, a launderette, and hookups.

FOOD

Right downtown, **Fundy Restaurant** (34 Water St., 902/245-4950; daily 8am-10pm; $13-25) is a large casual restaurant overlooking the scallop fleet. Seating is inside in a main dining room, in a solarium, or out on the balcony. Digby scallops are the specialty, prepared any way you'd like them or in combination with other seafood—the Fundy (scallop) omelet is an interesting breakfast choice, while the rest of the day, dishes such as scallop chowder and a platter of scallops cooked in various ways are good ways to sample this tasty treat.

One block back from the water, **Captain's Cabin** (2 Birch St., 902/245-4868; daily 11:30am-10:30pm; $11-18) is a locals' hangout, but it still specializes in seafood. Dishes are a little less creative. A half-lobster with a side of scallops is $25.

Check out ★ **Royal Fundy Fish Market**

Breakers Bed and Breakfast

(Prince William St., 902/245-6528; Mon.-Fri. 9am-5:30pm, Sat. 10am-5pm; lunches $9-15) for fresh seafood for those staying somewhere with cooking facilities. Otherwise, order pan- or deep-fried scallops, seafood chowder, fresh mussels and salmon, cooked lobster, and smoked cod, haddock, mackerel, and Digby chicks (smoked herring) to eat in or take out.

INFORMATION

Downtown, the **Digby Visitor Information Centre** (110 Montague Row, 902/245-5714) is open June-early October daily 9am-5pm. Along the road between the ferry terminal and town is the **Nova Scotia Visitor Information Centre** (237 Shore Rd., 902/245-2201; early May-Oct. daily 9am-5pm, July-Aug. daily until 7:30pm), which represents tourism regions throughout the province.

GETTING THERE

Lying outside the area's main roads, Digby is easily bypassed. Digby is 105 kilometers (1.5 hours) northeast of Yarmouth via Highway 101. It's 230 kilometers (2.5-3 hours) west of Halifax on Highway 101.

The terminus of the ferry from Saint John, *Princess of Acadia,* is through town near the mouth of the Annapolis Basin. Operated by **Bay Ferries** (902/245-2116 or 888/249-7245, www.ferries.ca), the large vessel plies the Bay of Fundy between Saint John (New Brunswick) and Digby (Nova Scotia) one or two times daily throughout the year. High-season one-way fares are adult $44, senior and youth $34, child under five $5, vehicle $88 plus a $20 fuel surcharge. The crossing takes 3.5 hours, and reservations are essential if you're traveling with a vehicle.

DIGBY NECK

The Digby Neck is a long spindly peninsula reaching like an antenna for almost 80 kilometers back down the Bay of Fundy from Digby. Beyond the end of the peninsula are two small islands. Off the main tourist path, the peninsula will appeal to those interested in nature and spending time in tiny coastal villages where the pace of life is much slower than elsewhere along the Fundy Coast.

From Digby, Highway 217 runs down the center of Digby Neck, through the villages of **Centreville, Sandy Cove,** and **Mink Cove.** At picturesque Sandy Cove, houses cling to the shoreline, while a nearby trail leads to Nova Scotia's highest waterfall. At East Ferry, a ferry departs every 30 minutes on the half-hour for **Long Island.** The trip across takes just five minutes and costs $5 per vehicle, including passengers.

★ Balancing Rock

Beyond Tiverton, the main town on Long Island, a two-kilometer (30-minute) each-way trail leads through a forest dotted with marshes, then descends over 200 stairs to wooden platform where the natural wonder of **Balancing Rock** presents itself in all its glory. This towering basalt column balances precariously above St. Mary's Bay, looking as if it will topple at any time.

Balancing Rock

Brier Island

A second ferry (also $5) connects Long Island to Brier Island, Nova Scotia's westernmost extremity. The island has a bustling little fishing port at **Westport** and a tourism business that revolves around spring wildflowers, summer whale-watching, and year-round bird-watching. The island's most famous inhabitant was Joshua Slocum (the two vehicle ferries are named for him and his famous sailing boat, *Spray*), who spent his childhood on the island before taking to the high seas and becoming the first person to sail around the world solo. A small monument on a headland south of Westport commemorates the feat.

★ Whale-Watching on the Bay of Fundy

Digby Neck is the base for a thriving whale-watching community. Companies generally offer half-day excursions between mid-June and early October, with regular sightings of finback, right, humpback, and minke whales, as well as Atlantic white-sided dolphins and porpoises. **Ocean Explorations,** based on Long Island at Tiverton (902/839-2417 or 877/654-2341, www.oceanexplorations.ca), is notable for guide Tom Goodwin, a well-known biologist who takes interested visitors

out into the bay aboard high-speed but stable inflatable Zodiac boats. In addition to the most common species, Goodwin searches out North Atlantic right whales when they gather in the middle of the bay (usually August). Estimated to number fewer than 300, these are the world's rarest whales, so named because they were the "right" whales to hunt. Rates are adult $65, child $45. Other operators include **Brier Island Whale and Seabird Cruises** (Westport, Brier Island, 902/839-2995 or 800/656-3660, www.brierislandwhalewatch.com) and **Mariner Cruises** (Westport, Brier Island, 902/839-2346 or 800/239-2189, www.novascotiawhalewatching.ca).

Accommodations and Food

Between the ferry and Westport (1 km from each), **Brier Island Lodge** (Northern Point Rd., 902/839-2300 or 800/662-8355, www.brierisland.com; May-early Oct.; $99-159 s or d) sits on a bluff overlooking the sea. The 40 motel-style rooms are spacious and bright; most have water views, and some have king beds. The lodge's pine-paneled restaurant (breakfast and lunch daily) is my favorite island dining room. You can order old-fashioned roast turkey dinner or local specialties such as smoked pollock chowder and steamed periwinkles.

whale-watching, Brier Island

Information

Stop by the **Nova Scotia Visitor Information Centre** (237 Shore Rd., 902/245-2201; early May-June and Sept.-Oct. daily 9am-5pm, July-Aug. daily 9am-7:30pm), between the ferry terminal and downtown Digby.

Annapolis Royal

The history of Annapolis Royal (pop. 500) spans four centuries, with much of the past preserved along a main street that is lined with the finest collection of pre-1800 buildings in Canada. The town and surrounding area has 150 registered historic buildings, three national historic sites, and Canada's oldest wooden building. Add to the mix one of the world's only tidal power-generating plants, Nova Scotia's largest fun park and its smallest pub, and a selection of gracious accommodations, and you find a town like no other place in the province.

History

In 1605, Samuel de Champlain and the survivors of the bitter winter in New Brunswick moved across the Bay of Fundy and established the fortified Port-Royal across Annapolis Basin from modern-day Annapolis Royal. It was the first permanent European settlement north of St. Augustine, Florida. After eight years, the settlement came to an abrupt end when it was attacked and destroyed by New Englanders. In the 1630s, the French governor Charles de Menou d'Aulnay built a new Port Royal on the south shore of the Annapolis Basin, attracting French settlers who came to be known as Acadians. The site would remain capital of Acadie for the next eight decades. The British captured the fort in 1710, renaming it Fort Anne and rechristening the town Annapolis Royal, in honor of their queen. It would serve as Nova Scotia's first capital until 1749, when it was succeeded by the new town of Halifax.

SIGHTS

It's easy to spend a half-day wandering through Fort Anne National Historic Site and the adjacent St. George Street, which curves downhill to the waterfront. For Annapolis Royal's other attractions, you'll need a vehicle.

Annapolis Tidal Station

It may not be the town's oldest attraction, but it contains the local tourist information center, so it makes a sensible starting place for your visit. Near the head of Annapolis Basin, signposted to the right as you come into town off Highways 1 or 101, the **Annapolis Tidal Station** (236 Prince Albert Rd.,

Annapolis Royal

To Bridgetown
0   400 yds
0   400 m
GRANVILLE FERRY
DUNROMIN WATERFRONT CAMPGROUND AND CABINS
GRANVILLE RD
To PORT-ROYAL NATIONAL HISTORIC SITE
ANNAPOLIS TIDAL STATION/VISITOR INFORMATION CENTRE
Annapolis Basin
ST. ANTHONY ST.
ALBERT RD
MAD HATTER BOOKS
YE OLDE TOWNE PUB
ST. GEORGE ST
PRINCE
ANNAPOLIS ROYAL
RESTAURANT COMPOSÉ
POST OFFICE
GARRISON HOUSE
© AVALON TRAVEL
FORT ANNE NATIONAL HISTORIC SITE
QUEEN ANN INN
GRANGE COTTAGE B&B
ST. GEORGE ST.
HISTORIC GARDENS
HILLSDALE HOUSE INN
KING GEORGE INN
SCHOOL ST
To Digby
To Hwy 101
8

902/532-0502; May-mid-Oct. daily 9am-5pm, July-Aug. 9am-8pm; free) is the only facility in North America that generates electricity from the tides. Originally built as an experiment, the plant still operates and is capable of generating 20 kilowatts of electricity (enough to power 4,000 homes). The facility harnesses the energy of the massive Fundy tides, which fill a head pond twice daily and then pass through a turbine as they flow back out toward the ocean. The plant's top floor is dedicated to describing the process, with windows allowing views down the bay and of the head pond.

★ Fort Anne National Historic Site

An 18th-century fort and grounds and Canada's first national historic site, **Fort Anne** (St. George St., 902/532-2397; June Tues.-Sat. 9am-5:30pm, July-Aug. daily 9am-5:30pm, Sept. Tues.-Sat. 9am-5:30pm; adult $4, senior $3.50, child $2), overlooks Annapolis Basin from the heart of Annapolis Royal. Considered the key stronghold for possession of Nova Scotia, as the British knew the region—it was Acadie to the French—the site had particular importance to both parties. It

has been fortified on at least eight occasions since Scots built Fort Charles in 1629. The earliest French fort, dating to 1630, was designed with a star-shaped layout. Earthwork from the French fort of 1702 remains today, impressively banked with sweeping verdant lawns. These are open to the public year-round. Interpretive boards describe features such as a parade ground, chapel site, and restored powder magazine. The British added an officers' garrison in 1797. This whitewashed building now houses a museum that tells the long and colorful story of the fort.

Historic Gardens

The **Historic Gardens** (441 St. George St., 902/532-7018; May-Oct. daily 9am-5pm, July-Aug. daily 8am-8pm; adult $12, senior $10, child $5) comprise four hectares of theme gardens, a restaurant, and a gift shop. The gardens are undeniably beautiful, but they are also interesting. The Acadian Garden, complete with an Acadian house and outdoor oven, replicates that of the earliest European settlers. Vegetables such as beets, carrots, parsnips, onions, and cabbages are surrounded by a hedge to keep out wild animals, and off to one side is a hedge-encircled

Fort Anne National Historic Site

orchard of apple and pear trees. Other high-lights include the Knot Garden, styled after a hedge garden of the Middle Ages; the Governor's Garden, laid out as a formal garden from the 1750s, when Annapolis Royal was the capital; and a striking Rose Garden with more than 200 varieties, including early English and modern hybrids. The gardens are at their most spectacular in summer, with roses peaking mid-July-September.

★ Port-Royal National Historic Site

The first lasting settlement north of Florida, the 1605 fort at the **Port-Royal National Historic Site** (902/532-2898; mid-May-mid-Oct. daily 9am-5:30pm; adult $4, senior $3.50, child $2) has been reconstructed at what is believed to be the original location. The original French settlement has been re-built from Samuel de Champlain's plan using 17th-century construction techniques; the rustic buildings—governor's house, priest's dwelling, bakery, guardroom, and others, furnished with period reproductions—form a rectangle around a courtyard within the palisaded compound. The original outpost boasted many historic firsts: Canada's first

play, *Le Théâtre de Neptune,* was written and produced here by the young Parisian lawyer Marc Lescarbot; the continent's first social club, l'Ordre de Bon Temps (the Order of Good Cheer) was founded here in 1606; and the New World's first grain mill was built here to grind meal from the first cereal crops. The story of these is brought to life by knowledge-able staff dressed in period costume. To get to Port-Royal, cross Annapolis Basin by the generating station and turn left at Granville Ferry. It's 10 kilometers along the road (two kilometers beyond Melanson Settlement National Historic Site).

RECREATION
Hiking

Delaps Cove, 24 kilometers west of Annapolis Royal (cross Annapolis Basin, head south toward Port Royal for 8 kilometers, and turn right on the unpaved road that ends at the Bay of Fundy), is a small fishing village that is the start of the **Delap's Cove Wilderness Trail,** one of the few longer hiking trails along this stretch of coast. From the wharf at the end of the road, the trail meanders southwest along the coast for 15 kilometers. It takes about eight hours round-trip, but you can hike for just an

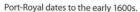
Port-Royal dates to the early 1600s.

hour or so before turning around if time is an issue.

Amusement Parks

Upper Clements Parks (2931 Hwy. 1, Upper Clements, 902/532-7557; mid-June-early Sept. daily 11am-7pm, entry $11, $5 per ride) is Nova Scotia's largest theme park. Its style is thoroughly Nova Scotian, featuring a train ride on a historic replica, a mini-golf course designed as a map of the province, and the re-creation of a fishing village. The park also has a roller coaster, a flume ride, a carousel, pedal boats, live entertainment, dinner theater Friday-Saturday evenings, a crafts area with demonstrations and a shop, and dining rooms. The adjacent **Adventure Park,** featuring 14 zip lines, obstacle courses, and suspended bridges, costs $34.50 for a full-day pass.

ACCOMMODATIONS AND CAMPING
$50-100

Aside from the cabins at **Dunromin Waterfront Campground and Cabins,** few places offer rooms for less than $100 in July and August. One option is **Grange Cottage** (102 Richie St., 902/532-7993; $75 s, $85 d), where the three guest rooms share one bathroom. The rear deck has river views and the front porch is a relaxing place to cool off on hot afternoons. Rates include a full breakfast.

King George Inn (548 Upper St. George St., 902/532-5286, www.kinggeorgeinn.20m.com; mid-May-mid-Nov.; $99-139 s or d) is a ship captain's home, built circa 1868 and furnished with Victorian-era antiques. It offers eight luxurious guest rooms, including a two-room family suite. Amenities include a library, pianos, free use of bicycles, and evening tea and coffee.

$100-150

The closest of the historic bed-and-breakfasts to downtown is **Garrison House** (350 St. George St., 902/532-5750 or 866/532-5750,

www.garrisonhouse.ca; mid-April-Oct.; $110-150 s or d), which is across the road from Fort Anne. Built in 1854 as a hotel, this gracious building holds seven guest rooms of varying configurations, as well as a downstairs restaurant open daily for dinner.

Hillsdale House Inn (519 St. George St., 902/532-2345 or 877/839-2821, www.hillsdalehouseinn.ca; May-Oct.; $120-170 s or d) is on a six-hectare estate that has been graced by kings and prime ministers. The main house has 11 air-conditioned guest rooms, and the adjacent coach house another three. Antiques fill public areas, including a cozy lounge. A cooked breakfast is included in the rates.

Set on two hectares of landscaped grounds, ★ **Queen Anne Inn** (494 Upper St. George St., 902/532-7850 or 877/536-0403, www.queenanneinn.ns.ca; May-Oct.; $129-229 s or d) is a restored 1865 Victorian mansion with a grand mahogany staircase that sweeps upstairs to 10 guest rooms outfitted with period furnishings. Room 10 is significantly smaller than the remaining nine, which are extra large ($159-189 s or d). Behind the main house, the carriage house contains two two-bedroom units, perfect for two couples traveling together or a family. Rates include a full three-course breakfast and afternoon tea.

Swimming, hiking, wagon rides, canoeing, and lawn games fill the day at **Mountain Top Cottages** (888 Parker Mountain Rd., 902/532-2564 or 877/885-1185, www.mountaintopcottages.com; May-Oct.; $120-150 s or d), in a forested setting atop North Mountain. Seventeen simple cottages with one or two bedrooms overlook a private lake. Each has a microwave and fridge as well as wireless Internet. To get there, cross Annapolis Basin at the tidal plant, follow Highway 1 through Granville Ferry, and take Parker Mountain Road off to the north.

Campgrounds

Running right down to a private beach on the Annapolis Basin, **Dunromin Waterfront Campground and Cabins** (902/532-2808, www.dunromincampsite.com; mid-May-mid-Oct., campsites $30-44) is the perfect place for families. With a fort-themed playground, an outdoor pool, mini-golf, lawn games, canoe rentals, and a café, the biggest problem will be dragging the children off for a day of sightseeing. The campground has 165 sites, most of them serviced. Canvas tepees with shared bathrooms are $50 s or d, and cabins range from $68 for shared bathroom to $115 for a two-bedroom waterfront cottage.

Enjoying an absolutely stunning location right on the Bay of Fundy, ★ **Cove Oceanfront Campground** (4405 Shore Rd., Parker's Cove, 902/532-5166, www.oceanfront-camping.com; mid-May-late Oct.; $30-100) has modern facilities including a pool, a playground, a games room, and a small café. But it's the views that make this an excellent choice, with grassy terraces ensuring everyone can see the water and the most expensive sites boasting absolute waterfront settings. To get to Parker's Cove, cross the Annapolis Basin at the generating station, turn right at Granville Ferry, and then take the first left, up and over the low wooded peninsula to Parker's Cove.

FOOD

St. George Street has many dining choices, including diner-style cafés and fine-dining restaurants. If you're staying at a campground or have chosen an accommodation with cooking facilities, head over North Mountain to Parker's Cove and pick up fresh seafood such as scallops, lobster, and crab from **R&R Shellfish** (902/532-7301), across the road from the water.

Facing Annapolis Basin from behind the main row of shops, **Restaurant Composé** (235 St. George St., 902/532-1251; Mon.-Sat. 11am-8pm, Sun. 1pm-8pm, $17-25) is easy to miss. This European-style eatery has evolved from a café into a popular restaurant, with the menu blending local seafood (namely scallops) with Continental cooking styles. The best place to enjoy the view is the water-facing solarium. The apple strudel is a great way to finish your meal.

Locals gather for afternoon beer and pub

Queen Anne Inn

grub on the outdoor patio or for nightcaps in the cozy interior of English-style **Ye Olde Towne Pub** (9 Church St., 902/532-2244; Mon.-Sat. 11am-11pm, Sun. noon-8pm; $11-21), beside the outdoor farmers market at the bottom end of St. George Street. Built in 1884 as a bank and reputed to be the smallest bar in Nova Scotia, its meals are typical pub fare, but the portions are generous. Look to the blackboard for seafood specials.

★ **Garrison House** (350 St. George St., 902/532-5501; daily from 6pm; $17-27) is a refined restaurant spread through three connected rooms of an 1854 inn. The chef is renowned for sourcing seasonal produce, while year-round specialties include fish cakes and Acadian jambalaya. With its impressive wine list and professional service, this is the best place in town for fine dining.

INFORMATION AND SERVICES

Annapolis Royal Visitor Information Centre (Hwy. 1, 902/532-5769; May-mid-Oct. daily 9am-5pm, July-Aug. daily 9am-8pm; free) is at the Tidal Power Plant, on the north side of downtown. Coming into town from Exit 22 along Highway 101, turn right before the historic main street.

Garrison House guest room

GETTING THERE

Annapolis Royal is 35 kilometers (30 minutes) from Digby along Highway 101. It's 200 kilometers (2.5 hours) west of Halifax on Highway 101.

Kejimkujik National Park

Deep in the interior of southwestern Nova Scotia, Kejimkujik (kedji-muh-KOO-jick, or "Keji" or "Kedge" for short) National Park lies off Highway 8, about midway between Liverpool and Annapolis Royal. Encompassing 381 square kilometers of drumlins (rounded glacial hills), island-dotted lakes (legacies of the last ice age), and hardwood and conifer forests, the park and the adjacent Tobeatic Game Sanctuary are an important refuge for native wildlife and town-weary Nova Scotians.

Wildlife enthusiasts visit the park for bird-watching (including barred owls, pileated woodpeckers, scarlet tanagers, great crested flycatchers, and loons and other waterfowl) and may also spot black bears, white-tailed deer, bobcats, porcupines, and beavers. The many lakes and connecting rivers attract canoeists and swimmers in warm weather, as well as anglers (particularly for perch and brook trout). Hikers can choose from a network of trails, some leading to backcountry campgrounds; some of the campgrounds are also accessible by canoe. In winter, cross-country skiers take over the hiking trails.

Kejimkujik National Park

0   4 mi
0   4 km

To South Milford and Annapolis Royal

Big Dam Lake

8

Maitland Bridge

Frozen Ocean Lake

VISITOR RECEPTION CENTRE

To Liverpool

West River

JEREMY'S BAY

JAKE'S LANDING

Kejimkujik National Park

Kejimkujik Lake

McGinty Lake

Peskawa Lake

Mountain Lake

Mersey River

Peskowesk Lake

© AVALON TRAVEL

RECREATION

The two most popular park activities are hiking and canoeing. The **Beech Grove Trail,** a two-kilometer loop, starts at the visitors center and wends along the Mersey River, where it climbs a drumlin hilltop swathed in an almost-pure beech grove. The **Farmlands Trail** is another drumlin variation, and the 45-minute hike makes its way up a drumlin to an abandoned farm on the hilltop. A little farther south along the park access road is the trailhead for the one-kilometer **Rogers Brook** loop, which passes through a forest of red maple and hemlock trees.

You can rent canoes, rowboats, and bicycles ($5 per hour, $24 per day) at Jakes Landing, on the northeast side of large Kejimkujik Lake; the adjacent stretch of the Mersey River is placid and suitable for beginning paddlers.

ACCOMMODATIONS AND CAMPING

Within the park, **Jeremy's Bay Campground** (mid-May-mid-Oct.; $27.50-31.50), on the north side of Kejimkujik Lake, has 360 sites, some with power hookups as well as washrooms and showers, fire pits and firewood ($8), a playground, picnic areas, and an interpretive program. Another 46 wilderness sites ($18) are scattered in the woodlands and offer toilets, tables, grills, and firewood. A percentage of sites can be booked through the **Parks Canada Campground Reservation Service** (519/826-5391 or 877/737-3783, www. reservation.pc.gc.ca) for $11 per reservation.

foggy morning in Kejimkujik National Park

Milford House (902/532-2617, www.milfordhouse.ca; from $155 s or d) is in South Milford, about 20 kilometers north of the park toward Annapolis Royal. The resort features a main lodge (rebuilt after it was destroyed by fire in 2014) and 28 lakeside cabins. All cabins have separate bedrooms, a wood-burning fireplace, and a full bathroom. Four hiking trails radiate out from the resort, some leading to lakes where canoes are available free of charge. Dinner and breakfast is a very reasonable $30 per person per day.

INFORMATION

The **Visitor Reception Centre** (902/682-2772; mid-June-Aug. daily 8:30am-8pm, Aug.-mid-June daily 8:30am-4pm) is just beyond the park entrance. This is the place to buy day passes (adult $6, senior $5, child $3) and fishing licenses ($10 per day, $35 annual) and pick up literature on the park, including hiking trail descriptions.

GETTING THERE

Although the park is just 50 kilometers from Annapolis Royal along Highway 8, allow about an hour to reach the entrance, as the road is narrow and winding.

From Halifax, take Highway 101 along the South Shore to Liverpool and then Highway 8 north. The total distance from Halifax to the park is 170 kilometers (two hours).

Annapolis Valley

The Annapolis Valley, which spreads along the Annapolis River east from Annapolis Royal, is a haze of white when its apple orchards bloom in late May to early June. The valley, extending northeast from Annapolis Royal, supports more than magnificent apple orchards, however; if you look closely, you'll also see hectares of strawberries, plums, peaches, pears, and cherries, as well as crops of hay, grain, and tobacco.

The Annapolis Valley has a legion of fans, among them the Mi'kmaq, who first settled this region. According to Mi'kmaq legend, Glooscap, a deity taking the form of a giant man, roamed the upper Fundy. He made his home atop the basalt cliffs of the peninsula—the lofty hook-shaped cape that finishes in sea stacks at Cape Split—and buried jewels on the Fundy beaches. (Today's tides still claw at the coastline to reveal agate, amethyst, and zeolite from Hall's Harbour to Cape Split's tip.)

ANNAPOLIS ROYAL TO CANNING

From Annapolis Royal, Highway 101 heads northeast, crossing the Annapolis River near Bridgetown and continuing east for 100 kilometers to Wolfville. You don't see a great deal from the highway, so plan to travel Highway 1 (cross the Annapolis Basin at Annapolis Royal to get going). Along this route, you pass through the villages and apple orchards now bypassed by Highway 101.

Bridgetown

This town has wide streets lined with grand old homes and stately trees. **James House Museum** (12 Queen St., 902/665-4530; mid-May-Sept. Mon.-Fri. 9am-5pm; free) is an 1835 residence sandwiched between modern shops along the main street.

Take Church Street north out of town and you reach **Valleyview Provincial Park** after five kilometers. This small park sits atop North Mountain, an ancient ridge of lava that forms a cap over softer shale and sandstone that has been gouged away to the south, forming the Annapolis Valley. From the park, views extend across the valley to the province's remote interior. The park campground (mid-June-mid-Oct.; $26) has just 30 sites, but it only ever fills on summer weekends. It has toilets and drinking water but no showers.

GETTING THERE

Bridgetown is 24 kilometers (20 minutes) northeast of Annapolis Royal along Highway 101. From Halifax, Bridgetown is 170 kilometers (two hours) west on Highway 101.

Kentville

The commercial hub of the Annapolis Valley is Kentville (pop. 6,100). The town is on the north side of Highway 101 and at the junction of Highway 12, which cuts south through the Nova Scotia interior to Mahone Bay and Lunenburg. In the historic heart of town is **King's County Museum** (37 Cornwallis Ave., 902/678-6237; Mon.-Fri. 9am-4pm; free), which contains a predictable collection of pioneer artifacts, as well as many interesting historical photographs within a two-story 1903 red-brick courthouse.

On the outskirts of town, you'll find a couple of inexpensive motels, including **Allen's Motel** (384 Park St., 902/678-2683, www.allensmotel.ns.ca; mid-Mar.-mid-Dec.; $74-160 s or d), two kilometers west of downtown. Here, 10 rooms are separated from the highway by well-tended gardens and a picnic area with a gas barbecue; larger units have separate bedrooms and full kitchens.

South Mountain Park (Hwy. 12, South Alton, 902/678-0152 or 866/860-6092, www.southmountainparkcampground.com; $39-46, cabins $76) fills with holidaying families through its mid-May to mid-October season. A few kilometers south of Kentville, it's not really set up for quick overnight stays. But if you have children and are looking for a break from touring, it's a great place to kick back for a few days. The activities offered could easily fill a week of fun—everything from fishing to tennis and wagon rides to walking paths. Amenities include a par-3 golf course, a games room, a TV room, a library with wireless Internet access, a large outdoor pool, and lots more. On the downside, campsites offer little privacy.

GETTING THERE

Kentville is about 95 kilometers (just over an hour) northeast of Annapolis Royal via Highway 101. It's 100 kilometers (1.5 hours) northwest of Halifax on Highway 101.

Starr's Point

Prescott House Museum (1633 Starr's Point Rd., 902/542-3984; June-mid-Oct. Mon.-Sat. 10am-5pm, Sun. 1pm-5pm; adult $4, senior and child $2.75) harks back to the valley's orchard beginnings, when horticulturist Charles Ramage Prescott imported species to add to the provincial store of fruit trees. His profits built this Georgian-style homestead. The restored mansion, constructed circa 1812, displays period furnishings and sits amid beautiful gardens. Its special events celebrate the fall harvest. It's along Highway 358, which leads north from Greenwich.

GETTING THERE

Starr's Point is about 110 kilometers (1.5 hours) northeast from Annapolis Royal, via Highway 101.

Canning

The east end of the Annapolis Valley has a smattering of emerging boutique wineries, including **Blomidon Estate Winery** (10318 Hwy. 221, 902/582-7565, http://blomidonwine.ca; June-Oct. daily 10am-6pm). This winery was the first in Nova Scotia to produce classic varietals such as chardonnay, pinot noir, and shiraz. The winery is two kilometers east of Canning along Highway 221.

GETTING THERE

Canning is about 115 kilometers (1.5 hours) northeast of Annapolis Royal along Highway 101. It's 105 kilometers northwest of Halifax on Highway 101.

BLOMIDON PENINSULA

The Blomidon Peninsula is at the northern end of North Mountain. Extending into the Minas Channel and with Minas Basin to its back, it features more fantastic Fundy scenery and a couple of good campgrounds.

The Look-Off

On the north side of Canning, **Look-Off Family Camping** (Hwy. 358, 902/582-3022, www.lookoffcamping.com; May-Sept.; $30-36, cabins $70 s or d) lives up to its name with a long list of activities—think hayrides, bingo, and fitness classes—and workshops such as kite-making and cookie painting. Other facilities include a café open daily at 9am, a playground, a pool, and a launderette. The namesake Look-Off (a Nova Scotian term for a lookout) is across the road and has wonderful views across the bucolic Annapolis Valley.

Blomidon Provincial Park

The dramatically positioned 759-hectare **Blomidon Provincial Park** (902/582-7319) is along the eastern side of the Blomidon Peninsula, facing Minas Basin. To get there, turn off Highway 358 three kilometers north of the Look-Off and follow the secondary road north for 14 kilometers. The red shale and sandstone that make the park so striking were laid down millions of years ago and then eroded by glacial and water action to form 180-meter-high bluffs that are topped by

coastal forest. Fundy tides sweep up to the cliff face twice daily, but as the water recedes, you can walk along the red-sand beach, searching for semiprecious stones such as amethyst and agate. The uplands area is covered in forests of sugar maple, beech, and birch, yet also present are alpine plants such as maidenhair.

The best place for a walk is along the beach, but check at the park office or information boards for tide times. Four official trails wind their way through the park. The best views are from the Look-Off Trail, an easy 1-kilometer walk to a lookout high atop the cliffs. The 5.6-kilometer **Jodrey Trail** fringes the cliffs, while the **Interpretive Trail** passes information boards describing the forest and its inhabitants. The main day-use area is where the access road enters the park. It's one of the few places along the Fundy Coast where the water gets warm enough for swimming.

Beyond the day-use area, the access road climbs to the campground (early June-early Oct.; $26), where sites are spread through the forest on two short loops. Facilities include showers, a playground, and drinking water.

To Cape Split

At the tip of the Blomidon Peninsula is Cape Split. To get there, continue north on Highway

Blomidon Provincial Park is notable for its high sea cliffs.

358 from the Look-Off to Scots Bay, where there's a small day use-only provincial park with a pebbly beach fronting Minas Channel. The road ends just beyond Scots Bay, from where it's 13 kilometers on foot to Cape Split. It's a long way to walk (and make the return trek) in one day, but there is no elevation gain and the rewards are total wilderness and sweeping views from the cliff top at the end of the trail.

Getting There

The Blomidon Peninsula is about 130 kilometers (1.5 hours) northeast of Annapolis Royal along Highway 101, and about 20 kilometers (20 minutes) north of Canning.

Wolfville and Vicinity

At the eastern end of the Annapolis Valley, the genteel town of Wolfville (pop. 3,700) began with the name Mud Creek, an ignoble tribute from the founding New England planters who wrestled with the Fundy coastal area once farmed by early Acadians. Now the town sits in the lushest part of the Annapolis Valley, and you won't want to miss it. Highway 1 runs through town as Main Street, where large houses with bay windows and ample porches sit comfortably beneath stately trees. Acadia University's ivy-covered buildings and manicured lawns lie along Main and University.

The town, just six blocks deep, has an uncomplicated layout alongside Highway 1 and Highway 101.

SIGHTS
Main Street

Wolfville's refined nature is apparent to anyone walking along Main Street, which is dotted with grand stone buildings and, at the eastern end, stately trees.

Randall House Museum (259 Main St., 902/542-9775; June-Sept. Tues.-Sat. 10am-5pm, Sun. 1:30pm-5pm; donation) is a historic home (built in 1815) with period furnishings and local artifacts from the 1760s to the 20th century.

Acadia University Art Gallery (Beveridge Arts Centre, at Highland Ave. and Main St., 902/585-1373; Tues.-Sun. noon-4pm; free) has a fine-arts collection of local and regional works, highlighted by Alex Colville's oils and serigraphs.

Waterfront

Most visitors miss Wolfville's waterfront, but the town does have one, one block north of the main street across Front Street. Trails and a small park have been developed at the mouth of the Cornwallis River, which was once lined with busy shipyards. Views extend across the Minas Basin to the red cliffs of Blomidon Provincial Park.

Along Front Street to the west is **Robie Tufts Nature Centre,** which is a series of covered interpretive boards describing the flora and fauna native to the area. The main purpose of the structure is to provide a home for chimney swifts, which make their home in the red-brick chimney rising through the roof.

SHOPPING

The **Harvest Gallery** (462 Main St., 902/542-7093; July-Oct. Mon.-Sat. 10am-5pm, Sun. noon-5pm, closed Mon. the rest of the year) displays the work of local artists. Especially eye-catching are the colorful oil paintings of Jeanne Aisthorpe-Smith.

Although apples get all the glory, lots of other farming happens in the Annapolis Valley. **Gaspereau Valley Fibres** (830 Gaspereau River Rd., 902/542-2656; closed Mon.) highlights the local wool industries, with knitting, weaving, and spinning, as well as raw materials sold as-is. The shop is on a

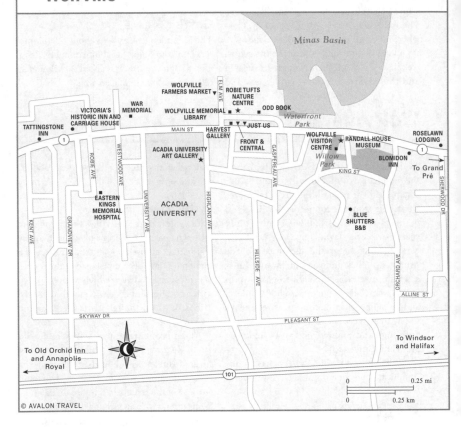

Wolfville

Minas Basin

WOLFVILLE FARMERS MARKET

ROBIE TUFTS NATURE CENTRE

ELM AVE

ODD BOOK

VICTORIA'S HISTORIC INN AND CARRIAGE HOUSE

WAR MEMORIAL

WOLFVILLE MEMORIAL LIBRARY

Waterfront Park

TATTINGSTONE INN

MAIN ST

HARVEST GALLERY

JUST US

WOLFVILLE VISITOR CENTRE

RANDALL HOUSE MUSEUM

ROSELAWN LODGING

ROBIE AVE

WESTWOOD AVE

ACADIA UNIVERSITY ART GALLERY

FRONT & CENTRAL

GASPEREAU AVE

Willow Park

BLOMIDON INN

To Grand Pré

SHERWOOD DR

KING ST

EASTERN KINGS MEMORIAL HOSPITAL

UNIVERSITY AVE

ACADIA UNIVERSITY

HIGHLAND AVE

BLUE SHUTTERS B&B

KENT AVE

GRANDVIEW DR

HILLSIDE AVE

ORCHARD AVE

ALLINE ST

SKYWAY DR

PLEASANT ST

To Old Orchid Inn and Annapolis Royal

To Windsor and Halifax

101

0   0.25 mi

0   0.25 km

© AVALON TRAVEL

farm on the south side of Highway 101; to get there from town, take Gaspereau Road south.

ACCOMMODATIONS

Most Wolfville accommodations are grand heritage homes, so there are few bargains.

$50-100

On the hill behind the information center, **Blue Shutters Bed and Breakfast** (7 Blomidon Terr., 902/542-3363, www.blueshuttersbnb.ns.ca; $80-110 s, $95-120 d) has three well-equipped guest rooms. Each has an en suite bathroom, a TV/DVD combo, wireless Internet, and an electric fireplace. Rates include a full breakfast.

Roselawn Lodging (32 Main St., 902/542-3420, www.roselawnlodging.ca; $90-185 s or d) is a modest motel on the east side of downtown. Facilities include an outdoor pool, a launderette, barbecues and picnic tables, a tennis court, and a playground. The 28 motel rooms are clean and comfortable, and 12 adjacent cottages come with kitchens.

$100-150

If you're a garden lover, you won't want to leave the expansive grounds of ★ **Blomidon Inn** (195 Main St., 902/542-2291 or 800/565-2291, www.blomidon.ns.ca; $109-269 s or d), which is surrounded by more than one hectare of cacti, roses, rhododendrons, azaleas, ponds, a croquet lawn, and a terraced vegetable garden that doubles as an outdoor eating area. The home itself, built in 1882 by a shipbuilder, reflects the wealth of its original owner. Mahogany and teak dominate, and local antiques are found throughout public areas and the 29 guest rooms. The least expensive rooms are on the small side, but all have en suite bathrooms. Rates include a continental breakfast and afternoon tea. Tennis courts, a restaurant, and a lounge round out this elegant accommodation.

A registered historic property built in 1893, **Victoria's Historic Inn and Carriage House** (600 Main St., 902/542-5744 or 800/556-5744, www.victoriashistoricinn.com; $138-245 s or d) combines a grand Victorian house with an adjacent carriage house. Rooms vary greatly in character; my favorite is the Hunt Room ($138 s or d), on the upper floor of the carriage house, which has a smart green and burgundy color theme and a vaulted cathedral ceiling. Like the other rooms, it has an en suite four-piece bathroom, TV, telephone, bathrobes, and a CD player. Rates include a cooked breakfast and afternoon tea.

Dating to 1874 and within walking distance of downtown, **Tattingstone Inn** (630 Main St., 902/542-7696 or 800/565-7696, www. tattingstone.ns.ca; $128-178 s or d) is casually formal, with nine guest rooms spread through the main house and adjacent carriage house. All are decorated with antiques and some have whirlpool tubs. The inn also offers a music room, dining room, steam room, heated outdoor pool, and tennis court. Rates include a cooked breakfast.

The **Old Orchard Inn** (153 Greenwich Rd., 902/542-5751 or 800/561-8090, www.oldorchardinn.com) is a sprawling resort near Exit 11 of Highway 101. It comprises more than 100 motel-style guest rooms ($105-155 s or d) and 29 cabins (May-Oct.; $150-225 s or d) spread through the forest. Tennis courts, an indoor pool, saunas, spa services, hiking trails, and a stone patio with sweeping valley views add to the appeal. The resort also has a dining room and lounge.

FOOD

For a small town, Wolfville has a surprising number of eateries, but my suggestion if you're in town on a Wednesday or Saturday is to head to ★ **Wolfville Farmers Market** (24 Elm St., 902/697-3344, May-Dec. Wed. 4pm-7pm, year-round Sat. 8:30am-1pm), which has a mouthwatering selection of choices from local producers, including many choices cooked on

Blomidon Inn

the spot such as Harbourville Schnitzelhaus, which sells authentic German dishes using lots of local produce. Many stalls sell items to go, such as baked goods, preserves, smoked meats, and wine.

Just Us! (450 Main St., 902/542-7731; Mon.-Fri. 7am-9pm, Sat. 8am-6pm, Sun. 10am-5pm; lunches $5-8) pours organic coffees and a wide range of teas from the front of a historic theater building, with seating spread through the lobby. Meals are very inexpensive ($5 for soup and sandwich), and the muffins are baked fresh daily.

In a restored 1860 home one block from Main Street, the kitchen at ★ **Front & Central** (117 Front St., 902/542-0588; Wed.-Mon. 5pm-9pm) prepares the most creative and well-presented cooking in the Annapolis Valley, all in the form of "small plates"—servings that are larger than typical tapas and range from $5 to $20 each. The menu features the latest trends in Canadian cooking but makes wonderful use of local seafood and produce. The tree-shaded patio fills on warmer evenings, so make reservations.

The dining rooms at the local inns are good bets for meals. One of the best of the dining rooms associated with local accommodations is the **Acadian Room** (Old Orchard Inn, 153 Greenwich Rd., 902/542-5751; daily 7am-9pm; $17-29), which draws diners to its large restaurant with stunning views and good food. Before 11am, the French toast with whipped cream and blueberry sauce is a delight. Local fare such as cedar-plank salmon basted with dark rum and maple syrup is an evening standout. Most dinner mains are less than $20. The wine list allows the opportunity to taste Nova Scotian wine by the glass.

INFORMATION AND SERVICES

At the east end of town is the **Wolfville Visitor Centre** (Willow Park, Main St., 902/542-7000, www.wolfville.ca; May-Oct. daily 9am-6pm).

Eastern Kings Memorial Hospital is at 23 Earnscliffe Ave. (902/542-2266). Call the **police** at 902/542-3817 or the **RCMP** at 902/679-5555.

Wolfville Farmers Market

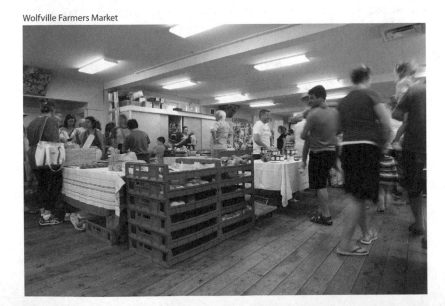

GETTING THERE

Wolfville is 120 kilometers (1.5 hours) east of Annapolis Royal along Highway 101. It's 90 kilometers (just over an hour) northwest of Halifax.

GRAND PRÉ

This small village was the epicenter of one of the most tragic events in Canadian history, the expulsion of the Acadians from their homeland. First settled in 1680 by an Acadian family who moved from the confines of nearby Port Royal, Grand Pré grew to become the largest Acadian settlement in Nova Scotia. The main attraction is Grand Pré National Historic Site, but also worth visiting is **Grand Pré Wines** (Hwy. 1, 902/542-1753; July-mid-Oct. Mon.-Sat. 10am-6pm, Sun. 11am-6pm, mid-Oct.-Dec. Wed.-Sun. 11am-5pm), where grapes are grown on 60 hectares of former Acadian farmland. In the main building you'll find a restaurant, wine shop, and crafts corner. Winery tours are offered through summer (daily 11am, 3pm, and 5pm).

★ Grand Pré National Historic Site

Commemorating the Acadian deportation, the **Grand Pré National Historic Site** (2242 Grand Pré Rd., 902/542-3631; mid-May-mid-Oct. daily 9am-5pm; adult $7.80, senior $6.60, child $4) brings Acadian history and the deportation to life. It wasn't until Henry Wadsworth Longfellow wrote the poem *Evangeline* in 1847 that the English-speaking world became aware of the expulsion, but by then nothing remained of Grand-Pré (Great Meadow), the setting for the story of the Acadian heroine separated from her lover by the deportation.

In 1922, an interested benefactor with Acadian roots built a small stone church on the presumed site of Grand Pré, and this became the foundation for the historic site of today. Visitors enter through a large museum complex, where there's a bookstore and gift shop, along with information panels describing Acadian life, the deportation, and the return of Acadians to Nova Scotia. Outside are sprawling grounds crisscrossed by pathways that lead to vegetable gardens, a

FUNDY COAST
WOLFVILLE AND VICINITY

Grand Pré National Historic Site

blacksmith shop, an orchard, a lookout over the diked farmland, and a statue of Henry Wadsworth Longfellow. In the middle of the site is a statue of Evangeline. Directly behind the statue is the 1922 church. It houses an exhibit of paintings that showcase the history of the people and a copy of the original expulsion order that was read to a congregation within the original church, as well as stained-glass windows with a story to tell. Guided tours of the grounds (included with admission) are highly recommended. A guide is also stationed within Église Saint-Charles to lead you through the story of each painting.

Accommodations and Food

The best choice of accommodations are in nearby Wolfville, but the centrally located **Evangeline Inn and Motel** (11668 Hwy. 1, 902/542-2703 or 888/542-2703, www.evangeline.ns.ca; May-Oct.; $109-139 s or d) provides comfortable accommodations right at the turnoff to the historic site. Choose from motel rooms or rooms in the adjacent boyhood home of Sir Robert Borden, prime minister of Canada for nine years in the early 20th century. All guests have use of the swimming pool. Also on the grounds is a restaurant open daily May to October 8am to 7pm, where cooked breakfasts are less than $7 and dishes such as haddock chowder with a warmed scone on the side are $6-10.

Stop at the headquarters of locally owned **Just Us!** (11865 Hwy. 1, 902/922; Mon.-Wed. 7am-5pm, Thurs.-Fri. 7am-6pm, Sat. 8am-6pm, Sun. 9am-6pm). Here, on the north side of the historic site, you'll find a roaster, a shop selling a thoughtful collection of coffee-related items, and a small museum (free entry) explaining the owners' dedication to free trade coffee and why it's important. Out back is a garden that visitors are free to wander through.

Getting There

To get to Grand Pré from Wolfville, head east on Highway 1 for about five kilometers, or take Exit 10 from Highway 101. From Halifax, head north on Highway 101 for 85 kilometers (one hour).

WINDSOR

If you've toured along the South Shore and then traveled along the Fundy Coast, the temptation may be to stay on the highway and give Windsor, just 60 kilometers northwest of Halifax, a miss. But this gracious town on the banks of the Avon River is worth the short detour from busy Highway 101. To get there from the main highway, take Exit 6, which leads into downtown. Before town is a small **information center** (902/798-2690; mid-May-mid-Oct. daily 9am-5pm).

Fort Edward National Historic Site

Dating to 1750, **Fort Edward National Historic Site** (King St., 902/542-3631; mid-June-late Sept. daily 10am-6pm; free) preserves the last 18th-century blockhouse in Nova Scotia. Fort Edward was one of the main assembly points for the deportation of the Acadians from the province in 1755. Although the building is open only during summer, touring the grounds will give a good feel for the location of the fort and the chance to see earthen mounds where the rest of the fort once stood.

Historic Homes

Haliburton House (414 Clifton Ave., 902/798-5619; June-early Oct. Mon.-Sat. 10am-5pm, Sun. 1pm-5pm; adult $4, senior and child $2.75) was owned by 19th-century author, humorist, historian, and judge Thomas Chandler Haliburton, who was born in Windsor in 1796. Among the sayings that originated in Haliburton's writings are "It's raining cats and dogs," "barking up the wrong tree," "facts are stranger than fiction," and "quick as a wink." The Victorian mansion on 10 hectares is open to the public, as

Holy Pumpkins!

Windsor may be famous as the birthplace of hockey, but no attraction is bigger than the pumpkins grown on the south side of town at **Howard Dill Enterprises** (400 College Rd., 902/798-2728; July-Aug. Mon.-Fri. 9am-5pm, Sept.-Oct. daily 9am-6pm). The Dill family is renowned in the giant pumpkin-growing business for developing seeds that go on to produce some of the world's largest pumpkins, some of which swell to over 700 kilograms (1,540 pounds).

You won't find the pumpkins grown from Dill's seeds on grocery store shelves. They are used for fall fairs and pumpkin-growing competitions, and as jack-o-lanterns by folks with strong porches. Most of the company's business is done online; at www.howarddill.com you can order the precious seeds and books such as *How to Grow World Class Giant Pumpkins* as well as download growing tips. At the Dill farm, visitors are encouraged to drop by and see Dill's own pumpkin patch, where even the smallest pumpkins are in the 180- to 230-kilogram (400- to 500-pound) range leading up to the late September-early October harvest.

are the surrounding gardens. For hockey fans, Haliburton's written memories of childhood have special meaning. In them, he reminisced about children "playing ball on ice" behind Haliburton House, which is the earliest mention of the game of ice hockey.

On Ferry Hill, **Shand House** (389 Avon St.) is another vintage beauty and marks the wealthy Shand family's prominence in Windsor. When it was built in the early 1890s, the Queen Anne-style mansion was one of the first residences in the area fitted with electric lights and indoor plumbing. Currently, there is no public access, but the grandeur can be admired from the grounds.

Getting There

Windsor is southeast of Wolfville, about 30 kilometers (25 minutes) away via Highway 1 or Highway 101. Windsor is about 60 kilometers (45 minutes) northwest of Halifax via Highway 101.

Central Nova Scotia

Halifax to Truro 132

Glooscap Trail 136

Sunrise Coast to Pictou 141

Pictou 144

Pictou to Cape Breton Island . . . 147

Marine Drive. 150

Central Nova Scotia extends north from Halifax to Truro (the geographical center of the province) and then west to the New Brunswick border and east to the causeway leading to Cape Breton Island. This region, at once the

most-traveled and least-known part of the province, is perfect for those looking for low-key attractions as varied as ancient fossils, beautiful beaches, and remote parks.

The region can be divided roughly into manageable sections—each very different in look and feel. The TransCanada Highway slices through the region's northwest corner and extends to Cape Breton Island in the east. But this route promises little besides uninterrupted speed. Detour south to explore an area that was once the realm of Glooscap, the mythical Mi'kmaq god who roamed this part of Nova Scotia in the form of a man as large as Gulliver among the Lilliputians. According to legend, Glooscap slept stretched out over the region's northern portion and used Prince Edward Island as his pillow. While the Northumberland Strait has long been the domain of vacationing locals—attracted by warm water and long stretches of beautiful beach—other visitors on a fast track often

see the region as a flash of landscape from the TransCanada Highway. The other option for reaching Cape Breton Island from Halifax is to drive along the Eastern Shore, which is as rugged as the Northumberland Strait shore is tame. This super-scenic road unfurls itself at a leisurely pace, and it's worth slowing down and taking two or three days to travel its length. Passing tiny fishing ports reminiscent of seafaring life of decades ago and rock-bound coves where the forest grows right down to the sea, the road's services are few and far between (Canso, with a population of 950, is the largest town), so plan ahead by making accommodation reservations and keeping your gas tank full.

PLANNING YOUR TIME

Central Nova Scotia is not a destination like Cape Breton Island, where you would plan your visit around an itinerary that lasted a certain length of time. Instead, you will surely

Previous: Waterside Beach; historic boat at dock. **Above:** Balmoral Grist Mill.

Look for ★ to find recommended
sights, activities, dining, and lodging.

Highlights

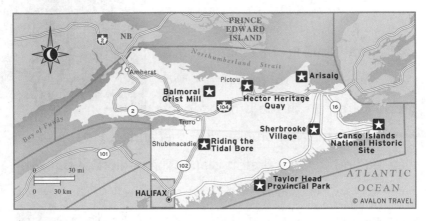

© AVALON TRAVEL

★ **Riding the Tidal Bore:** The tidal bore phenomenon occurs in only a few places in the world. Locals call it the Total Bore, and while admittedly it's not exactly exciting to watch from the sidelines, riding the wave on a raft is a once-in-a-lifetime experience (page 132).

★ **Balmoral Grist Mill:** Surrounded by rich green foliage, the reflection of this bright-red building in an adjacent pond creates a scene of tranquility (page 143).

★ **Hector Heritage Quay:** Step aboard a full-size replica of the *Hector,* upon which Pictou's first settlers arrived, to get a taste of the hardships that were once endured crossing the Atlantic Ocean (page 144).

★ **Arisaig:** The unassuming cliffs at Arisaig are filled with fossils that have helped scientists understand the evolution of life on earth 400 million years ago (page 148).

★ **Taylor Head Provincial Park:** Marine Drive passes dozens of protected areas, but Taylor Head stands out for its ease of access and interesting geology (page 152).

★ **Sherbrooke Village:** History comes alive at this living museum. For the full effect, join the Hands on History program and dress up in period costume (page 154).

★ **Canso Islands National Historic Site:** The focus of this attraction is Grassy Island, once home to a thriving fishing community in the early 1700s. But the best part for budget-conscious travelers will be the price—just $5 including a boat trip (page 156).

Central Nova Scotia

NEW BRUNSWICK

PRINCE EDWARD ISLAND

CHARLOTTETOWN

Minas Channel

Chignecto Bay

Cape Chignecto Provincial Park

Advocate Harbour

Glooscap Trail

Joggins

Southampton

Parrsboro

Nappan

Amherst

Economy

Five Islands Provincial Park

Springhill

Oxford

Linden

Pugwash

Wallace

Tidnish

Tidnish Provincial Park

Amherst Shore Provincial Park

Northport Beach Provincial Park

Heather Beach Provincial Park

Northumberland Strait

Minas Basin

Wolfville

Windsor

To Halifax

Glooscap Trail

Cobequid Bay

Maitland

Urbania

Shubenacadie River

Shubenacadie

RIDING THE TIDAL BORE

SHUBENACADIE WILDLIFE PARK

Tatamagouche

JOST VINEYARDS

BALMORAL GRIST MILL

Balmoral Mills

Denmark

Matagash

Malagash

Tatamagouche Bay

Caribou/Monroes Island Provincial Park

Seafoam

Pictou

Caribou

HECTOR HERITAGE QUAY

Wood Islands

Caribou Provincial Park

Arisaig

ARISAIG

Truro

To Lawrencetown

Musquodoboit Harbour

Oyster Pond

Ship Harbour

Clam Harbour PP

Spry Bay

Sheet Harbour

TAYLOR HEAD PROVINCIAL PARK

Tangier

Liscomb Game Sanctuary

Caledonia

Liscomb Mills

Sherbrooke

SHERBROOKE VILLAGE

Marie Joseph

Aspen

New Glasgow

Stellarton

Antigonish

Cape George

St. Georges Bay

Ballantynes Cove

Cape George

Auld's Cove

Pomquet

Port Bickerton

Isaac's Harbour

To Canso

CANSO ISLANDS NATIONAL HISTORIC SITE

ATLANTIC OCEAN

© AVALON TRAVEL

0 15 mi
0 15 km

find yourself passing through central Nova Scotia on more than one occasion—for example, driving from New Brunswick through to Halifax and then again on the way to Cape Breton Island. If you've been touring through New Brunswick, you'll already be well aware of the massive Fundy tides. In central Nova Scotia, you can **ride the tidal bore** on the Shubenacadie River. Along Northumberland Strait, beaches lapped by warm water will tempt you to linger, while historic attractions such as **Balmoral Grist Mill** and Pictou's **Hector Heritage Quay Museum** keep the past alive. From Halifax, you could plan on spending two days reaching Cape Breton Island via the above-mentioned attractions, which would also allow time for a detour to **Arisaig,** a fossil hot spot protected by a small provincial park. If you have an extra day or two, consider taking Marine Drive to or from Cape Breton Island. The distance

(320 kilometers) is deceiving when planning how long the drive will take. Add a ferry trip to a winding, often narrow road that passes through dozens of small townships, and you should expect the journey to take at least six hours. From Canso, it will take another 90 minutes to reach Port Hastings, the gateway to Cape Breton Island. But of course, this estimate of 7.5 hours to complete the Marine Drive is sans stops, and if you're only interested in reaching Cape Breton Island from Halifax, the Highway 102/104 route via Truro takes about half as long. Leaving Halifax in the morning, an ideal scenario would be to spend one night en route and to plan on reaching Cape Breton Island later the following day. This would allow time to explore **Taylor Head Provincial Park,** to step back in time at **Sherbrooke Village,** and to take the boat trip to **Canso Islands National Historic Site.**

Halifax to Truro

As you head north from Halifax, suburbia is quickly left behind, as divided Highway 102 speeds north to Truro, which is easily reached in an hour from downtown. Highway 2, the original route between these two cities may look appealing on the map, but the scenery is no different from what you'll see from Highway 102—it simply takes around 30 minutes longer.

SHUBENACADIE

If you're willing to try something new, or you have an animal-loving family, there are two good reasons to visit Shubenacadie.

★ Riding the Tidal Bore

The **Shubenacadie River,** which drains into the Bay of Fundy at Cobequid Bay, is not just a good place to view the tidal bore but also to *ride* it. **Tidal Bore Rafting Park** (Hwy. 215, Urbania, 902/758-4032 or 800/565-7238, www.raftingcanada.ca) operates

two- and four-hour Zodiac raft excursions May-September. You board the rafts at low tide and head downstream, just in time to catch the tidal bore back upriver. The driver rides the wave, then doubles back to blast through its face, finding rapids along the way to keep the adrenaline pumping. Rates range $60-75 depending on the extremity of the tide. Departures are dependent on the tides; check the website for times.

Shubenacadie Wildlife Park

Families will enjoy **Shubenacadie Wildlife Park** (149 Creighton Rd., 902/758-2040; mid-May-mid-Oct. daily 9am-6:30pm, mid-Oct.-mid-May Sat.-Sun. 9am-3pm; adult $4.50, child $2), a provincially-operated zoo well signposted from Highway 102 (take Exit 10 or 11). Throughout the spacious grounds are Canadian animals you are unlikely to see in the wild (fishers, otters, and more), ones that you don't want to meet face to face (bears,

peacock at Shubenacadie Wildlife Park

right on the Shubenacadie River is **Wide Open Wilderness Campground** (Urbania, 902/261-2228 or 866/811-2267, www.wow-camping.com; mid-May-mid-Oct.; campsites $27-35, cabins $80 s or d). You can watch the tidal bore, walk marked hiking trails, relax around the pool, try your hand at the horseshoe pits, or join in the many scheduled activities.

Getting There
To get to Shubenacadie from Halifax, take Exit 10 from Highway 102. It's a 60-kilometer, 45-minute drive.

MAITLAND
Maitland, at the mouth of the Shubenacadie River, was where Canada's largest wooden ship, the three-masted *William D. Lawrence*, was built. Documentaries, ship portraits, and memorabilia are kept at the shipbuilder's former homestead, the **Lawrence House Museum** (8660 Hwy. 215, 902/261-2628; June-early Oct. Mon.-Sat. 10am-5pm, Sun. 1pm-5pm; adult $4, senior and child $2.75), which overlooks Cobequid Bay. The actual 1874 launching is commemorated on the middle Saturday of each September with a parade of period-dressed locals, a symbolic launch, and seafood suppers hosted throughout the village.

Getting There
To get to Maitland from Halifax, it's a 90-kilometer, 70-minute drive starting with Highway 118 and ending with Highway 215.

If you've been moseying eastbound along the Bay of Fundy and don't particularly want to detour back through Halifax, turn at Windsor (take Exit 5 from Highway 101) and follow Highway 215 along the edge of Minas Basin to Maitland, crossing the Shubenacadie River to meet busy Highway 102 at Truro. Between Windsor and Truro it's 90 kilometers (1.5 hours)—you won't save any time, but the scenery is better than via Halifax (120 kilometers, 1.5 hours).

cougars, wolves, and lynx), and those you'll see only at Christmas (reindeer). The Sable Island horses may look like regular horses, but they are one of the world's few wild horse populations.

Accommodations and Camping
★ **Rafters Ridge Cottages** (Hwy. 215, Urbania, 902/758-4032 or 800/565-7238, www.raftingcanada.ca; $145-195 s or d) is part of the Tidal Bore Rafting Park complex, so it's no surprise that many guests come for the rafting (rooms are discounted when a rafting package is purchased). In the riverside location, you can also rent canoes or hang out around the outdoor pool. Lodging is in one- and two-bedroom cottages. The cottages have decks, barbecues, and pleasant views across a tree-sprinkled hillside. The facility also has a restaurant open daily for breakfast and dinner.

In the vicinity of the rafting park and also

TRURO

Situated at the convergence of the province's major expressways and served by VIA Rail, Truro (pop. 12,500) is called the hub of Nova Scotia. It is the province's third-largest population center, with an economy based on shipping, dairy products, and the manufacture of clothing, carpets, plastic products, and wines. Truro's academic side includes a teachers' college in town and an agricultural college on the outskirts.

Sights

The access road leading into 400-hectare **Victoria Park** (corner of Brunswick St. and Park Rd.) ends at a wide-open day-use area where beds of tulips flower through June, a colorful highlight of the town. At other times of year, the park is still worth visiting—forests of spruce, hemlock, and white pine are spliced with hiking trails that lead along a deep canyon and past two waterfalls.

In a quiet residential area, the **Colchester Society Museum** (29 Young St., 902/895-6284; June-Aug. Mon.-Fri. 10am-5pm, Sat. 1pm-5pm, shorter hours Sept.-May; adult $4, child $2) does a fine job entwining exhibits on Fundy eccentricities and the area's natural history.

WATCHING THE TIDAL BORE

Tidal bores only occur in a few places in the world, and one of the most accessible is at the

Truro

Salmon River, which flows through Truro. Best described as a small wave, the bore is particularly high along the Salmon River, as it is at the head of Cobequid Bay, where the incoming tide pushing up the Bay of Fundy is forced into a narrow funnel. At Truro, the lead wave travels up the river as it pushes toward town beneath the Highway 102 overpass. If you want a close-up look at the tidal bore, take Robie Street west out of town beyond Highway 102 (or, from Hwy. 102 take Exit 14) and take the signed road that leads to the **Tidal Bore Observation Deck.** Tidal bore arrival times are listed at the deck, in the *Truro Daily News,* and at the Truro Welcome Centre (Commercial St.).

Accommodations

Lodgings in Truro are plentiful and reasonably priced. Motels line all the main routes into town, and you shouldn't have a problem finding a room at short notice.

As usual, the **Super 8** (85 Treaty Trail, 902/895-8884 or 877/508-7666, www.super-8truro.com; $155 s or d) is close to a main artery and is filled with clean, comfortable air-conditioned rooms packed with amenities.

Here you also get an indoor pool with a waterslide and hot tub. A light breakfast is included, and you can walk next door to the Capricorn Restaurant for dinner. Call for last-minute specials.

Food

In a nondescript strip mall near the heart of downtown, ★ **Murphy's** (88 Esplanade, 902/895-1275; daily 11am-7pm; $9-18) serves some of the best-priced seafood anywhere in this part of the province. I had the deep-fried haddock and chips—cooked to perfection—for just $10. A variety of fish is offered—pan-fried, poached, or "Texas style"—amid bright nautical-themed decor.

Another favorite is **Nook and Cranny** (627 Prince St., 902/895-0779; Mon. 11am-9pm, Tues.-Thurs. 11am-11pm, Fri. 11am-1am, Sat. 9am-11pm, Sun. 9am-11pm; $16-24). While locals often stop by just for a craft beer on the outdoor tables, the lunch and dinner menu provides good value, with most dishes featuring local produce and game.

Information

The **Truro Welcome Centre** (Commercial

looking out from the Tidal Bore Observation Deck

St., 902/893-2922; mid-May-mid-Oct. daily 9am-5pm, July and Aug. 9am-7:30pm) is at the heart of downtown overlooking Victoria Square; ask for a map of the tree-trunk sculptures scattered through town and check your email using the free wireless Internet.

Getting There

True to its nickname, the Hub of Nova Scotia, Truro is centrally located within the province at the junction of Highways 102 and 104. It's an easy one-hour run between Halifax and Truro (100 kilometers apart), and even less from Halifax Airport (66 km south). Baddeck on Cape Breton Island is 252 kilometers to the northeast (allow three hours) and Moncton, New Brunswick, is 172 kilometers (90 minutes) to the west.

Glooscap Trail

Named for the mighty Glooscap, a mythical Mi'kmaq figure who controlled the tides, this region is far enough from the main highway that it is missed by most visitors. It's a shame, because it is dotted with interesting seaside villages, has beaches that occasionally give up precious gemstones, and has been the site of some amazing dinosaur discoveries. The Glooscap Trail extends along the Bay of Fundy from as far west as Windsor; this section covers the best of Highway 2, which follows the coast west from Truro to Cape Chignecto and then north to Amherst.

TRURO TO PARRSBORO

Take Exit 14A from Highway 102, and you'll quickly find yourself on Highway 2, heading west along Cobequid Bay. En route to Parrsboro are a string of small fishing villages, lookout points, and a couple

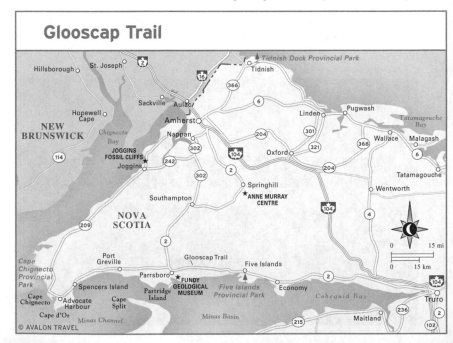

Glooscap Trail

of spots where beach access is possible at low tide.

Five Islands Provincial Park

As the name suggests, **Five Islands Provincial Park** does protect five islands, but it also encompasses more than 600 hectares of the mainland between Economy and Parrsboro. Among the park's coastal extremes are high cliffs and beaches, the latter revealing gems such as agate, amethyst, and jasper as the huge Fundy tides sweep across the bay. The five-kilometer (round-trip; allow 90 minutes) **Red Head Trail** reaches almost a dozen lookouts, including the Old Wife, a point of land that enjoys views across to the five islands.

PARRSBORO

The sea's erosive force has opened a window on the ancient world here along the coastlines of Chignecto Bay and Minas Basin. Archaeological digs have yielded 100,000 fossilized bone fragments of ancient dinosaurs, crocodiles, lizards, sharks, and primitive fish.

Sights
FUNDY GEOLOGICAL MUSEUM

Cross the bridge from downtown via Two Island Road to reach **Fundy Geological Museum** (162 Two Islands Rd., 902/254-3814; mid-May-mid-Oct. daily 9:30am-5:30pm; adult $8, senior $6.50, child $4.50). It highlights the Bay of Fundy, with displays describing how the tides have eroded the bedrock to expose numerous geological wonders, such as precious gemstones and the fossilized remains of dinosaurs.

PARRSBORO ROCK AND MINERAL SHOP AND MUSEUM

Parrsboro Rock and Mineral Shop and Museum (349 Whitehall Rd., 902/254-2981, May-Dec. daily 10am-6pm; free) is famed local geologist Eldon George's pride. The museum displays dinosaur, reptile, and amphibian footprint fossils. The shop stocks fossil and gem specimens, rock hound supplies, books, and maps.

OTTAWA HOUSE MUSEUM

Through town, beyond the mineral shop, is **Ottawa House Museum** (902/254-2376; June-Sept. daily 10am-6pm; adult $2), a 21-bedroom waterfront home dating to 1775. All that remains on the beach in front of the home are broken-down pylons, so it's hard to believe that this was once an important shipbuilding port. Now cared for by the local historical society, Ottawa House has two floors of historic displays and a tearoom.

Linked to the mainland by a narrow strip of rocky beach that begins below Ottawa House you'll find Partridge Island; archaeological evidence points to Mi'kmaq occupation of the island 10,000 years ago. A rough road ends just before the island, from where a hiking trail winds to the summit and allows views across the Minas Basin to Cape Split (30 minutes round-trip).

Accommodations

Riverview Cottages (3575 Eastern Ave., 902/254-2388 or 877/254-2388, www.riverviewcottages.ca; mid-May-mid-Oct.; $60-100 s or d) lie along Farrells River on the east side of town. They are older and only a few have cooking facilities, but canoes are available for guest use, and the price is right.

Within walking distance of downtown, the ★ **Maple Inn** (2358 Western Ave., 902/254-3735, www.mapleinn.ca; $99-179) smoothly combines two historic homes into an accommodation with 11 regular rooms and a spacious two-bedroom suite. The building was originally a hospital, so the inn has special meaning to those visitors returning to the town where they were born (Room 1 was the delivery room). The inn is surrounded by well-tended gardens, while inside is a lounge with a TV and a library of books. Rates include a full breakfast served in a cheery dining room.

The rooms at **Gillespie House Inn** (358 Main St., 902/254-3196 or 877/901-3196, www.

gillespiehouseinn.com; May-Oct.; $119-139 s or d) ooze old-world charm, and each has an en suite bathroom. The Elderkin Room has a wooden sleigh bed and looks over the front garden, which catches the morning sun.

Food
As you cruise the main street, **Glooscap Restaurant** (758 Upper Main St., 902/254-3488; daily breakfast, lunch, and dinner; $12-17) is obvious, but a better choice is the **Harbour View Restaurant** (476 Pier Rd., 902/254-3507; summer daily 11am-9pm; $14-27), which has uninterrupted water views off Two Island Road. It's a friendly place, with all the usual seafood choices, including daily specials that are sourced from seasonal catches. The lobster dinner is a favorite.

Getting There
Parrsboro is just over 90 kilometers (1.5 hours) from Truro via Highway 2. It's 180 kilometers (2.5 hours) via Highway 102 and 2 through Truro.

WEST TO CAPE CHIGNECTO
At Parrsboro, most travelers head north to Springhill on Highway 2, but Highway 209 along Minas Channel makes for a pleasant drive. It's 50 kilometers to the last village of any consequence, Advocate Harbour. At the halfway mark is Port Greville, once home to four shipbuilding companies. Today, take Wagstaff Street to the cliff edge and you can peer down at the river mouth that 100 years ago would have been filled with ships in various stages of construction. Across the water, Cape Split is plainly visible.

Advocate Harbour
At Spencers Island, Highway 209 turns inland to **Advocate Harbour,** a quiet corner of the province first visited by Europeans in 1604, when Samuel de Champlain came ashore. Just before town, take the signposted road to Cape d'Or, where a light-keeper's residence has been converted into ★ **The Lighthouse at Cape d'Or** (902/670-0534, www.capedor.ca; May-mid-Oct.; $80-110 s or d). Perched on high cliffs overlooking the Bay of Fundy, this four-room lodge is a wonderful place to kick back and do absolutely nothing at all. One room has an en suite bathroom, while the other three share two bathrooms, and the common room is stocked with books and board games. The attached restaurant (closed Wednesday; cash only) serves light lunches and creative dinners ($13-30).

Cape Chignecto Provincial Park
As the crow flies, **Cape Chignecto Provincial Park** isn't far from the TransCanada Highway or the city of Saint John (New Brunswick), but it is a world away from civilization, protecting an arrow-shaped headland jutting into the Bay of Fundy. Cliffs up to 185 meters high are lapped by the world's highest tides, which pour into Chignecto Bay on one side and Minas Basin on the other. No roads penetrate the park. Instead, from the end of the road at Red Rocks, just beyond the village of West Advocate and 46 kilometers from Parrsboro, a hiking trail leads around the cape and loops back through the forested interior. Most backpackers complete the circuit in three days, packing their own food and water and pitching their tents at backcountry campgrounds. Cabins along the way at Arch Gulch and Eatonville provide an alternative to camping (call 902/392-2085 for reservations). All hikers should be experienced in backcountry travel and totally self-sufficient.

JOGGINS
This town on the Chignecto Bay coast is 40 kilometers southwest of Amherst.

Joggins Fossil Cliffs
Declared a UNESCO World Heritage Site in 2008, **Joggins Fossil Cliffs** have yielded thousands of fossils from the Carboniferous period (350 million to 280 million years ago).

Plants are most common, but a forest of upright petrified tree stumps is what the site is best known for. First noted in the 1850s, the hollow stumps contained the fossilized remains of *Hylonomus,* the earliest reptile ever discovered. It is supposed that these 30-centimeter-long critters fell inside and were unable to escape. The site has also revealed a two-meter-long arthropod with 30 sets of legs, as well as dinosaur footprints.

In conjunction with the UNESCO designation, the opening of the **Joggins Fossil Centre** (100 Main St., off Hwy. 302, 902/251-2727; mid-April-June and Sept.-Oct. daily 10am-4pm, July-Aug. 10am-5:30pm; adult $8, senior and child $6) in 2008 cemented the town as an important stop in central Nova Scotia. In addition to displays of ferns, fish scales, reptile footprints, and gastropods, visitors can watch lab technicians at work. Daily two-hour guided tours to Coal Mine Point ($10.50 per person) are dependent on the tides.

Getting There
From Parrsboro, take Highway 2 north to Southampton and then follow Highways 302 and 242 north and then west for 40 kilometers (40 minutes) until you reach Joggins. From Halifax, take Highway 102 north to Truro, then Highway 104 west to Amherst where Highway 302/Highway 242 leads to Joggins. Allow 2.5 hours for the 225-kilometer drive from Halifax.

SPRINGHILL
The sultry voice of crooner Anne Murray is known the world over, but the folks in the small town of Springhill, on a slight rise just off Highway 104, take special pride in this local girl who has gone on to sell 50 million albums and win more awards than any other female vocalist.

Anne Murray Centre
You probably already guessed that Springhill would provide a home for the **Anne Murray Centre** (36 Main St., 902/597-8614; mid-May-mid-Oct. daily 9am-4:30pm; adult $7, senior and student $6). The museum pays tribute to the beloved local warbler who hit the Top 40 in the 1970s with "Snow Bird" and is still going strong. Exhibits include photos, clothing, and other memorabilia, and an audiovisual display catalogs Murray's career.

Getting There
Springhill is 45 kilometers (45 minutes) northeast of Parrsboro via Highway 2. It's 180 kilometers (two hours) north then west of Halifax via Highways 102 and 104.

AMHERST AND VICINITY
Amherst (pop. 9,500) is built on high ground above Amherst Marsh—part of the larger 200-square-kilometer Tantramar Marshes—on the isthmus joining Nova Scotia to the mainland of Canada. The fertile marshes were first diked and farmed by the Acadians in the 1600s and are still productive today, mainly as hayfields.

Sights
Amherst is at its architectural best along Victoria Street, where the profits of industry and trade were translated into gracious houses, commercial buildings, and churches garnished in Tudor, Gothic, and Queen Anne Revival styles (the red sandstone **First Baptist Church** on Victoria Street in the heart of downtown is particularly impressive). A few blocks south of the historic district, **Cumberland County Museum** (150 Church St., 902/667-2561; Feb.-Dec. Tues.-Fri. 9am-5pm, Sat. noon-5pm; adult $3) is in an 1838 residence. The museum does an impressive job of tracking the past, with exhibits on early Acadian settlements, Amherst's Anglo background, and spicy tidbits relating to Russian revolutionary Leon Trotsky, who was interned in an Amherst POW camp in 1917.

Amherst Point Migratory Bird Sanctuary, a few kilometers from town at the end of Victoria Street, spreads out over

Amherst's First Baptist Church

190 hectares with trails through woodlands, fields, and marshes, and around ponds. The sediment-rich Cumberland Basin lures 200 bird species, including Eurasian kestrels, bald eagles, hawks, and snowy owls.

Accommodations and Food

Amherst Wandlyn Inn (Victoria St., off Hwy. 104 at Exit 3, 902/667-3331 or 800/561-0000, www.wandlyninns.com; from $115 s or d, includes a light breakfast), the town's largest lodging, has 88 air-conditioned rooms with wireless Internet and an indoor pool. The hotel dining room (daily 7am-9pm; $16-30), with sweeping views across the marsh, has inspired offerings by a creative chef who likes grilled salmon with a maple butter glaze and Caesar salad tossed at the table.

Information

The **Nova Scotia Visitor Information Centre** (90 Cumberland Loop, 902/667-8429; daily 8:30am-4:30pm, July-Aug. 8am-8pm) is a large complex well signposted from Highway 102 as you enter the province from New Brunswick to the west. Adjacent is a promenade describing driving routes through the province, with picnic tables overlooking Tantramar Marshes. In a rail carriage on the same side of town, the **Amherst Tourist Bureau** (51 La Planche St., 902/667-0696, www.amherst.ca; May-Aug. Mon.-Sat. 10am-6pm) specializes in the region, with lots of information for those heading south to the Glooscap Trail.

Getting There

Staying on Highway 2, Amherst is 25 kilometers (20 minutes) northwest of Springhill. Taking Highway 102 then Highway 104, Amherst is 200 kilometers (two hours) northwest of Halifax.

Sunrise Coast to Pictou

The quickest way to reach Pictou from Amherst is to take Highway 104 via Truro, but Highway 6 is more scenic. Throughout the region, the land dips and sweeps in manicured farmlands extending to the red beaches and cliffs of Northumberland Strait. The villages are small, and the backcountry roads are scenic. This is rural Nova Scotia at its best. Allow three hours, plus stops.

TIDNISH AND VICINITY

Highway 366 branches off Highway 6 a few kilometers northeast of Amherst and reaches the Northumberland Strait at Tidnish, which lies right on the provincial border between Nova Scotia and New Brunswick.

Tidnish Dock Provincial Park

Across the Tidnish River from town is **Tidnish Dock Provincial Park.** This small day-use park protects the northern terminus of an ambitious railway construction project that was designed to transport vessels across the isthmus between the Bay of Fundy and Northumberland Strait. The initial proposal had been for a canal link, but the government decided constructing a rail line would be easier. The plan called for the construction of hydraulic presses at either end to lift the boats into cradles that were to be pulled across the 28-kilometer rail line by locomotives. In 1891, nearing completion, the entire project was abandoned; the dock and a short length of the rail bed remain.

Continuing East Along Highway 366

Head east from Tidnish to **Amherst Shore Provincial Park.** From the day-use area, a short trail follows Annebelles Brook to a short beach, while on the other side of the highway is a campground (mid-May-mid-Sept.; $26) with flush toilets, showers, and fire pits. Continue east for seven kilometers

to **Northport Beach Provincial Park,** renowned for its excellent beach and water warmed by shallow sandbars. Next up, and equally popular for swimming, is **Heather Beach Provincial Park.**

Getting There

Tidnish is about 30 kilometers (30 minutes) northeast of Amherst. From Highway 6, take Highway 366 until you reach Tidnish. From Halifax, Tidnish is 215 kilometers (2.5 hours) northwest via Highways 102, 104, 6, then 366.

PUGWASH

Recognized mostly for its delightful name, Pugwash (from the Mi'kmaq word *pagweak,* meaning "shallow water") lies at the mouth of Pugwash Basin, 50 kilometers east of Amherst. Durham Street (Highway 6) is the main drag. Here you find a summer-only information center and the usual array of small-town businesses. Across the water to the south of downtown is a salt mine. Current production is 90,000 tons annually (10 percent of Nova Scotia's total mineral value). The best opportunity to get an idea of the operation's scope is to watch the freighters being loaded at the downtown dock.

Accommodations and Food

Downtown, the vaguely Irish-themed **Inn the Elms** (10340 Durham St., 902-243-2885, www.inntheelms.com; June-mid-Oct.; $80-95 s or d) has a distinctive green and red exterior and four guest rooms with older furnishings. The dining room is open Wed.-Sun. 9am-2:30pm; breakfast is included for all paying guests. It also opens Friday evening for dinner until 8pm with simple mains all under $15.

Chatterbox Café (10163 Durham St., 902/243-4059; Mon.-Sat. 9:30am-5pm; lunches $7.50-11) has tables along a covered veranda and a menu of healthy choices, as well excellent coffee.

Getting There

Pugwash is 50 kilometers (45 mintues) east of Amherst via Highway 6. It's 40 kilometers (40 minutes) from Tidnish to Pugwash, for those traveling along Highway 366. From Halifax, it's a 200-kilometer, 2.5-hour drive northwest.

PUGWASH TO PICTOU

It's 110 kilometers (1.5 hours) between Pugwash and Pictou along Highway 6, but there are many worthwhile detours; the first, Gulf Shore Road, starts from downtown Pugwash.

Along Gulf Shore Road

From downtown's Durham Street, Gulf Shore Road spurs north and then follows the edge of Northumberland Strait in an easterly direction before rejoining Highway 6 at Wallace. About four kilometers from Pugwash is **Gulf Shore Picnic Park,** a day-use area with fireplaces and picnic tables spread across a grassed area that slopes to a red-sand beach.

Near where Gulf Shore Road loops south to Wallace is **Fox Harb'r Golf Resort and Spa** (1337 Fox Harbour Rd., 902/257-1801 or 866/257-1801, www.foxharbr.com). While the resort and its facilities wouldn't look out of place in Arizona or on the Atlantic Coast, it's certainly unique in rural Nova Scotia. At $225 for a round of golf (only members and resort guests can play), the greens fee is high, but it's a beautiful course. Other facilities include an Olympic-size indoor pool, spa services, guided kayaking, and formal dining (jacket required) in the Great Room. Guests soak up pure luxury in suites (from $475 s or d) contained within chalets that line the fairways and look out over Northumberland Strait.

Jost Vineyards

About 34 kilometers west of Pugwash, **Jost Vineyards** (48 Vintage Ln., 902/257-2636; mid-June-mid-Sept. daily 9am-6pm, the rest of the year daily 9am-5pm) is signposted off Highway 6. The creation of the Jost (pronounced "yost") family from Europe's Rhineland, this 18-hectare (44-acre) vineyard produces fine white wines that are sold throughout the province, including at many better restaurants. The best-known blends are the Jost ice wines. To produce this style, grapes are left on the vines until after the first frost, then gently pressed to produce just a few drops of concentrated juice from each grape. The result is an intensely sweet wine that is perfect as an after-dinner treat. Free guided tours are given daily in summer at noon and 3pm, and a deli is stocked with picnic treats—the perfect complement to Jost wines.

Thinker's Lodge

Recognized mostly for its delightful name, Pugwash (from the Mi'kmaq word *pagweak,* meaning "shallow water"), 50 kilometers east of Amherst, is best known as the origin of the **Pugwash Conferences on Science and World Affairs** (www.pugwash.org). The first of these took place in 1955 in Pugwash after Albert Einstein called for a meeting to discuss the dangers of a nuclear war. Cyrus Eaton, who had made his fortune in the United States as an industrialist, offered to sponsor the event on the condition it was held in his hometown. And so in 1957 it came to be that 13 Cold War nuclear scientists, including three from the USSR, met at what became known as the Thinker's Lodge, a large but otherwise unremarkable residence on the Pugwash foreshore. It was the first of many such gatherings, which now take place annually in London, Washington, Rome, Tokyo, and even still in Pugwash. Weapons of mass destruction are still discussed, but topics have broadened to include breaking down international borders, the environment, and economic prosperity. To get to **Thinker's Lodge** (249 Water St., info@thinkerslodge.org; July-Aug. Tues.-Sun. 10am-5pm by appointment only; free), follow Durham Street to its eastern end and turn right down Water Street.

Balmoral Grist Mill

★ Balmoral Grist Mill

Best known for its 1864 gristmill, the town of Balmoral Mills lies along Highway 311, 10 kilometers south of Tatamagouche and 38 kilometers north of Truro. Nestled at the base of a wooded vale, bright red **Balmoral Grist Mill** (660 Matheson Brook Rd., 902/657-3016; June-early Oct. Mon.-Sat. 9:30am-5pm, Sun. 1pm-5pm; adult $4, senior and child $2.75) is a photographer's ideal setting. Wheat, oats, and barley are still ground using 19th-century methods at this historic gristmill-cum-museum built in 1874. Milling demonstrations are at 10am and 2pm. The mill is busiest the first Sunday in October—an Open Day drawing a crowd of hundreds with activities such as milling demonstrations and popular taste-testing of oatmeal cakes.

Seafoam

At the coastal village of **Seafoam,** 24 kilometers east of Tatamagouche, you find the **★ Seafoam Campground** (Harris Ave., 902/351-3122, www.seafoamcampground.ca; mid-May-Sept.; $32-39), a large facility with direct access to the beach and warm swimming water. Amenities include lawn games, a playground, showers, and a laundry. On the west side of the campground, a side road leads to an abandoned dock, where a concrete wall has created a barrier for shifting sand. The result is a wide stretch of beach, perfect for lazing away a few hours on a warm summer day.

Pictou

Pictou (PIC-toe), 160 kilometers west of Amherst and 14 kilometers north of Exit 22 from Highway 104, is a historic port town of 3,800 on Northumberland Strait. It is also the ferry gateway to Prince Edward Island, meaning plenty of traffic passes through.

Nearly everything in Pictou happens at the waterfront, which is home to the main museum, restaurants, and historic accommodations. Some of the older buildings have a distinct Scottish vernacular style, designed to reflect local lineage. The residential streets also have numerous fancier styles; you'll see examples of stone Gothic and Second Empire designs along Water, Front, and Church Streets.

History

In 1773, 33 families and 25 unmarried men arrived from the Scottish Highlands aboard the *Hector,* and Pictou quickly became known as the "birthplace of New Scotland." The flamboyant Presbyterian minister and doctor Thomas McCulloch, en route to ministerial duties on Prince Edward Island, arrived here with his family by accident in 1803 when a storm blew his ship into Pictou Harbour. Local immigrants asked him to stay, and McCulloch agreed. In addition to providing medical care to the immigrants, McCulloch tried to reform the province's backward educational system.

SIGHTS
★ Hector Heritage Quay

At the heart of the downtown waterfront, **Hector Heritage Quay** (33 Caladh Ave., 902/485-4371; May-June daily 11am-5pm, July-Aug. daily 9am-7pm, Sept.-Oct. daily 11am-5pm; adult $7, senior and student $6, child $3) is home to a three-floor interpretation center detailing the Scottish immigrants'

Climbing aboard this replica of the *Hector* is a highlight of visiting Pictou.

arrival and early years. An elevated outdoor walkway overlooks the harbor. Admission includes access to the *Hector,* a replica of the sailing ship that transported Scottish settlers from across the Atlantic.

Take time to look over the *Hector.* The three-masted black-and-off-white replica is a splendid vessel, wide-hulled and round-ended. From the shape of the ship, though, you'll easily see that the voyage from Scotland was not so splendid. The ship's hull is unusually wide, and indeed the *Hector,* owned by the Dutch and chartered by the Scots for the voyage, was built as a freighter and modified only slightly to carry human cargo. Remarkably, the 200-plus immigrants from the Highlands survived, and Nova Scotia owes its Scottish heritage to those seaworthy voyagers.

Northumberland Fisheries Museum

The fascinating **Northumberland Fisheries Museum** (71 Front St., 902/485-4972; mid-June-Sept. daily 10am-6pm; adult $5, senior $4, child $2) is within a red-brick railway station, away from the redeveloped waterfront precinct and easy to miss. Displays tell the story of the local fishing industry through a vintage lobster boat, an aquarium holding local marine species, a mock fisherman's bunkhouse, period photos, and other memorabilia.

McCulloch Heritage Centre

The next worthwhile attraction is east of downtown along Old Haliburton Road. The main building at **McCulloch Heritage Centre** (86 Old Haliburton Rd., 902/485-4563; June-mid-Oct. Mon.-Sat. 9am-5pm; adult $5) showcases fine arts as part of the national arts exhibit circuit. The site is also one of the province's best genealogical libraries. A path leads uphill from the main building to McCulloch House, the early 1800s home of Thomas McCulloch. With distant water views, it holds period antiques and a small library. The print of a Labrador falcon downstairs was a gift to McCulloch from artist-naturalist John James Audubon.

ENTERTAINMENT

The local performing arts scene is based at **deCoste** (85 Water St., 902/485-8848, https://decostecentre.ca), a modern waterfront entertainment complex that puts on upward of 100 shows each year. In July and August, the center hosts the Summer Sounds of Nova Scotia series. These concerts highlight top Celtic dancers, singers, and fiddlers, who hit the stage Tuesday-Thursday at 8pm. Tickets are generally under $20.

ACCOMMODATIONS AND CAMPING

Pictou has cheap motels such as the **Rustic Anchor Motel** (132 W. River Rd., 902/485-4423, www.rusticanchormotel.com; $84-119 s or d), with 17 spacious rooms and free wireless Internet, but I encourage you to take advantage of the wonderful choice of historic lodgings below, many within walking distance of the waterfront and all well priced.

$50-100

In the heart of downtown and close to the waterfront, the 1865 **Auberge Walker Inn** (34 Coleraine St., 902/485-1433 or 800/370-5553, www.walkerinn.com; $89-139 s or d) has 11 guest rooms, some with harbor views, and a dining room where guests gather for a light breakfast each morning.

$100-150

Right on the water and within walking distance of downtown, the ★ **Customs House Inn** (38 Depot St., 902/485-4546, www.customshouseinn.ca, $119-149 s or d) dates to 1870. It's a historic building overlooking the harbor constructed of red brick and sandstone that was, as the name suggests, originally a customs house. The restored inn has eight guest rooms, all air-conditioned and some with exposed brickwork and water views. Rates include Internet access and a light breakfast.

Dating to the 1920s, **Pictou Lodge Beach Resort** (172 Braeshore Rd., 5 km east of town, 902/485-4322 or 800/495-6343, www.pictoulodge.com; mid-May-mid-Oct.; $125-435 s or d) sits on a 67-hectare oceanfront estate overlooking Northumberland Strait. The roomy lodge has been restored with rustic comforts

the Customs House Inn

and features a long outside porch, dining in the high-ceilinged rotunda, and a nearby pond with canoes. Lodging choices include oceanfront villas, three-bedroom chalets, suites of various sizes and configurations, and standard motel rooms. All units have private baths, and many have fireplaces, kitchens, and separate living rooms. Resort amenities include canoe rentals, an outdoor pool, and a playground.

Camping

Caribou/Munroes Island Provincial Park (mid-June-mid-Oct.; $26) has 87 campsites (Loop B is closest to the beach), cooking shelters, flush toilets, and fire pits. It fronts a long red-sand beach, which at low tide links Munroes Island to the mainland. The park is six kilometers west of town, signposted from Highway 6.

FOOD

For waterfront ambience, head to the **Saltwater Cafe,** next to Hector Heritage

Quay (67 Caladh Ave., 902/485-2558; daily 11am-8:30pm; $14-21). Sit inside or out on the screened waterfront deck while enjoying the house specialty—seafood, moderately priced. Across the road from the harbor, **Lobster Bar Restaurant** (50 Caladh Ave., 902/382-8527; Mon.-Thurs. 11:30 9pm, Fri.-Sat. 11:30am-10pm, Sun. 11:30am-8pm; $15-24) is owned and operated by a longtime local family. As the name suggests, the menu is inspired by the ocean, with lots of traditional choices such as haddock cakes and, of course, lobster dinners.

Five kilometers out of town, the dining room at the ★ **Pictou Lodge Beach Resort** (172 Braeshore Rd., 902/485-4322; mid-May-mid-Oct. daily 7am-9pm; $18-31) is a woodsy, old-fashioned space. You'll enjoy strait views from an intimate setting, with tables centered around a massive stone fireplace. The menu features entrées such as Indian-spiced lamb shank, cedar-planked salmon, and smoked maple pork belly with grilled scallops. Sunday brunch (11am-2pm) attracts hordes of locals for a buffet that includes everything from sushi to smoothies.

INFORMATION AND SERVICES

At the Pictou Rotary (where Highway 106 meets Highway 6), the **Nova Scotia Visitor Information Centre** (902/485-6213 or 800/565-0000; May-Sept. daily 9am-5pm, from 8:30am in summer) is primarily in place for those arriving in Nova Scotia via the ferry from Prince Edward Island, but it is also a good source of local information. The website www.townofpictou.com may also help you plan your trip to the town.

Sutherland-Harris Hospital is at 1059 Haliburton Road (902/485-4324). Locals do their banking in style at the architecturally resplendent **Bank of Nova Scotia**, in a Second Empire-style building at the corner of Front and Colerain Streets (902/485-4378). The **post office** is at 49 Front Street.

GETTING THERE

If you're combining your travels through Nova Scotia with a visit to Prince Edward Island, you have the choice of driving across the Confederation Bridge or catching the ferry. From Caribou, a short drive north of Pictou, **Northumberland Ferries** (902/566-3838 or 800/565-0201, www.ferries.ca) operates 5-9 sailings May-mid-December daily to the eastern side of Prince Edward Island. The trip takes just over an hour, and the fare is $69 round-trip per vehicle, regardless of the number of passengers (you pay when leaving the island).

From the west, it's 110 kilometers (1.5 hours) along Highway 6 to Pictou from Pugwash. Heading north from Halifax, Pictou is 165 kilometers (two hours) along Highways 102, 104, and 106.

Pictou to Cape Breton Island

The TransCanada Highway promises little besides uninterrupted speed on its route across the northeastern mainland. The best vistas, beaches, camping, and other attractions lie off the expressway, along the strait's coastal roads between Tatamagouche and Cape Breton. Shallow pools of seawater among sandbars turn warm in the sun, making for comfortable wading and swimming at Rushton's Beach Provincial Park, Tatamagouche Bay, and Melmerby Beach Provincial Park, east of Pictou.

CAPE GEORGE SCENIC DRIVE

The route to fossil hunting at Arisaig and Cape George's ruggedly beautiful eastern coastline lies along Highways 245 and 337 between New Glasgow and Antigonish, via a 110-kilometer, two-hour drive. From Exit 27 east of New Glasgow, allow half a day to reach Antigonish, which is enough time to visit all the sights detailed here.

★ Arisaig

Like many other places in Nova Scotia, Arisaig, 57 kilometers northeast of New Glasgow, is an unassuming place that is much more interesting than the casual visitor might imagine. The cliffs on the west side of the village tell the story of a 4-million-year period of life on earth 400 million years ago—one of the only places in the world where such a long period of time is exposed in a single layered cliff line. Four hundred million years ago, this area was a shallow sea, and as the layers of sediment built up on its floor, brachiopods (shells), nautiloids (related to squid), trilobites (ancient crabs), crinoids (filter-feeders that attached themselves to the sea bed), and bryozoans (coral) were buried. As ocean levels dropped, cliffs were formed along the shoreline, and as erosion broke the sediment down further, fossils from the Silurian Period were exposed, perfectly preserved in bands of rock that represent specific time periods all those millions of years ago. Added to the mix is the upper cliff face, which is topped with up to four meters of sand and gravel left behind when glaciers retreated across the area at the end of the last ice age. Geologists have studied the site since the mid-1800s, and as the erosion process continues and more fossils are uncovered, interest continues.

You can walk to the cliffs from the harbor at Arisaig, but the official access is from **Arisaig Provincial Park,** on the west side of the town. The advantage of using the park access is that there are interpretation panels beside the parking lot, which help visitors appreciate the geology down at sea level. From these panels, steps descend to the beach far below, from where it's a short stroll westward along the beach to Arisaig Brook, where the

Arisaig

largest concentration of fossils is found. It is illegal to dig at the cliff face, but scavenging through fallen rock is permitted.

Cape George

At Malignant Cove, Highway 337 branches north from Highway 245 and climbs steadily before peaking at an elevation of 190 meters at Cape George. The setting is a bicyclist's favorite scene and a just reward after the steep coastal climb. The panorama from the lighthouse at the cape's tip takes in the manicured farmlands of the Pictou-Antigonish highlands to the south as well as the misty vision of Prince Edward Island across the strait.

Along Cape George's eastern side, Highway 337 peels down from the peak alongside St. George's Bay. Nestled below the cape is **Ballantynes Cove.** From the town wharf, a rough walking trail climbs back to the lighthouse. The 1.8-kilometer route takes less than an hour each way and makes reaching the cape more satisfying than simply driving to its summit.

ANTIGONISH

First impressions of Antigonish (an-tee-guh-NISH), from a Mi'kmaq name meaning "place where the branches are torn off by bears gathering beechnuts," are not promising. As it passes through town, the highway is a thicket of fast-food restaurants and service stations—but the town is not without its charms. Dig deeper and you'll find a bustling university town with nearby beaches and hiking trails, a good choice of places to stay and eat, and two popular festivals.

Sights

In a 1908 red-brick railway building on the north side of downtown, the **Antigonish Heritage Museum** (20 E. Main St., 902/863-6160; Mon.-Sat. 10am-5pm; free) tells the town's story through donated items and historical photographs. Back toward the historic heart of town is the **County Courthouse** (168 Main St.), still in use even though it has been designated a National Historic Site. Although no tours are offered, the landscaped grounds of gracious **St. Francis Xavier University** (take Exit 32 north from Highway 104) are pleasant for a stroll, especially in summer when the campus is deserted.

Festivals and Events

The second week of July, the town hosts the **Antigonish Highland Games** (902/863-4275, www.antigonishhighlandgames.ca)—the longest-running in North America, celebrated since 1863. Highlights include Celtic music, pipe bands, dancing, heavy sports such as caber tossing, and a kilted golf tournament. Throughout July and August, the **Festival Antigonish** (902/867-3333 or 800/563-7529, www.festivalantigonish.com), Nova Scotia's largest and most successful

professional summer theater program, features a variety of drama, musicals, comedies, cutting-edge improv, and children's entertainment at the university campus.

Accommodations

Maritime Inn Antigonish (158 Main St., 902/863-4001 or 888/662-7484, www.maritimeinns.com; $130-185) is open year-round. It has 32 modern units and a restaurant open daily for breakfast, lunch, and dinner. Directly across the road, **Antigonish Victorian Inn** (149 Main St., 902/863-1103 or 800/706-5558, www.antigonishvictorianinn.ca; $130-175 s or d) is a splendid bed-and-breakfast occupying a dark burgundy-colored William Critchlow Harris-designed Queen Anne-style mansion. Each of the 12 guest rooms has a private bath and TV. Rates include full homemade breakfast.

Food

Antigonish offers a surprising number of good dining options. **Ruchi Indian Restaurant** (332 Main St., 902/863-5851; Wed.-Mon. 11am-9pm; $13-24) has a homey atmosphere and a good menu of inexpensive East Indian fare, including a number of choices for vegetarians, as well as locally inspired dishes such as curried lobster.

Being close to the university, **Piper's Pub** (33 College St., 902/863-2590; Mon.-Sat. 10am-2am, Sun. 11am-2am; $12-18) is a popular student hangout. The typical pub grub is well priced, and bands play Saturday night.

Getting There

The most direct route to Antigonish from New Glasgow is along Highway 104, about 60 kilometers (40 minutes). Via the Cape George scenic drive, it's about 110 kilometers (two hours) from New Glasgow to Antigonish. Antigonish is 215 kilometers (2.5 hours) north then east from Halifax via Highways 102 and 104.

Marine Drive

Marine Drive extends 320 kilometers along the Eastern Shore from Halifax to Canso, at the eastern tip of mainland Nova Scotia. From Canso, it's another 80 kilometers to the Canso Causeway, gateway to Cape Breton Island. The Marine Drive is a scenic alternative to Highways 102 and 104 via Truro. It's longer (allow 5-6 hours, not counting stops) and beyond the main tourist path, but it features delightful bays, sandy beaches, and interesting fishing villages around every bend.

LAWRENCETOWN

Begin the Marine Drive by following Cole Harbour Road from Exit 7 of Highway 111 in Dartmouth to **Lawrencetown Beach,** one of Canada's best-known surf spots. Easily reached in 30 minutes from Dartmouth, this long stretch of sand backed by high dunes is an enjoyable stop even if you don't plan to take to the water.

Surfing at Lawrencetown Beach

The waves of "L-town," as it's known to locals, break along the length of the beach and off a rocky headland that breaks the main beach in two. They are best November-May, when winter swells provide large and consistent waves. These waves also coincide with the coldest ocean temperatures. But even with water temperatures of 0°C (32°F) and air temperatures that drop to -20°C (-4°F), it's not unusual to see footprints leading down a snow-covered beach to the breakers beyond. Summer is not devoid of waves. They are just likely to be smaller and less consistent. Hardy locals swim in the ocean in the warmer months, when water temperatures rise to 15°C (59°F), but for surfing, be prepared with a wetsuit. The beach's southern headland provides an ideal vantage point for watching the action.

Kannon Beach (4144 Lawrencetown Rd., 902/471-0025; Mon.-Fri. 9am-6pm, Sat.

9am-5pm) is a full-service surf shop in a renovated house on the hill between Lawrencetown and Stoney Beaches. Surfboard and wetsuit rental packages (complete with gloves and booties) are $40 per day, and stand-up paddleboard rentals cost $50 per day. Lessons are also offered. From an unlikely spot in the heart of Dartmouth, **DaCane Surf Shop** (300 Prince Albert Rd., Dartmouth, 855/434-8900, www.dacanesurfshop.com; daily 9am-5pm) rents surfboards ($30 for 24 hours), wetsuits ($25), stand-up paddleboards ($50), and bodyboards ($15).

Accommodations

Ocean views from **Moonlight Beach Suites** (Hwy. 207, north end of Lawrencetown Beach, 902/827-2712, www.moonlightbeachinn.com; $139-350 s or d) are nothing short of stunning. The three guest rooms are decorated in a nautical theme, and each has a private deck, jetted tub, and TV/DVD combo, while thoughtful extras include binoculars and beach towels. The largest of the three rooms is massive and has a huge private deck with sweeping water views. Rates include a full breakfast.

Getting There

Lawrencetown is about 15 kilometers (20 minutes) east of Dartmouth (a suburb of Halifax) via Highway 207.

MUSQUODOBOIT HARBOUR TO TANGIER

With just 900 people, Musquodoboit Harbour is nevertheless the largest community between Dartmouth and Canso. The only real attraction in town is the **Musquodoboit Railway Museum** (Hwy. 7, 902/889-2689; June-Aug. daily 9am-4pm; free), housed within a 1918 railway station and three vintage rail cars. The **tourist information center** is in the same building. Ten kilometers south of Musquodoboit Harbour on East Petpeswick

Fabled Sable Island

Just under 200 kilometers off Nova Scotia's eastern coastline is a 40-kilometer-long sliver of sand that was known to generations of seafarers as the Graveyard of the Atlantic. Protected today as a national park, **Sable Island** is inhabited by a herd of horses that have taken on almost mythical proportions.

The island is made up entirely of sand. The sand is part of a terminal moraine left behind by the receding ice cap at the end of the last ice age 11,000 years ago. Hardy marram grass stabilizes the central part of the island, while seals and birds are also native. The island's most famous residents are horses; they were introduced in the late 1700s. Some say it was to feed shipwreck victims, while others claim they were aboard ships that came to grief. Today, Sable Island is home to about 400 horses. They are of special interest since they are one of the world's few truly wild horse populations, without feral intruders (such as domestic horses gone wild), and they are free to roam, feed, and reproduce without human interference.

Since Sable Island was first mapped in the late 1500s, more than 350 vessels have been wrecked along its fog-shrouded shore (the last was a small yacht, the *Merrimac*, in 1999). In 1801 a station manned with a lifesaving crew was established on the island. This government-operated service soon expanded to five stations and continued until 1958. Today, the island has a year-round population of fewer than 20 people—mostly scientists who study the weather and monitor the island's environment.

Only about 200 intrepid travelers visit Sable Island each year, most arriving by air charter or private vessel and staying for just the day. The season runs from June through October, but June and July are often foggy. If you'd like to visit, the first step is to register with Parks Canada (902/426-5080, www.pc.gc.ca/sable). You will then need to arrange fixed-wing air charters from Halifax through **Maritime Air** (902/873-3330, www.maritimeair.com), which charges $6,200 for the round-trip, inclusive of taxes; Parks Canada also charges a $500 per flight landing fee (collected by the airline). These flights take up to seven passengers, so the best way to reduce costs is to check the company website for a link to a Facebook page dedicated to sharing costs of reaching the island. The best source of island information is the website of the **Friends of Sable Island Society** (www.sableislandfriends.ca).

Road, **Martinique Beach Provincial Park** protects the southern end of Nova Scotia's longest beach. The beach is often windy, but it's still a relaxing place for a long, easy walk.

Salmon River Bridge

Cross the bridge for which the village of Salmon River Bridge, 13 kilometers east of Musquodoboit Harbour, is named and you reach a neat little lodge nestled between a forested hill and the river. Dating to 1850 and operating as a guesthouse since 1920, **Salmon River Country Inn** (9931 Hwy. 7, 902/889-3353, www.salmonrivercountryinn. ca; $95-130 s or d) has seven guest rooms, all with en suite bathrooms and some with water views, and a riverfront cottage with a fireplace. Part of the inn is a seafood restaurant

(Apr.-Nov. daily 8am-9pm; $12-28), with seats that spill outside to a large riverfront deck. Lobsters kept in the tank are often larger than three pounds, but there's a wide choice of less-expensive seafood, including delicious fish-and-chips.

Drive three kilometers beyond Salmon River Bridge and then four kilometers north to reach ★ **Webber Lakeside Park** (738 Upper Lakeville Rd., 902/845-2340 or 800/589-2282, www.webberslakesideresort. com), which is filled with the opportunity for activities that include lake swimming with a floating dock, canoe and boat rentals, a playground, and a games room with table tennis. The two-bedroom cottages ($145 s or d) have kitchens and wide decks, and the campground (mid-May-mid-Oct.; $27-36) has full hookups and hot showers. Being just an hour's drive from Halifax, this place fills up every summer weekend, so you'll need reservations.

Oyster Pond

Turn south off Highway 7 just beyond Salmon River Bridge to visit the small but interesting **Fisherman's Life Museum** (58 Navy Pool Loop, 902/889-4209; June-early Oct. daily 10am-5pm; adult $4, senior and child $2.75). Rather than a collection of artifacts, this museum within a small homestead re-creates the simple self-sufficient lifestyle of a fisherman, his wife, and their 13 children.

Clam Harbour Provincial Park and Vicinity

Clam Harbour Provincial Park, along the south-facing side of Clam Bay protects a long stretch of hard white sand. The beach has supervised swimming in summer, as well as changing rooms and picnic areas, but no camping (from the end of the access road, turn right to reach the nicest picnic area, where tables are nestled in windswept coastal forest).

Members of the Murphy family have lived in Murphy Cove for seven generations, and have been involved through time in everything from rum running to fishing. Now they operate ★ **Murphy's Camping on the Ocean** (308 Murphy's Rd., 902/772-2700, www.murphyscamping.ca; mid-May-mid-Oct.; $27-39), which sprawls across a grassy headland. The campground has all the usual facilities—showers, boat and kayak rentals, a laundry, a playground, and more—but it's Brian's evening storytelling, boat tours (two hours for $23), clam-digging trips, and mussel bakes that make this place stand apart.

TANGIER

Tangier is best known for the smokehouse of ★ **J. Willy Krauch and Sons** (signposted off Hwy. 7, Tangier, 902/772-2188; Mon.-Fri. 8am-6pm, Sat.-Sun. 10am-6pm), whose smoked salmon you'll find in better restaurants throughout the province and beyond .

Willy Krauch was a Danish immigrant who settled in Tangier in the 1950s. Krauch's sons still use the traditional Scandinavian recipe: the fish is cold-smoked (salted and then smoked at low temperatures for one week), creating a divine-tasting treat of the most delicate texture. The smokehouse's retail shop stocks smoked salmon, mackerel, and eel, ready to eat or packed to travel. If you've planned well by bringing crackers and cheese from the city, stop by for a selection of salmon and continue to Taylor Head Provincial Park for a seafood snack by the seaside.

Coastal Adventures (84 Mason's Point Rd., 902/772-2774, www.coastaladventures. com) pushes off into the cove on full-day kayak excursions that include a visit to uninhabited islands; $110 per person includes lunch. Kayak rentals are $70 per day for a single and $90 for a double. The same people operate ★ **Paddler's Retreat Bed and Breakfast** ($65-80 s or d), which is an excellent spot to spend one or more nights. Most guests staying in this restored 1860s fisherman's home do so as part of a kayaking instruction package or before or after participating in a day trip. Three of the four rooms share bathrooms, while the fourth has an en suite bathroom and private entrance. Rates include a full breakfast.

Getting There

Tangier is about 85 kilometers (1.5 hours) east of Dartmouth via Highway 7.

TANGIER TO SHERBROOKE

★ Taylor Head Provincial Park

Turn off at Spry Bay, 15 kilometers beyond Tangier, to reach the interesting oceanside **Taylor Head Provincial Park,** which protects a narrow peninsula extending six kilometers to Taylor Head. The west-facing side of the spit is rugged and windswept, with stunted white spruce trees clinging precariously to the rocky ground, while the east side is characterized by sandy coves lapped by calm waters. A five-kilometer unpaved road from Highway

Psyche Cove, Taylor Head Provincial Park

7 hugs the west side of the peninsula before crossing to protected **Psyche Cove.** At the end of the road is a series of small parking lots with beach access. You can walk along the beach back toward the mainland to Bob Bluff

or head in the opposite direction to a headland with sweeping views up and down the peninsula and of island-dotted Mushaboom Harbour. Taylor Head itself is four kilometers by hiking trail from the end of the road. If you return via rocky Spry Bay, you'll have walked 10 kilometers (allow four hours).

Spry Bay to Liscomb Mills

Marine Drive between Spry Bay and Liscomb Mills passes a string of fishing villages with delightful names such as Ecum Secum (a Mi'kmaq word of unknown origin) and Spanish Ship Bay (named for a nearby headland that resembles a Spanish galleon). Linked to Highway 7 by a short bridge, Sober Island's name has a more cynical origin (the first residents bemoaned the lack of alcohol).

In Liscomb Mills, **Liscombe Lodge Resort** (Hwy. 7, 902/779-2307 or 877/375-6343, www.liscombelodge.ca; mid-May-mid-Oct.; from $170 s or d) boasts an idyllic setting along the Liscomb River. Amenities include an indoor pool; a sauna; hot tubs; a fitness center; hiking trails; tennis courts; a small marina with boat, canoe, and fishing-equipment rentals; and a comfortable dining room overlooking the river (where children eat free).

Liscombe Lodge Resort

MARINE DRIVE

CENTRAL NOVA SCOTIA

SHERBROOKE

Highway 7 leaves the coast at Liscomb, turning north to Sherbrooke, from which it continues north to Antigonish and the Marine Drive spurs east, continuing along the Eastern Shore as Highway 316. Sherbrooke (pop. 400) was founded at the farthest navigable point of the St. Mary's River in the early 1800s. By 1869 gold had been discovered in the area, and the town was booming. In addition to mining, mills were established to process lumber for export, and local farms depended on the town for services. By 1890 the gold rush was over, and the population began slipping away.

★ Sherbrooke Village

By the late 1960s, Sherbrooke was a shadow of its former self. Gold rush-era buildings remained in varying states of disrepair, but the only visitors were anglers chasing salmon along the river. At this point, a local trust stepped in, and under the guidance of the Nova Scotia Museum, an ambitious restoration project took place. Today, **Sherbrooke Village** (42 Main St., 902/522-2400; June-early Oct. daily 9:30am-5pm; adult $12, senior $10, child $6) comprises more than 80 restored buildings that are integrated with the town itself. About 20 buildings are open to the public, including an ambrotype photography studio, the colonnaded courthouse, a jail, a water-powered sawmill, the Sherbrooke Hotel, a drug store, a blacksmith shop, a church, and a farmyard. The site is brought alive by costumed interpreters who wander the village streets, tend to their crops, and go about operating each business as folks would have done in the late 1800s. To fully immerse yourself in the experience, consider participating in the Hands on History program (July-Aug. only), where the costume department will dress you in period clothing and you can spend the day helping in the kitchens, trying your hand at pottery, or learning skills from the blacksmith. The Courthouse Concert Series takes place 2-3 nights a week through the summer season; entertainment varies from traditional Celtic ceilidhs to musical comedies. Starting time is usually around 7:30pm. The main parking lot and entrance are off Court Street (turn left at the end of the modern-day main street).

Accommodations and Food

For overnight stays, Sherbrooke offers several choices. **St. Mary's River Lodge** (21 Main St., 902/522-2177, www.riverlodge.ca; Apr.-Dec.; $76-106 s or d) is across the road from

Sherbrooke Village

the river and steps from Sherbrooke Village. It has five guest rooms, each with an en suite bathroom. A cooked breakfast is included in the rates. On the east side of town, a 10-minute walk from the village, is **Sherbrooke Village Inn** (7975 Hwy. 7, 902/522-2235 or 866/522-3818, www.sherbrookevillageinn.ca; May-Oct.; $100-120 s or d). The medium-size motel rooms are plain but comfortable, and the on-site restaurant is open daily for breakfast, lunch, and dinner.

In the Sherbrooke Hotel, within the historical village, the ★ **What Cheer Tea Room** (June-mid-Oct. daily 9:30am-5pm; lunches $6-12) is a countrified restaurant with friendly staff and basic but tasty dishes that will set you up for more historical sightseeing. You can try traditional rural dishes such as fish cakes and homemade baked beans on freshly baked bread. **Sherbrooke Village Inn Restaurant** (7975 Hwy. 7, 902/522-2235; May-Oct. daily 7:30am-9pm; $15-26) is a small wood-paneled restaurant on the east (Halifax) side of town. The emphasis is on simple presentations of local seafood. You could start with fish chowder and then choose between dishes such as deep-fried scallops and strip loin or a lobster from the tank. Save room for the homemade pie with ice cream.

GETTING THERE

Sherbrooke is about 195 kilometers (three hours) east of Dartmouth along Highway 7.

SHERBROOKE TO CANSO

It's only a little more than 100 kilometers between Sherbrooke and Canso, but the drive will take at least two hours, plus any time you wait for the ferry at Country Harbour.

Bickerton Lighthouse Interpretive Centre

There could be no better location for a lighthouse display than in a restored light-keeper's home at the end of a windswept, often fog-enshrouded peninsula—which is exactly where the **Bickerton Lighthouse Interpretive**

Centre (Lighthouse Rd., Port Bickerton, 902/364-2000; mid-June-mid-Sept. daily 10am-5pm; adult $3) is situated. Built in 1901 and deactivated in 1962, the two-building complex now holds a display describing the lonely life of Nova Scotian light-keepers and their families, the original foghorn, and a directory of Nova Scotia's lighthouses. Stairs lead to an observation tower. Outside, a trail leads past clumps of tasty blueberries and cranberries to a sandy beach. From the turnoff in Port Bickerton, 25 kilometers beyond Sherbrooke and seven kilometers before the ferry across Country Harbour, it's three kilometers to the interpretive center, the last two along an unpaved road.

Country Harbour

The **Country Harbour ferry,** along Highway 316, seven kilometers north of Port Bickerton, departs from the east side (Halifax side) of the bay on the half-hour and the west side on the hour. During the laughably named "rush hour" (9am-10am and 5pm-6pm), ferries operate more frequently. The ferry has room for just 12 passenger vehicles or a limited number of trucks and RVs, and the fare is $5.50 (cash only), which is paid to the attendant upon loading. From the west side of the bay, it's 86 kilometers to Canso. Aside from the short detour to Tor Bay, it's worth slowing down to admire the village of Isaacs Harbour, which on a calm day is reflected across the bay of the same name from Goldboro.

Tor Bay

Named for granite knolls that dot the region, Tor Bay is lined by three small communities established by Acadians after their deportation by the English in 1755. For visitors, the highlight is **Tor Bay Provincial Park,** on an isthmus along a peninsula that forms the southern boundary of the bay. This small day-use park has one of the few sandy beaches this far east along the Marine Drive. A boardwalk leads to the beach, from where a short trail leads to a rocky headland where covered interpretive boards describe the geology that led to the creation of the beach.

CANSO

The remote town of Canso, 320 kilometers along Marine Drive from Halifax, is the jumping-off point to an interesting historic site that protects Canada's oldest fishing village. In more recent times, Canso was an important link in trans-Atlantic communications. The most striking reminder of this era is the 1884 **Hazel Hill Cable Station,** just outside town. It was from here that the distress signal from the sinking *Titanic* and news of the 1929 stock market crash were transmitted to the rest of the world.

★ Canso Islands National Historic Site

Archaeological digs point to European settlement as early as the 1500s on the small island that comprises the **Canso Islands National Historic Site,** one kilometer offshore from Canso. These visitors' time on the island was only temporary, and no obvious signs of this era remain today. Two hundred years later, the French and British were fighting for control of North America, with ownership of the Canso Islands in dispute even after the signing of the Treaty of Utrecht in 1713. In 1718 the French were displaced, and the same year, fearing a reprisal attack by the French, the British built a small fort on Grassy Island to protect access to cod stocks that were being harvested at the amazing rate of 10 million pounds per year. Grassy Island grew into a prosperous community, complete with wealthy merchants who built solid stone homes. The village was destroyed by a French invasion from Louisbourg in 1744 and was never rebuilt.

The site comprises a visitors center (Union St., 902/366-3136; July-Aug. daily 10am-6pm; $5 donation) on the Canso waterfront and the island itself. Mainland exhibits include a scale model of the settlement, fragments of French pottery dated to the early 1700s, and a short documentary. Boats run on demand between the visitors center and the island. Once safety regulations are described, the small craft is off, and you'll be on the island within 15 minutes. A mowed trail passes eight information boards describing the settlement and what remains—cellar pits, mounds of rubble from residences, and terraced vegetable plots—before looping back down to the dock. Allow about 30 minutes to walk the trail. If visitation is slow, the boat will be waiting at the wharf for your return; otherwise, expect a wait of up

Canso Islands National Historic Site

to 30 minutes while it transports more visitors across. The only services on the island are pit toilets and a shelter, so bring warm clothes and water. The suggested donation at the visitors center includes the boat ride to the island.

Stan Rogers Folk Festival

On the first weekend of July, the population of Canso increases 10 times as music fans descend on the town for **"Stanfest"** (888/554-7826, www.stanfest.com), a folk-music festival of 50 acts from around the world performing on six stages. In addition to the music, the festival features a food fair, craft show, and beer garden. Most visitors camp at the Acoustic Campground, set up by the organizers within walking distance of the main stage. Other temporary campgrounds take the overflow, with shuttle buses running to the grounds and to showers at the local high school. A camping pass is $60-75, and entry to the concert is $120 for the entire weekend.

Accommodations and Camping

Canso is most definitely not a tourist town. The **Last Port Motel** (Hwy. 16, 902/366-2400, www.lastportmotel.ca; $90-100) is just before town. It offers 13 basic rooms with wireless Internet access, as well as a restaurant open daily at 7am. A better option for those looking for a memorable stay is ★ **DesBarres Manor Inn** (90 Church St., 902/533-2099, www.desbarresmanor.com; $199-259 s or d), 56 kilometers east in Guysborough. Dating to

1837, the three-story inn has been beautifully restored and the grounds remain in immaculate shape. The 10 guest rooms are stylish and come with niceties like 600-thread-count sheets on super-comfortable mattresses, plus luxurious bathrooms. Rates include a gourmet continental breakfast, with dinner available with advance reservations.

Ten kilometers west of Canso along Highway 16 is **Seabreeze Campground and Cottages** (230 Fox Island Rd., Fox Island, 902/366-2352, www.seabreezecampground.com; mid-May-mid-Oct.; camping $25-35, cottages $100-110 s or d), where modern facilities, full hookups, and views across Chedabucto Bay keep the 51 campsites full through July and August. One- and two-bedroom cottages have basic cooking facilities, a lounge area with TV, and separate bedrooms. Other resort amenities include coin-operated showers, a laundry, firewood sales, a playground, canoe rentals, and even a lobster pound, where you can buy live lobster.

Information

Whitman House (1297 Union St., 902/366-2170; June-Sept. daily 9am-5pm; donation), a handsome three-story 1885 house with displays illustrating local history, doubles as an information center.

Getting There

Canso is about 320 kilometers (5-6 hours) east of Dartmouth, a suburb of Halifax, via Highway 7.

CENTRAL NOVA SCOTIA
MARINE DRIVE

Cape Breton Island

Port Hastings to Baddeck 162

Baddeck and Vicinity 166

Chéticamp..................... 172

Cape Breton Highlands
  National Park................. 174

Ingonish and Vicinity 178

The Northeast 182

Alexander Graham Bell, perhaps Cape Breton Island's most renowned transplant, once wrote, "I have seen the Canadian and American Rockies, the Andes and the Alps, and the Highlands of Scotland; but for simple beauty, Cape Breton outrivals them all."

Linked to the mainland by a two-lane causeway, nearly every coastal and inland backcountry road on the western half of the island leads eventually to the Cabot Trail, the scenic highway rimming the unforgettable landscape of northwestern Cape Breton. The dramatic coastal scenery alone qualifies the Cabot Trail as one of the world's great drives, but you can also spend time soaking up local Acadian culture, hiking through pristine forests of the Cape Breton Highlands, or simply relaxing on white-sand beaches. The most spectacular section of the route is in the far northern part of the island, through magnificent Cape Breton Highlands National Park, which stretches from coast to coast and is as wild and remote as the highlands of Scotland. Green, steeply pitched highlands begin at the sea in the south and sweep north, cut by salmon-filled rivers. As the elevation increases, the Acadian and boreal forests give way to a taiga tableland of stunted, windswept trees.

The Northumberland Strait opens into the Gulf of St. Lawrence on the western coast, while the Atlantic washes the opposite shore. The 1,098-square-kilometer Bras d'Or Lakes forms the island's heart. The saltwater "Arm of Gold," though barely influenced by tidal cycles, is an inland arm of the Atlantic consisting of a sapphire-blue main lake with numerous peripheral channels, straits, and bays.

PLANNING YOUR TIME

Although you can fly into the airport at Sydney, most visitors drive to Cape Breton from Halifax, reaching the causeway linking the island to the mainland in less than four hours. From the causeway, a choice of routes present themselves, including the

Previous: Cabot Links; Keltic Lodge. **Above:** Le Bloc Beach.

Look for ★ to find recommended
sights, activities, dining, and lodging.

Highlights

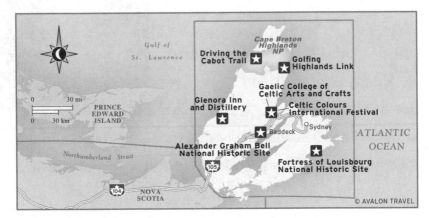

★ **Glenora Inn and Distillery:** Tucked into a quiet glen along the remote west coast is North America's only single-malt whiskey distillery, complete with a restaurant and guest rooms for those looking to linger longer (page 164).

★ **Alexander Graham Bell National Historic Site:** Dedicated to one of the world's most prolific inventors, this museum will interest all ages (page 167).

★ **Driving the Cabot Trail:** This spectacular 300-kilometer circuit traverses varying landscapes, but the highlight is the section through Cape Breton Highlands National Park—the main reason for visiting the island (page 175).

★ **Golfing Highlands Links:** Where else can you walk the fairways of one of the world's finest golf courses, knowing that what you've

paid to play is less than at many regular city courses (page 178)?

★ **Gaelic College of Celtic Arts and Crafts:** No, you don't need to sign up for a course. Instead, take in music recitals and demonstrations such as weaving (page 181).

★ **Celtic Colours International Festival:** Hosted at venues across Cape Breton Island, this October festival draws crowds for the opportunity to enjoy traditional music while soaking up the colors of fall (page 181).

★ **Fortress of Louisbourg National Historic Site:** It may be a little off the tourist path, but sprawling across 10 hectares of a remote headland is this reconstruction of a French town destroyed by the British 250 years ago (page 184).

Cape Breton Island

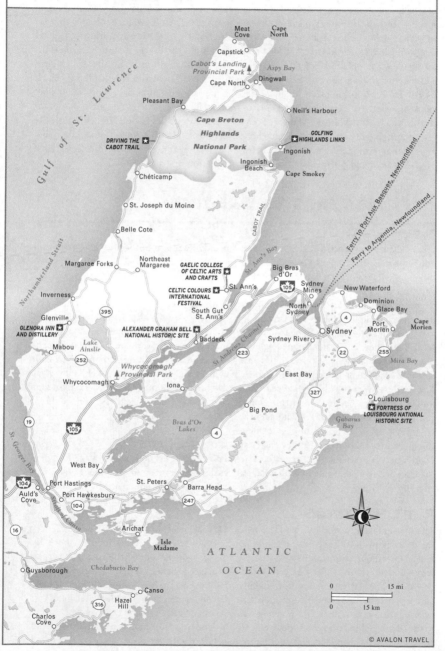

Meat Cove
Cape North
Capstick
Cabot's Landing Provincial Park
Aspy Bay
Cape North
Dingwall
Pleasant Bay
Neil's Harbour
Cape Breton Highlands National Park
GOLFING HIGHLANDS LINKS
DRIVING THE CABOT TRAIL
Ingonish
Chéticamp
Ingonish Beach
Cape Smokey
St. Joseph du Moine
CABOT TRAIL
Belle Cote
Margaree Forks
Northeast Margaree
GAELIC COLLEGE OF CELTIC ARTS AND CRAFTS
St. Ann's Bay
Big Bras d'Or
CELTIC COLOURS INTERNATIONAL FESTIVAL
St. Ann's
105
Sydney Mines
New Waterford
Inverness
South Gut St. Ann's
North Sydney
Dominion
Glace Bay
Glenville
395
ALEXANDER GRAHAM BELL NATIONAL HISTORIC SITE
4
Sydney
Port Morien
Cape Morien
GLENORA INN AND DISTILLERY
Baddeck
223
Sydney River
22
255
Mabou
252
Lake Ainslie
Whycocomagh Provincial Park
St. Andrew's Channel
East Bay
Mira Bay
Whycocomagh
Iona
327
Big Pond
Louisbourg
FORTRESS OF LOUISBOURG NATIONAL HISTORIC SITE
Bras d'Or Lakes
4
Gabarus Bay
19
105
West Bay
St. Peters
Barra Head
Port Hastings
104
Port Hawkesbury
247
Auld's Cove
104
16
Arichat
Isle Madame
ATLANTIC OCEAN
Guysborough
Chedabucto Bay
Canso
0   15 mi
0   15 km
316
Hazel Hill
Charlos Cove

Gulf of St. Lawrence

Northumberland Strait

St. George's Bay

Strait of Canso

Ferry to Port Aux Basques, Newfoundland
Ferry to Argentia, Newfoundland

© AVALON TRAVEL

little-traveled route up the west coast, which passes the **Glenora Inn and Distillery.** The geographic and tourist hub is Baddeck. Plan to spend at least one full day at this resort town, which is enough time to visit the **Alexander Graham Bell National Historic Site** and take to the waters of Bras d'Or Lakes. Baddeck is also a good starting point for beginning the **Cabot Trail,** a 300-kilometer highway that loops through the wilderness of **Cape Breton Highlands National Park.** The park scenery is the highlight of the drive, but along the way, plan on browsing the **arts and crafts of Chéticamp** and **golfing** at Cabot Links and Highlands Links. If your travels correspond with the October **Celtic Colours International Festival,** plan on taking in as many concerts as you can. At other times of the year, St. Ann's **Gaelic College of Celtic Arts and Crafts** is the place to immerse yourself in Celtic culture. To hit all the highlights mentioned above, you should allow yourself at the very least three days from Halifax, but preferably four or five. The main reason for veering from the Cabot Trail is to visit the **Fortress of Louisbourg,** a lesser-known but impressive attraction that re-creates a French town from the mid-1700s.

Port Hastings to Baddeck

Canso Causeway, easily reached in four hours from Halifax, links Cape Breton to the mainland. From this point, Highways 104 and 105 (the TransCanada) and Highway 19 fan out across the island. Highway 19 follows the west coast up to Mabou and Inverness, and then links up with the Cabot Trail in the Margaree Valley. The TransCanada Highway lies straight ahead, leading through the center of the island to Baddeck and on to Sydney. The endless stream of buses packed with tourists makes a beeline along this route, connecting with the Cabot Trail at Baddeck. Highway 4 branches off to the east (or take the more direct Highway 104 for the first 28 kilometers), passing the turnoff to Isle Madame and then following Bras d'Or Lakes, en route to Sydney.

PORT HASTINGS

The main reason to stop in Port Hastings, the gateway town to Cape Breton Island, is to load up with brochures at the well-stocked **Nova Scotia Visitor Information Centre** (902/625-4201; May-June and Sept.-Dec. daily 9am-5pm, July-Aug. 9am-8:30pm), on the right as the TransCanada Highway crosses to the island. Behind the center, views extend back across to the mainland, and information boards describe the processes involved in constructing the causeway.

Accommodations

Through town toward Port Hawkesbury, **Canada's Best Value Inn MacPuffin** (313 Hwy. 4, 902/625-0621 or 800/867-2212, www. macpuffin.com; Apr.-late Dec.; $99-159 s or d) has 46 air-conditioned rooms, each with comfortable beds, coffeemakers, and wireless Internet. Bonuses include a small indoor pool, a playground, a fitness room, and free breakfast.

Getting There

Port Hastings is 60 kilometers (45 minutes) east of Antigonish via Highway 104. It's 275 kilometers (three hours) north then east from Halifax via Highways 102 and 104.

ISLE MADAME

Settled by French fishermen in the early 1700s, this was one of the first parts of the province to be settled, and it's one of the oldest fishing ports in North America. Isle Madame has four main communities—Arichat, West Arichat, Petit Grat, and D'Escousse.

The wooded island is a popular weekend getaway, with two provincial parks (**Lennox**

Passage to the north and **Pondville Beach** on the east side) and plenty of picnicking, swimming, and vista spots. In Arichat, on the waterfront, **LeNoir Forge Museum** (708 Veteran's Memorial Dr., 902/226-9364; June-Aug. daily 10am-6pm; donation) is a restored working 18th-century forge open to visitors.

L'Auberge Acadienne Inn (2375 Hwy. 206, Arichat, 902/226-2200, www.acadienne. com) is designed as a 19th-century Acadian-style inn, with eight inviting rooms, one with a jetted tub, in the main building ($105 s, $115 d) and nine adjacent motel units ($85 s, $95 d). The dining room serves Acadian breakfast and dinner dishes in a casual, country-style atmosphere.

Getting There

Take Highway 104 for 30 kilometers (30 minutes) east from Port Hastings, and then Highway 320 south over Lennox Passage Bridge to reach this 43-square-kilometer island.

BRAS D'OR LAKES SCENIC DRIVE

The **Bras d'Or Lakes scenic drive** traces the shoreline of Bras d'or Lakes. To see the southern portion of the route, it's an easy two-hour drive (148 kilometers) from the Canso Causeway to Sydney via Highway 4 along the southeastern shore of Bras d'Or Lakes. The highway steers away from the water until passing St. Peters, with nearby **Dundee Resort** (368 Shore Rd., Baddeck, 902/295-3500 or 800/565-5660, www.capebretonresorts.com; mid-May-Oct.) a destination in itself. The resort, 12 kilometers from Highway 4, is set on 223 hectares overlooking Bras d'Or Lakes. It features an 18-hole golf course (greens fee $68), an outdoor pool, a marina with all manner of watercraft for rent, an arcade activities center, summer programs for the kids, and a restaurant. Motel rooms, most with balconies, range $149-209, while cottages with limited cooking facilities and up to three bedrooms are $149-239.

St. Peters and Vicinity

Photography buffs should check out the **MacAskill House Museum** (7 MacAskill Dr., 902/535-2531; mid-June-Sept. daily 9:30am-5:30pm; donation), in the restored childhood home of Wallace MacAskill, one of the world's preeminent marine photographers. The museum exhibits a collection of his best photographs as well as historic cameras.

Overlooking Bras d'Or Lakes, 1.5 kilometers east of St. Peters, **Joyce's Motel and Cottages** (902/535-2404, www.joycesmotel. com; June-Sept.; $70-120 s or d) offers the choice of regular motel rooms or larger but dated one-bedroom cottages. Attractions include a laundry, boating, fishing, and an outdoor swimming pool. **Battery Provincial Park** (off Hwy. 4, 1 km east of town, 902/535-3094; mid-June-early Sept.) has hiking trails and ocean views. The 52 open, wooded, unserviced campsites rent for $26.

GETTING THERE

The small St. Peters lies 12 kilometers (10 minutes) beyond the turnoff to Isle Madame and 55 kilometers (40 minutes) from Port Hastings. St. Peters is 320 kilometers (3.5 hours) from Halifax via Highways 102 and 104.

Big Pond

From St. Peters, the run to Sydney takes a little more than an hour, with Highway 4 paralleling Bras d'Or Lakes for much of the way. A good halfway-point lunch stop is **Rita's Tea Room** (902/828-2667; summer daily 9am-7pm; lunch $8-12), in a converted schoolhouse at Big Pond. Opened by singer Rita MacNeil, who grew up in Big Pond and who continued to promote Cape Breton Island around the world until her death in 2013, the café serves specially blended teas, sandwiches, and salads in a country setting. An adjacent room is devoted to her distinguished career.

GETTING THERE

Big Pond is 50 kilometers (45 minutes) northeast of St. Peters along Highway 4 and 370 kilometers (four hours) from Halifax via Highways 102, 104, and 3.

HIGHWAY 19: THE CEILIDH TRAIL

The least traveled of the three routes north from the Canso Causeway, Highway 19 hugs the coastline and passes many small villages that haven't changed much in decades. This stretch of coastline is a bastion of Celtic music, hence the nickname Ceilidh Trail. Natalie MacMaster and the Rankins, as well as a new generation of stars headed by Chrissy Crowley, were all born and raised in the area.

Mabou

The town of Mabou (pop. 400) is the center of Gaelic education in Nova Scotia (the language is taught in the local school) and the location of Our Lady of Seven Sorrows Pioneers Shrine. The Mabou Gaelic and Historical Society Museum, or **An Drochaid** (902/945-2311; July-Aug. Tues.-Sun. 9am-5pm) focuses on crafts, local music and poetry, genealogical research, and Gaelic culture.

The Mabou Mines area, near the coast, has some excellent hiking trails into a roadless section of the **Mabou Highlands.**

GETTING THERE

Mabou is a 60-kilometer (40-minute) drive north up Highway 19 from the Canso Causeway. It's 335 kilometers (3.5 hours) from Halifax via Highways 102, 104, and 19.

★ Glenora Inn and Distillery

The **Glenora Inn and Distillery** (Hwy. 19, Glenville, 902/258-2662 or 800/839-0491, www.glenoradistillery.com; tours May-Oct. daily 9am-5pm; adult $7) is North America's only single-malt whiskey distillery. (It can't be called Scotch whiskey, as it's not from Scotland.) The final product is marketed as Glen Breton Rare, with 250,000 liters distilled annually. Built in 1990 using impressive post-and-beam construction and traditional copper pots for the distilling process, the complex is open for tours daily on the hour 9am-5pm. Better still, it's also a country inn with nine comfortable rooms ($179-189 s or d) and six spacious log chalets ($225-325) that sleep up to six people. Also at the distillery is **Glenora Dining Room and Pub** (May-Oct. daily 11:30am-9pm; $16-32), which serves hearty lunches and dinners accompanied by live Celtic music.

Fiddling the Night Away

A ceilidh (KAY-lee) was originally an informal gathering, usually on a Friday or Saturday night, that would bring together young people to dance the night away to lively Celtic music in a local hall. These social gatherings originated in Gaelic-speaking regions of Scotland and Ireland, with the tradition introduced to the New World by immigrants in the 1700s. Although nightclubs and pubs may have replaced the ceilidh in popularity in the city, along the west coast of Cape Breton Island and in other rural areas they remain an important part of the social scene. Most important, the music has retained its original roots, with progressive dancing in which the woman moves along a ring from man to man or everyone dancing in formation (similar to line dancing). The most skilled dancers break away from the formations to step dance.

Highway 19 is known as the **Ceilidh Trail,** and for good reason, as ceilidhs take place in towns and villages along the route year-round. Everyone is welcome, with many of the summer events especially tailored for visitors. At Mabou, the Mabou Community Hall fills with the sound of fiddle music every Tuesday through summer, while the following night, the foot-stomping fun happens down the road at the local museum. Passing through on Thursday? Plan for a lively evening of entertainment at the Inverness Fire Hall ceilidh.

Glenora Inn and Distillery

GETTING THERE

Glenville is 12 kilometers north of Mabou on Highway 19.

Inverness

Golfers know this Scottish settlement (pop. 2,000), the largest town along Highway 19, for **Cabot Links** (Beach Rd. #2, 902/258-4653; greens fee $185), one of North America's few links courses and rated one of the world's top 100 golf courses. Located between the town and the ocean, the location alone makes the effort to reach Inverness worthwhile. Overlooking the course, **Cabot Links Lodge** (Beach Rd. #2, 902/258-4653, www.cabotlinks.com; May-Oct.; $245-325 s or d) features 48 modern hotel-style rooms in five configurations, as well as a restaurant and lounge. If you're not a golfer, spend your time beyond the course, walking along the seemingly endless sandy beach below the golf course. Back up the hill in town, the **Ned Macdonald Museum** (62 Lower Railway St., 902/258-3291; June-Oct. daily 10am-6pm; adult $1) focuses on the region's mining history and pioneer families.

Ten kilometers north of Inverness on Highway 19 is ★ **MacLeod's Beach Campsite** (Dunvegan, 902/258-2433, www.macleods.com; June 15-Oct. 15; $32-35), which slopes down to a delightful beach that rarely gets crowded. Amenities include washrooms, showers, fire pits, a store, a launderette, a games room, volleyball, basketball, horseshoes, and more.

GETTING THERE

Inverness is about 20 kilometers north of Mabou on Highway 19.

HIGHWAY 105 TO BADDECK

From the Canso Causeway, it's 90 kilometers to Baddeck along Highway 105 (the TransCanada Highway). This is the main route north to Sydney and the Cabot Trail.

Iona

Where it intersects with Highway 105, Highway 223 crosses Little Narrows to Iona, then follows the shoreline of St. Andrews Channel all the way to Sydney. It's the least traveled of the many up-island highways, but no less interesting than the other options. The route is posted as Bras d'Or Lakes Drive.

Set on 16 hectares overlooking the narrow body of water between Bras d'Or Lakes and St. Andrews Channel, Iona's **Highland Village Museum** (Hwy. 223, 902/725-2272; June-mid-Oct. daily 10am-5pm; adult $11, senior $9, child $5) features 10 historic buildings as well as many examples of working farm equipment.

GETTING THERE
From the intersection of Highway 105 and Highway 223, it's 25 kilometers to Iona along Highway 223.

Baddeck and Vicinity

Baddeck (from *abadak,* or "place near an island," as the Mi'kmaq called it, referring to Kidston Island just offshore) is a picturesque town of 1,000 that lies on the misty wooded shore of St. Patrick's Channel, a long inlet of Bras d'Or Lakes. Baddeck also marks the traditional beginning and ending point for the Cabot Trail.

SIGHTS AND RECREATION
Many visitors plan a stop in Baddeck for its heritage accommodations and fine dining, but there are also a few things to see and do, including a national historic site that everyone should visit.

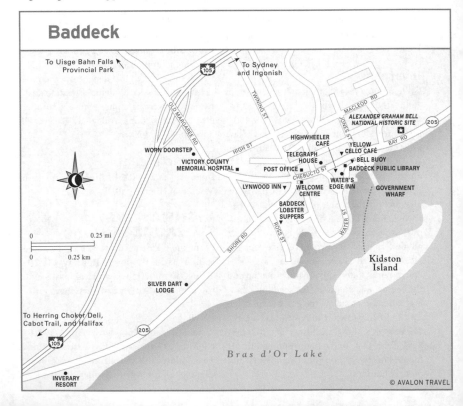

Baddeck

To Uisge Bahn Falls Provincial Park

To Sydney and Ingonish

OLD MARGAREE RD

TWINING ST

JONES ST

MACLEOD RD

ALEXANDER GRAHAM BELL NATIONAL HISTORIC SITE

BAY RD

HIGH ST

HIGHWHEELER CAFÉ

YELLOW CELLO CAFÉ

WORN DOORSTEP

TELEGRAPH HOUSE

BELL BUOY

VICTORY COUNTY MEMORIAL HOSPITAL

POST OFFICE

CHEBUCTO ST

BADDECK PUBLIC LIBRARY

LYNWOOD INN

WELCOME CENTRE

WATER'S EDGE INN

GOVERNMENT WHARF

WATER ST

ROSS ST

BADDECK LOBSTER SUPPERS

SHORE RD

0   0.25 mi

0   0.25 km

Kidston Island

SILVER DART LODGE

To Herring Choker Deli, Cabot Trail, and Halifax

205

105

INVERARY RESORT

Bras d'Or Lake

© AVALON TRAVEL

Alexander Graham Bell

Alexander Graham Bell National Historic Site

Once a major shipbuilding center, Baddeck claims as its most famous resident not a sailor but an inventor—Alexander Graham Bell. The landscape, language, and people all reminded the Scotsman of his native land. He built a grand summer home, Beinn Bhreagh (pronounced Ben Vreeah), across the inlet from Baddeck (it is still owned by his descendants and is not open to the public). While the telephone is his most famous invention, Bell possessed an intellectual curiosity that is almost impossible to comprehend in today's world.

At Beinn Bhreagh, he studied heredity by breeding sheep and seeking to increase twin births. Even when separated from the rest of the world at Baddeck, he maintained friendships in high places—after the attempted assassination of President Garfield in 1881, Bell was hastily commissioned to invent an electromagnetic device to find the bullet. When his son died after experiencing breathing problems, he developed a breathing device that was the prototype of the iron lungs used to help polio victims. More than anything else, Bell was captivated by flight. He tested propeller-driven kits as early as the 1890s, and in 1909, four years after the Wright brothers' famous flight, the great inventor took to the air over Bras d'Or Lakes in the **Silver Dart.** But he wasn't done yet: In 1919, at the age of 72, Bell and his estate manager, Casey Baldwin, invented the hydrofoil, which set a water-speed record of more than 70 miles per hour. Bell died three years later and was buried at Beinn Bhreagh.

★ Alexander Graham Bell National Historic Site

At the east end of Baddeck (within walking distance of downtown) is the **Alexander Graham Bell National Historic Site** (902/295-2069; June-Oct. daily 9am-5pm; adult $7.80, senior $6.55, child $3.90), a tremendously satisfying museum with displays on Bell's life, his family, and his seemingly inexhaustible curiosity about science. The multimedia exhibits include working models of

Bell's first telephones and a full-size reproduction of his speed-record-setting HD-4 hydrofoil, but some of the most interesting displays are information panels describing how Bell's interest in teaching the deaf to speak led to the invention of the telephone. The inventor always had a soft spot for children, and the love of the younger generation is reflected in the museum's Children's Corner, a large space where kids of all ages can make and decorate kites, do experiments, and generally have fun in an educational environment. Allow at least two hours, more if you have children.

Kidston Island

A free ferry runs from Government Wharf (Jones St.) out to **Kidston Island,** just 200 meters from the mainland, which has a beach with supervised swimming. The wooded island also has numerous short walking trails, including one that leads to a lighthouse that has been guiding vessels on Bras d'Or Lakes for more than a century. The ferry operates every 20 minutes July-August (Mon.-Fri. 10am-6pm, Sat.-Sun. noon-6pm). The trip takes less than five minutes.

Boat Tours

The *Amoeba* (902/295-2481; June-mid-Oct.; adult $25, child $10), a 67-foot concrete-hulled yacht built by the owner's father during a 10-year period, provides an inexpensive way to enjoy the Bras d'Or Lakes. Ninety-minute trips depart from Government Wharf three or four times daily mid-May through mid-October. In addition to enjoying the lake, you'll pass Alexander Graham Bell's estate and often spot bald eagles perched atop shoreline trees.

ACCOMMODATIONS AND CAMPING
$50-100

A 10-minute walk from town, the ★ **Worn Doorstep** (43 Old Margaree Rd., 902/295-1997; $90 s or d) has a rooftop deck and four delightful en suite rooms, each with a private entrance, air-conditioning, basic cooking facilities, and a TV.

Owned by the same family for five generations, **Telegraph House** (479 Chebucto St., 902/295-1100; $90-130 s or d) combines basic rooms in the grandly historic original 1861 home with a row of modern motel units. The lodge has two historic links of note—it was once home to a telegraph office that sent some of the first transatlantic messages, and Alexander Graham Bell was a frequent guest. The room that Bell called his own looks exactly like it would have in the 1880s ($120 s or d); others have been given a modern look while retaining the historic feel through antique furnishings. Amenities include a library, a sitting room, and a dining room open daily for breakfast, lunch, and dinner. Telegraph House is also one of the few downtown accommodations open year-round.

Over $100

Direct water access is a major draw at ★ **Inverary Resort** (Exit 8 from Hwy. 105, 902/295-3500 or 800/565-5660, www.capebretonresorts.com; May-Nov.; $135-385), a large complex that offers accommodations varying from homey B&B-style rooms to modern two-bedroom suites. Down on the waterfront, rent canoes and kayaks from the activity center. Elsewhere on the grounds are an indoor pool, game rooms, a playground, spa services, two dining rooms, and a pub.

Named for Alexander Graham Bell's famous airplane, **Silver Dart Lodge** (257 Shore Rd., 902/295-2340 or 888/662-7484, www.maritimeinns.com; mid-May-mid-Oct.; $145-230 s or d) sits on a 40-hectare hillside overlooking the lake. Amenities include a heated outdoor pool and putting green, as well as lake cruises, boat rentals, a beach, and hiking trails. Oatcakes and hot drinks (no extra charge) are served for early risers, followed by a buffet breakfast ($14 per person). Picnic lunches are available with notice, and the restaurant is also open for dinner.

Water's Edge Inn (22 Water St., 902/295-3600 or 866/439-2528, www.thewatersedgeinn.com; June-mid-Oct.; $155-185 s or d) is across the road from the lake and also within easy walking distance of downtown restaurants. Four of the six rooms have lake views and private balconies. All six are heritage-themed yet stylishly outfitted with modern touches such as air-conditioning and TV/DVD combos.

Campgrounds
Bras d'Or Lakes Campground (5 km west

of Baddeck on Hwy. 105, 902/295-2329, www.brasdorlakescampground.com; mid-June-Sept.; campsites $32-61, cabins $59-89 s or d) has almost 100 unserviced and hookup sites. The only local campground actually on the lake, it has showers, washrooms, a launderette, wireless Internet throughout, and an outdoor swimming pool.

In the vicinity, **Adventures East Campground** (between Exits 7 and 8 of Hwy. 105, 902/295-2417 or 800/507-2228, www.adventureseast.ca; early June-mid-Oct.; campsites $29-36, cabins $125-155 s or d) also has all the necessary amenities—showers, laundry, a pool, fishing, a restaurant, and tours.

FOOD

Cafés and restaurants line Baddeck's main street, but most open only through the warmer months, and by mid-October, choices become very limited.

Casual Dining

For breakfast, sandwiches, pizzas, and light meals, the **Yellow Cello Cafe** (525 Chebucto St., 902/295-2303; May-mid-Oct. daily 8am-11pm; $11-17) is centrally located and well priced, with an indoor dining room and

veranda in front. The calzones are delicious, the beer selection is good, and the people-watching can't be beat.

For the best coffee in town, head to the **Highwheeler Café** (484 Chebucto St., 902/295-3006; May-mid-Oct. daily 7am-6pm, until 10pm in summer; lunch $8-12). This café has an in-house bakery, so you know everything is fresh, including daily soup specials and healthy sandwiches made to order.

Lakeside Café (Exit 8 from Hwy. 105, 902/295-3500; Apr.-Nov. daily from 11am; $16-29) is set on the waterfront within the Inverary Resort complex. The food is simple and unsurprising, but the prices are reasonable and the setting a delight when the sun is shining and you find yourself seated at an outdoor table.

With a welcoming, woodsy ambience, ★ **Herring Choker Deli** (Hwy. 105, 902/295-2275; summer daily 8am-8pm, shorter hours in spring and fall; lunches $7-10) overlooks the water from 11 kilometers west of town. Instead of greasy cooked breakfasts, tuck into a scrambled egg, ham, and cheese panini ($7). The lunchtime highlight: thick gourmet sandwiches packed with goodies on bread baked each morning.

Inverary Resort

Lobster Supper

Lobster suppers originated as local gatherings held in church basements and community halls. Today, they have become a little more commercialized, but they are still a fun and inexpensive way to enjoy this succulent seafood treat. One of the few regularly scheduled in Nova Scotia (Prince Edward Island is a hotbed of lobster suppers) is **Baddeck Lobster Suppers** (17 Ross St., 902/295-3307; early June-mid-Oct. daily 4pm-9pm) in a community hall just off Main Street. A 1- to 1.5-pound lobster with all-you-can-eat chowder, mussels, trimmings, dessert, and nonalcoholic drinks costs $35 per person. If you're not a lobster fan, substitute for salmon, crab, or steak.

Other Restaurants

Watching the sun set over Bras d'Or Lakes from a window table at the ★ **Bell Buoy Restaurant** (536 Chebucto St., 902/295-2581; mid-May-June daily 4pm-9pm, July-mid-Oct. daily 11:30am-9pm; $16-30) is worth the price of dinner alone. A menu highlight is the seafood chowder, which comes chock-full of haddock, salmon, mussels, and even lobster, as well as a slab of homemade oatmeal bread as a side. Mains vary from pastas to whole lobsters, with a number of vegetarian and gluten-free options also offered.

Of many local lodges with dining rooms that welcome nonguests, none is better than the **Lynwood Inn** (24 Shore Rd., 902/295-1995; mid-May-mid-Oct. noon-8:30pm; $16-30), a grand 1868 home that has been converted into an inn and restaurant. The smallish dining room is tastefully decorated in Victorian-era style. The menu is less expensive than you may imagine.

INFORMATION AND SERVICES

At the east end of the main street, the **Baddeck Welcome Centre** (corner of Chebucto St. and Shore Rd., 902/295-1911, www.visitbaddeck.com; June-Sept. daily 9am-5pm) is indeed welcoming. Friendly staff will

Baddeck Welcome Centre

help out with finding accommodations and, as always, love handing out maps and brochures.

For emergencies, dial 911 or **Victoria County Memorial Hospital** (902/295-2112).

GETTING THERE

Halfway between the Canso Causeway and Sydney, Baddeck is 350 kilometers from Halifax (allow at least four hours driving time).

MARGAREE RIVER VALLEY

Eight kilometers west of Baddeck, the Cabot Trail branches off the TransCanada Highway northwest through the hills and into the valley of the Margaree River, a renowned salmon-fishing stream and the namesake of seven small communities.

The peak time for fishing is mid-June to mid-July and September to mid-October; many guides are available locally. Near North East Margaree, **Margaree Salmon Museum** (60 E. Big Intervale Rd., 902/248-2848;

Cabot Trail: Planning Your Drive

Looping around the northern end of Cape Breton Island by driving the 311-kilometre **Cabot Trail** is always a highlight of my travels through Nova Scotia, but understanding the route is key to making the most of your travel time. It is possible to drive the entire Cabot Trail in less than five hours—but don't. Instead, plan on immersing yourself in the destination for at least two full days. Offering a mix of historic and resort-style accommodations and dining options, Baddeck is an ideal base. Those equipped for camping will appreciate the numerous campgrounds through Cape Breton Highlands National Park, or for unequalled historic ambience, make reservations at the Keltic Lodge, which is perched high above the ocean overlooking Ingonish Beach.

Unlike every other highway in the province, the Cabot Trail does not have a specific number designation; instead it is a combination of numbered highways (also called "routes" by the locals). Nor does the Cabot Trail have an official start or finish point, although many start their journey by veering off Highway 105 at Whycocomagh, 50 kilometers north of the Canso Causeway, and heading north on Highway 395. From Whycocomagh, key driving distances (and minimum driving times) are:

- **Whycocomagh to Margaree Forks:** 48 kilometres (50 minutes). Highway 395 from Whycocomagh leads north through lush valleys and prime angling territory.

- **Margaree Forks to Cheticamp:** 39 kilometres (30 minutes). Heading north from Margaree Forks, the Cabot Trail follows the Margaree River to the Gulf of St. Lawrence, then hugs the ocean to the Acadian village of Cheticamp.

- **Cheticamp to Ingonish:** 105 kilometres (80 minutes). This section through Cape Breton Highlands National Park is the highlight of the Cabot Trail, with seeming endless ocean views before crossing the rugged interior to emerge at the white sand beaches of Ingonish.

- **Ingonish to St. Anns:** 73 kilometres (90 minutes). It's only 85 kilometers from Ingonish south to St. Anns, but the road is narrow and there are many tight corners, so allow at least 90 minutes, plus any time spent at the numerous lookouts en route.

- **St. Anns to Baddeck:** 21 kilometres (30 minutes). Heading south from St. Anns, the Cabot Trail is extremely narrow and winding. At South Haven, you reach the main island highway and can head south to Baddeck or north to Sydney.

- **Baddeck to Whycocomagh:** 25 kilometres (20 minutes). The final leg of the Cabot Trail is along Highway 105, the main route up-island to Sydney.

mid-June-mid-Oct. daily 9am-5pm; adult $2, child $1) tells the story of the river and its fishy inhabitants.

Accommodations

Even though it's away from the ocean, the Margaree River Valley is a popular spot to get away from it all. Near the village of Margaree Valley, **Normaway Inn** (691 Egypt Rd., 902/248-2987 or 800/565-9463, www.thenormawayinn.com; $159-229 s or d) is typical of the many accommodation options. This elegantly rustic 1920s resort is nestled on 100 hectares in the hills. The main lodge has nine guest rooms, and the grounds hold 19 one- and two-bedroom cabins. Activities include nightly films or traditional entertainment, tennis, walking trails, bicycling, weekly barn dances, and fiddling contests. The dining room (open for breakfast and dinner) serves dishes of Atlantic salmon, lamb, scallops, and fresh fruits and vegetables. The Normaway is about 30 kilometers along the Cabot Trail from Highway 105, and then three kilometers along Egypt Road.

On Lake O'Law, **The Lakes Resort** (902/248-2360 or 888/722-2112, www.thelakesresort.com; May-Oct.; $135 s or

d) comprises eight two-bedroom cottages overlooking the lake. Each cottage has a bathroom, microwave, living area, and outdoor barbecue. Recreational opportunities include boating, fishing, canoeing, mini-golf, and go-karting, while the resort restaurant specializes in lobster dinners. To get there, turn off the Cabot Trail at North East Margaree.

Getting There

The Margaree River Valley is about 50 kilometers northwest of Baddeck via the southern portion of the Cabot Trail.

Chéticamp

Along the Cabot Trail, Chéticamp is an Acadian fishing village (pop. 1,000) set along a protected waterway that opens to the Gulf of St. Lawrence. Deep-sea fishing and whale-watching charter boats leave from the central Government Wharf, and the entrance to Cape Breton Highlands National Park is five kilometers north of town.

The village was first settled by Acadians expelled from the Nova Scotia mainland in the 18th century. Today, the weeklong **Festival de l'Escaouette,** in early August, celebrates aspects of Acadian culture with a parade, arts and crafts, and music.

SIGHTS

The first stones for **St. Pierre Catholic Church** were laid in 1893, but it took almost 20 years to finish. Its tower pierces the sky at a height of more than 50 meters and can be seen from far up and down the coast. On the south side of town, the **Acadian Museum** (744 Main St., 902/224-2170; mid-May-mid-June daily 9am-5pm, mid-June-Aug. daily 8am-9pm, Sept.-Oct. daily 9am-5pm; donation) displays artifacts from early settler days, with an emphasis on the area's sheepherding past, including weaving, spinning, and rug-hooking demonstrations.

RECREATION

At Government Wharf, **Whale Cruiser** (902/224-3376) takes guests out on three-hour whale-watching trips three times daily July to mid-September and less frequently in May, June, and late September. Fare is adult $50, child $30.

One of the major cottage industries of this area is the production of hooked rugs, a craft developed by Acadians centuries ago. In the late 1930s, a group of Chéticamp women formed a rug-hooking cooperative that still thrives. The Co-op Artisanale de Chéticamp gives demonstrations and displays its wares at the Acadian Museum. You can also see beautiful hooked rugs and tapestries at **Les Trois Pignons** (15584 Main St., 902/224-2642; mid-May-mid-Oct. daily 9am-5pm, the rest

St. Pierre Catholic Church

of the year weekdays only; adult $5, senior and child $4), a striking red-roofed building at the northern end of Chéticamp. The building also houses the visitor information center.

A number of galleries and shops hereabouts also sell locally produced folk arts—brightly colored, whimsical carvings and paintings of fish, seabirds, fishermen, boats, or whatever strikes the artists' fancy. One kilometer north of the visitors center, the **Sunset Art Gallery** (15856 Cabot Trail, 902/224-1831; mid-May-mid-Oct. daily 9am-6pm) features the colorfully painted woodcarvings of William Roach.

ACCOMMODATIONS

If you're traveling on a budget, a choice of older, inexpensive motels along the main street makes Chéticamp a good base for day trips into Cape Breton Highlands National Park. Best of the bunch is **Albert's Motel** (15086 Cabot Trail, 902/224-2077; mid-May-mid-Oct.; $70-85 s or d), which has remarkably comfortable rooms for the price.

Overlooking the ocean a few kilometers south of town, ★ **Chéticamp Outfitters Inn B&B** (13938 Cabot Trail, Point Cross, 902/224-2776; Apr.-mid-Dec.; $85-120 s or d) is a large, modern home with six guest rooms and common areas that include a deck with sweeping ocean views. The less expensive rooms share two bathrooms, while all rates include a full breakfast. The hosts operate a charter fishing business, so this is a good base for anglers.

At the north end of the main street, ★ **Ocean View Chalets** (15569 Cabot Trail, 902/224-2313 or 877/743-4404, www.oceanviewchalets.com; motel rooms $125-140 s or d, cabins $150-190 s or d) has a delightful oceanfront setting, with a wide strip of green space separating the cabins from the water. Each

unit has a kitchen, a separate bedroom, and a wood barbeque out front.

Behind the main street and linked to the local golf course by a short trail, **Cabot Trail Sea and Golf Chalets** (902/224-1777 or 877/244-1777, www.seagolfchalets.com; mid-May-mid-Oct.; $159-299 for up to four people) is a complex of spacious and modern freestanding units, each with a bathroom, kitchen, deck, and barbecue.

FOOD

At the north end of town, **Hometown Kitchen** (15559 Main St., 902/224-3888; summer daily 8am- 8pm; $13-19) has a few outdoor tables with water views. The food is simple but tasty and a good value.

Dine at the ★ **Restaurant Acadien** (774 Main St., 902/224-3207; May-Oct. daily 11am-7pm, summer 7am-10pm; $14-23) for authentic Acadian food: *fricot* (souplike stew), meat pies, fresh fish, blood pudding, and butterscotch pie. **Evangeline** (15150 Main St., 902/224-2044; daily 7am-9pm; $11-19) is a family restaurant specializing in homemade soups and meat pies.

INFORMATION

On the north side of town, **Chéticamp Visitor Information Centre** (15584 Main St., 902/224-2642; mid-May-mid-Oct. daily 9am-5pm) has information on tours, accommodations, and campgrounds. For national park information, continue north through town to the large visitors center complex.

GETTING THERE

Chéticamp is 90 kilometers (just over an hour) northwest of Baddeck via the Cabot Trail. The trip north from Halifax is 400 kilometers and takes five hours.

Cape Breton Highlands National Park

Protecting a swath of wilderness at the northern tip of Cape Breton Island, this national park is one of the finest in Canada. While outdoor enthusiasts are attracted by opportunities to hike and bike, anyone can enjoy the most spectacular scenery simply by driving the Cabot Trail, which spans the length of the park from Chéticamp in the west to Ingonish in the east.

The Land

Heath bogs, a dry rocky plateau, and a high taiga 400 meters above sea level mark the interior of the 950-square-kilometer park. Rugged cliffs characterize the seacoast on the west side, where the mountains kneel into the Gulf of St. Lawrence, and gentler but still wildly beautiful shores define the eastern side.

Nova Scotia's highest point, 532-meter White Hill, is simply a windswept hump, far from the nearest road and with no formal access trail reaching it.

Typical Acadian forest, a combination of hardwoods and conifers, carpets much of the region. Wild orchids bloom under the shade of thick spruce, balsam fir, and paper birch. The **Grand Anse River** gorge near MacKenzie Mountain is the Acadian forest's showpiece. Its terrain—with sugar maples, yellow birches, and rare alpine-arctic plants—has been designated an international biological preserve. The park is also a wildlife sanctuary for white-tailed deer, black bears, beavers, lynx, mink, red foxes, snowshoe hare, and more than 200 bird species, including eagles and red-tailed hawks.

Cape Breton Highlands National Park

© AVALON TRAVEL

The Cabot Trail is one of the world's great scenic drives.

Park Entry

Cape Breton Highlands National Park is open year-round, though campgrounds and the two information centers operate only mid-May-October. A **National Parks Day Pass** (adult $7.80, senior $6.80, child $3.90, maximum of $19.60 per vehicle). It is valid until 4pm the day after its purchase. Passes can be bought at both park information centers, Chéticamp and Ingonish campgrounds, or at the two park gates.

★ DRIVING THE CABOT TRAIL

The Cabot Trail extends well beyond park boundaries along its 300-kilometer length, but the most spectacular stretch is undoubtedly the 110 kilometers through the park between Chéticamp and Ingonish. By allowing a full day for the drive, you will have time to walk a trail or two, stop at the best lookouts, and even head out on a whale-watching trip. This section describes the drive itself, with recreational opportunities discussed next.

You can of course follow the Cabot Trail in either direction, but I've laid out the drive from Chéticamp to Ingonish (clockwise), meaning you pass the main park information center at the beginning of the drive and that you're driving on the safer inland side of the road the entire way.

Thousands of outdoor enthusiasts tackle the Cabot Trail under pedal power each summer. The trip is not particularly long, but it is very strenuous in sections, and lack of a wide shoulder can make for some hair-raising moments.

Chéticamp to Pleasant Bay

Make your first stop inside the park at the **Cheticamp Visitor Centre** (902/224-2306; mid-May-mid-Oct. 9am-5pm, July-Aug. 8:30am-7pm). Pick up a map, ask about hiking opportunities, browse the natural history displays, and hit the highway. You can pay for park entry here or at the tollgate a little farther up the road.

This is the most impressive stretch of one of the world's most spectacular drives, with the highway clinging to the shoreline and then climbing steeply along oceanfront cliffs to a viewpoint 18 kilometers north of the information center.

Continuing Around the Cape

From Pleasant Bay, the park's northwestern corner, the highway turns inland and wraps upward to 455-meter-high **French Mountain.** From this point, a level stretch barrels across a narrow ridge overlooking deeply scooped valleys. The road climbs again, this time to **MacKenzie Mountain,** at 372 meters, and then switchbacks down a 10-12 percent grade. Another ascent, to **North Mountain,** formed more than a billion years ago, peaks at 445 meters on a three-kilometer summit. The lookout opens up views of a deep gorge and the North Aspy River.

Cape North and Vicinity

The northernmost point on the Cabot Trail is Cape North, the name of a small service town (as well as a geographical feature to the north). Here a spur road leads 22 kilometers north to Meat Cove. Although outside the park, this road traverses complete wilderness before reaching the open ocean at St. Lawrence Bay. En route, **Cabot's Landing Provincial Park,** the supposed landing site of English explorer John Cabot, offers a sandy beach on Aspy Bay (good for clam digging) and a picnic area and marks the starting point for hikes up 442-meter-high Sugar Loaf Mountain.

The East Coast to Ingonish

From Cape North, it's 45 kilometers east and then south to the resort town of Ingonish. Aside from tucking into a seafood feast at Neil's Harbour, you should make time for a stop at **Black Brook Cove.** Backed by a short stretch of beach, the cove is an extremely popular spot for picnicking and swimming. To escape the summertime crowd, walk to the north end of the beach and follow the Jack Pine Loop through open coastal forest.

waterfalls at the north end of Black Brook Cove

RECREATION
Hiking

The park offers 26 established hiking trails, varying from simple strolls shorter than half a kilometer to challenging treks leading to campgrounds more than 20 kilometers away. Many of the trails are level; a few climb to awesome viewpoints. Some hug the rocky shoreline; others explore river valleys. No matter what your abilities may be, you'll be able to enjoy the park at your own speed. For details on hiking in the park, browse the many books sold at Les Amis du Plein Air, the bookstore within the Park Information Centre.

The following hikes have been arranged in a clockwise direction.

On the light side, the self-guiding **Le Buttereau Trail** leads 1.9 kilometers to wildflowers and good bird-watching opportunities. The trailhead is just north of the park gate north of Chéticamp.

For the more hardy, the seven-kilometer (two hours one-way) **Skyline Loop** climbs a headland, from which the lucky can spot pilot

whales; along the way, look for bald eagles, deer, and bears. The trail begins where the Cabot Trail heads inland at French Mountain.

On overcast or wet days, **Benjie's Lake Trail** provides an ideal break from driving. From a trailhead six kilometers beyond the start of the Skyline Loop Trail, this easy walk takes about 30 minutes each way.

Serious backpackers gravitate to the **Fishing Cove Trail** (16 km round-trip), a rugged journey to a campground and beach. You can reach the end of the trail in two hours, but allow at least three for the strenuous return trip back up to the highway.

Whale-Watching

From Pleasant Bay, one of two whale-watching spots in Nova Scotia (the other is the Bay of Fundy), a number of operators depart daily through summer. The region boasts a high success rate when it comes to spotting pilot, humpback, and minke whales, simply because of the high numbers close to the coastline. **Captain Mark's** (902/224-1316 or

888/754-5112) is easily recognized down at the harbor by his booth shaped like a lighthouse. This company offers the option of stable exfishing boats (adult $40, child $20) and rigid-hulled Zodiacs (adult $50, child $25). The advantage with the latter is that the whales are reached much more quickly. You should book by phone in advance for July and August sailings.

ACCOMMODATIONS AND CAMPING

Since it's a national park, there are no hotel accommodations within the park boundary. Instead, visitors stay at Chéticamp for its Acadian heritage, at Ingonish for its beaches and golfing, or at one of the following choices in between the two.

Under $50

HI-Cabot Trail Hostel (23349 Cabot Trail, 902/224-1976, www.cabottrailhostel.com; dorm $29, $58 s or d) is within walking distance of Pleasant Bay, 38 kilometers north of Chéticamp on the park's western side. The facility is small but friendly and comfortable, with 18 dorm beds in two rooms and an adjacent bunkhouse. Guests have use of communal washrooms, two kitchens, a deck with barbecue, and wireless Internet access.

$100-150

Just more than 40 kilometers north of Chéticamp, the Cabot Trail exits the park for a short distance at Pleasant Bay. Here, the distinctively salmon pink **Midtrail Motel & Inn** (23475 Cabot Trail, 902/224-2529 or 800/215-0411, www.midtrail.com; mid-May-Oct.; $105-125 s or d) offers 20 bright but basic motel rooms, some with ocean views, as well as a family-friendly seafood restaurant, a launderette, and a couple of Adirondack chairs perched high above the motel on a knob of land offering sweeping ocean views.

Set on 25 hectares of oceanfront property, **Markland Beach Cottages** (802 Dingwall Rd., Dingwall, 902/383-2246, www.themarkland.com; May-mid-Oct.; $125-235 s or d) is 52 kilometers north of Ingonish (signposted off the Cabot Trail between Cape North and South Harbour). Although it is a resort, the emphasis is on the outdoors, with most guests spending their time on the adjacent beach or lazing around the outdoor pool. The cottages (from $175 s or d) are an excellent value. The resort restaurant features the freshest of fresh seafood combined with seasonal produce such as fiddleheads and wild mint.

Campgrounds

Cape Breton Highlands National Park is the most popular camping destination in Nova Scotia. Parks Canada operates seven campgrounds within the park.

Chéticamp Campground (5 km north of Chéticamp) is behind the main park information center. Amenities include showers, flush toilets, kitchen shelters, playgrounds, and an outdoor theater hosting a summer interpretive program. Only some sites have fire pits. Tent sites are $25.50 per night, serviced sites $38.20. Chéticamp Campground is the park's only campground that accepts reservations. Sites can be reserved through the **Parks Canada Campground Reservation Service** (519/826-5391 or 877/737-3783, www.pccamping.ca) for $11 per reservation. If you're traveling in the height of summer and require hookups, this booking system is highly recommended.

Continue north from the park gate for 10 kilometers to ★ **Corney Brook Campground** (mid-May-early Oct.; $23.50), which is not much more than a parking lot with 20 designated sites, but incredible ocean views more than make up for a lack of facilities. Beyond Pleasant Bay, the 10 sites at **MacIntosh Brook Campground** (mid-May-early Oct.; $21.50) fill quickly. Ten kilometers farther east is **Big Intervale Campground** (mid-May-early Oct.; $18), also with 10 sites. Neither of these two campgrounds have drinking water. With 256 sites, **Broad Cove Campground** (mid-May-early

Oct.; $25.50), on the ocean just north of Ingonish, is the park's largest campground. Campers have use of showers, flush toilets, kitchen shelters, playgrounds, and an outdoor theater. **Ingonish Campground** (late June-early Sept.; $25.50) is within a finger of the park that extends to the ocean along the Ingonish coastline. Although it's close to the resort town of Ingonish, the wooded setting is quiet and private and within walking distance of a sandy beach with safe swimming. It has showers, flush toilets, and kitchen shelters.

INFORMATION

Turn right as soon as you cross into the park north of Cheticamp for the excellent **Cheticamp Visitor Centre** (902/224-2306; mid-May-mid-Oct. 9am-5pm, July-Aug. 8:30am-7pm). It features natural-history exhibits, weather reports, an activities schedule, and helpful staff.

Parks Canada also operates a smaller information center in Ingonish for those entering the park from the east. It's open mid-May-mid-October 9am-5pm, extended to 8:30am-7pm in July and August.

Ingonish and Vicinity

Ingonish (pop. 500), 110 kilometers east of Chéticamp and 100 kilometers north of Baddeck, is a busy resort center at the eastern entrance to Cape Breton Highlands National Park. The town is a lot more than somewhere simply to rest your head: It is fringed by beautiful beaches, has one of Canada's premier golf courses, and offers a delightful choice of seafood restaurants. If you are allowing yourself some rest time on your Nova Scotia travels, this is the place to book two or more nights in the same accommodation.

SIGHTS AND RECREATION

Ingonish has no official attractions as such. Instead, beach lovers gather on **Ingonish Beach,** where a lifeguard watches over swimmers splashing around in the shallow water that reaches enjoyable temperatures July-August.

Drag yourself away from one of Canada's finest beaches and you'll find the **Freshwater Lake Loop,** a two-kilometer circuit that encircles a shallow lake where beavers can often be seen hard at work in the evening. The trailhead is the parking lot at Ingonish Beach.

Even if you're not a guest at the **Keltic Lodge,** the grounds are a pleasant place for a stroll. Beyond the end of the lodge access road,

a walking trail leads two kilometers to the end of Middle Head Peninsula.

★ Highlands Links

Highlands Links (3 km north of Ingonish Beach, 902/285-2600 or 800/441-1118) is generally regarded as one of the world's top 100 golf courses, and relative to other courses of similar reputation the greens fees are a steal—$103 in.high season, with twilight rates from just $54. Power carts are an additional $35. The course, which opened in 1939, was designed by Stanley Thompson, the same architect commissioned to design famous courses in Banff and Jasper National Parks.

ACCOMMODATIONS

Accommodations are spread along the Ingonish coastline, but demand is high in July and August, so book well ahead. Also note the given open dates, as very few places are open year-round.

$50-100

Sea Breeze Cottages and Motel (8 km north of the east park gate, 902/285-2879 or 888/743-4443, www.seabreezecottagesandmotel.com; mid-Apr.-mid-Dec.) overlooks the ocean and boasts a playground that children will love. Accommodation options include

Ingonish Beach

through quiet offshore waters, or working out in the fitness room. There are also lawn games, tennis, volleyball, and bike rentals. At the end of the day, you can relax with a glass of wine in one of the shoreline Adirondack chairs or try a Nova Scotian brew at the resort pub. Accommodation options are motel rooms up by the highway, older-style cottages (some right by the ocean), and my favorite rooms in all of Cape Breton Island—casual but stylish kitchen-equipped suites with private balconies.

Over $200

The Cabot Trail has its devoted fans, and so does the **Keltic Lodge** (902/285-2880 or 800/565-0444, www.kelticlodge.ca; mid-May-mid-Oct.; from $225 s or d), on Middle Head Peninsula. The access lane from the Cabot Trail meanders through thick stands of white birches and finishes at the lodge. The long, low, wood-sided lodge—painted bright white and topped with a bright red roof—is as picturesque as a lord's manor in the Highlands of Scotland. The main lodge has 32 rustic rooms off a comfortable lobby, furnished with overstuffed chairs and sofas arranged before a massive stone fireplace. Another 40 rooms are in the adjacent newer White Birch Inn. In addition, nine cottages with suite-style layouts (nice for families) are scattered across the grounds. Well-marked hiking trails meander through the adjacent national park woodlands and ribbon the coastal peninsula. An outdoor pool (a bit chilly), tennis courts, and a spa facility are also available.

Affiliated with one of the region's finest restaurants, ★ **Seascape Coastal Retreat** (36083 Cabot Trail, Ingonish, 902/285-3003 or 866/385-3003, www.seascapecoastalretreat. com; Apr.-Oct.; $239-259 s or d) is suited to couples looking for a quiet getaway in romantic surroundings. Within the walls of this very private resort are 10 wooden cottages, each air-conditioned and with a private deck overlooking the ocean and a separate bedroom. Bathrobes, jetted tubs, and TV/DVD combos add to the appeal. Outside, paths lead through

basic motel rooms ($98 s or d) or cottages ($115-168 s or d).

$100-150

Open year-round, **Ingonish Chalets** (36784 Cabot Trail, Ingonish Beach, 902/285-2008 or 888/505-0552, www.ingonishchalets.com; $123-199 s or d) has access to the beach and hiking trails. Nine two-bedroom log chalets start at $169, while five motel-style rooms cost $123. The rooms are furnished in a very woodsy way, with pine paneling extending from the handcrafted furniture to the wall linings. These units also come with basic cooking facilities—microwave, kettle, and so on.

It would be difficult to claim boredom at ★ **Glenghorm Beach Resort** (36743 Cabot Trail, Ingonish, 902/285-2049 or 855/285-4631, www.glenghormbeachresort.com; May-Oct.; $135-435 s or d), a sprawling complex that extends from the Cabot Trail to a long arc of sandy beach. Things to do include walking along the beach, relaxing around the outdoor pool, renting kayaks and paddling landscaped gardens to an herb garden and courtyard where guests gather in the evening. Rates include a full breakfast, and dinner is available with advance reservations in a smart, stylish dining room overlooking the ocean. A three-course meal is $45 per person.

FOOD

Occupying a weathered wooden building on the high headland at Neil's Harbour is the ★ **Chowder House** (902/336-2463; June-Sept. daily 11am-8pm; $10-18). Order at the inside window and wait for your number to be called. Then tuck into creamy clam chowder ($5), fish-and-chips ($8), a lobster burger ($10), or a full crab ($17). Dollar for dollar, you're doing well if you find better value than the food at this always-busy establishment.

Keltic Lodge

The **Keltic Lodge** (Middle Head Peninsula, 902/285-2880) is home to two very different restaurants. Along the access road is the **Atlantic Restaurant** (mid-May-mid-Oct. daily 11am-9pm; $14-29), a big family-style restaurant with seafood for all tastes and budgets: beer-battered fish-and-chips, grilled salmon ($20), and lobster. An excellent add-on is the salad bar ($10). The tables along the east side have stunning ocean views. The smart-casual **Purple Thistle Dining Room** (late May-mid-Oct. daily 7am-10am and 6pm-9pm) has one of Nova Scotia's finest reputations, especially in seafood. Meals are five courses (about $55) rather than à la carte, with an emphasis on lobster in varied creations and other seafood. If you're tooling along Cabot Trail and hope to stop here for dinner, reservations are very wise.

GETTING THERE

Ingonish lies on the Cabot Trail 110 kilometers (1.5 hours) east of Chéticamp and 100 kilometers (1.5 hours) north of Baddeck. To get to Ingonish from Halifax, it's 440 kilometers (five hours) northwest.

Keltic Lodge sits atop high cliffs jutting into the Atlantic Ocean.

SOUTH FROM INGONISH

South of Ingonish Beach, the Cabot Trail descends hairpin turns. Stop at 366-meter-high **Cape Smokey** for a picnic or hiking along the cliff top, which has wonderful views. The steep and twisting road finishes in a coastal glide with views of the offshore Bird Islands. Lying off the northwest side of the cape at the mouth of St. Ann's Bay, these two islands are the nesting site of a multitude of seabird species.

ST. ANN'S

During the 1850s, about 900 of St. Ann's residents, dissatisfied with Cape Breton, sailed away to Australia and eventually settled in New Zealand, where their descendants today make up a good part of the Scottish population. Despite this loss of nearly half its population, St. Ann's, 80 kilometers south of Ingonish and 30 kilometers north of Baddeck, is today the center of Cape Breton's Gaelic culture.

A good place to eat in this area is the

Lobster Galley (51943 Cabot Trail, 902/295-3100; daily 7:30am-10pm; $12-28), at the head of St. Ann's Harbour. Fish cakes and Caesar salad are just $12, a filled lobster roll $18; or try the full lobster dinner for $28.

★ Gaelic College of Celtic Arts and Crafts

The only institution of its kind in North America, the **Gaelic College of Celtic Arts and Crafts** (51779 Cabot Trail, 902/295-3411) was established in 1938. Programs include Highland dancing, fiddling, piping, Gaelic language, weaving, and other subjects. The summer session attracts Gaelophiles from around the world. The **Great Hall of the Clans** (July-Aug. daily 9am-5pm), on the campus, examines the course of Scottish culture and history, including the migrations that brought Highlanders to Cape Breton. Activities include weaving and instrument-making demonstrations, as well as music and dance performances (July-Aug. Mon.-Fri.). The campus gift shop sells a predictable collection of kilts and tartans.

★ Celtic Colours International Festival

The popular **Celtic Colours International Festival** (902/567-3000 or 888/355-7744, www.celtic-colours.com) takes place the second full week of October. It celebrates Cape Breton's Gaelic heritage through concerts held at venues around the island, but the Gaelic College of Celtic Arts and Crafts is a focal point, especially for its nightly Festival Club, where musicians get together for an unofficial jam after performing elsewhere. The festival proper features six or seven concerts nightly, usually in small town halls, with visitors enjoying the brilliant colors of fall as they travel from venue to venue.

Getting There

St. Ann's is 80 kilometers (over an hour) south of Ingonish and 30 kilometers (25 minutes) north of Baddeck. To get to St. Ann's from Halifax, it's 400 kilometers (five hours) northwest.

Gaelic College of Celtic Arts and Crafts

The Northeast

SYDNEY

Cape Breton Island's only city is Sydney (pop. 30,000), set around a large harbor on the island's northeast corner. In the early 1800s, it was the capital of the colony of Cape Breton. At the turn of the 20th century the Sydney area boomed, ranking as one of Canada's major steel production centers.

Sights

Historic buildings constructed of stone quarried at nearby Louisbourg dot the streets north of downtown. One of these, the 1828 **St. Patrick's Church Museum** (87 Esplanade; June-Aug. Mon.-Fri. 10am-3pm; donation), is Cape Breton's oldest Roman Catholic sanctuary. **Cossit House** (75 Charlotte St., 902/539-7973;

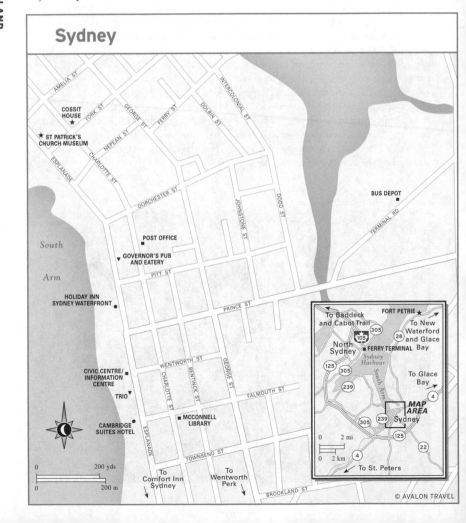

Sydney

© AVALON TRAVEL

June to mid-Oct. Tues.-Sat. 9am-5pm, Sun. 1pm-5pm; adult $2, senior and child $1) is almost as old as Sydney itself. The 1787 manse has been restored to its original condition.

Accommodations

Motel rooms in Sydney are generally more expensive than they should be. Use the websites to search out package rates or wait until the last minute and start calling around for deals.

Comfort Inn Sydney (368 Kings Rd., 902/562-0200, www.comfortinn.com; $130-150 s or d) overlooks the waterfront two kilometers south of downtown. The midsize rooms have contemporary style and modern necessities such as high speed Internet access.

My pick in Sydney is the modern **Cambridge Suites Hotel** (380 Esplanade, 902/562-6500 or 800/565-9466, www.cambridgesuitessydney.com; $165 s or d), which comprises 150 spacious self-contained units, each with a kitchen and wireless Internet access. On the roof level are a pool, sauna, exercise room, and sundeck.

Right downtown, **Holiday Inn Sydney Waterfront** (300 Esplanade, 902/562-7500 or 877/660-8550, www.ihg.com; $200 s or d) is a well-designed comfortable high-rise with more than 150 rooms, a restaurant with water views, an indoor pool and waterslide, a whirlpool, a sauna, an exercise room, and a gift shop. The rack rates of $200 are too high, but the $150 I was quoted for a water-view room in early June seemed about right.

Food

The best coffee in town is poured at **Wentworth Perk** (697 George St., 902/270-3355; Mon.-Sat. 7:30am-8pm, Sun. 11am-5pm; lunches $7-10), a modern café with the usual range of drink choices as well as wraps, sandwiches, and pastries. It's located in a converted residence on the south side of downtown.

★ **Trio** (Cambridge Suites Hotel, 380 Esplanade, 902/563-7009; daily 7-9:30am, daily 5pm-10pm; $14-29) stands out as the best place in town for a healthy, well-priced meal in contemporary surroundings. Breakfast is served buffet-style, while in the evening tasty temptations include blackened haddock, an East Coast hot pot, and rib eye steak.

Away from the hotel dining scene, ★ **Governor's Pub & Eatery** (233 Esplanade, 902/562-7646, daily 11am-11pm; $13-30) has two bustling patios, a pub-style room, and a restaurant. The food is surprisingly good, with seafood and steak the specialties. You could start with maple mandarin salad and then choose from mains such as beer-battered fish-and-chips with hand-cut fries or slow-cooked pork back ribs.

Information and Services

Sydney Visitor Information Centre is well signposted as you enter town from the south (20 Keltic Dr., Sydney River, 902/539-9876, www.cbisland.com; June-mid-Oct. Mon.-Fri. 8:30am-5pm).

Cape Breton Regional Hospital is at 1482 George Street (902/567-8000). For the **RCMP,** call 564-7171, or 911 in emergencies.

Getting There and Around

It's just more than 400 kilometers between Halifax and Sydney—easily driven in under five hours.

The main reason to fly in would be the ease of getting to Cape Breton Highlands National Park, a two-hour drive northeast of town. **Sydney Airport** (YQY, 280 Silver Dart Way, 902/564-7720, http://sydneyairport.ca) is 14 kilometers northeast of the city center. A taxi to town costs $22, or rent a car through Avis, Budget, Hertz, or National, all of which have rental desks at the airport. Sydney is served by **Air Canada** (902/539-7501 or 888/247-2262) with daily direct flights (40 minutes) from Halifax.

HIGHWAY 28 TO GLACE BAY

From Sydney, the New Waterford Highway (Highway 28) spurs north off Prince Street and follows the eastern side of Sydney Harbour for 26 kilometers to the industrial town of New Waterford. Along the way is **Fort**

Petrie (3479 Hwy. 28, 902/862-8367; May-Nov. 10am-6pm; free), one of seven such forts constructed to protect local coal and steel production facilities from attack during World War II. Not much remains, but an interpretive display tells the story of the fort, and views of the harbor make the stop worthwhile.

Glace Bay

At Glace Bay, 21 kilometers northeast of Sydney, **Cape Breton Miners' Museum** (17 Museum St., 902/849-4522; June-Aug. daily 10am-6pm, Sept.-May Mon.-Fri. 9am-4pm; adult $12, child $10) is the main attraction for visitors. Retired miners guide you on an underground tour of a real mine, the Ocean Deeps Colliery, to show the rough working conditions under which workers manually extracted coal. Above the mine is an exhibit gallery where the highlight is a simulated, multimedia trip into the workings of a modern mine, using laser-disc projection and other special effects. On selected Tuesday evenings through summer (usually at 8pm), the Men of the Deeps, a local singing group composed of miners dressed in their coveralls, gives concerts at the museum. Also in the main building is Miners' Village Restaurant (mid-Apr.-Oct. daily noon-8pm), where the food is both tasty and well priced.

LOUISBOURG

This small fishing town (pop. 1,200), 32 kilometers southeast of Sydney, is famous for its historic links to France and for its reconstruction of an entire walled town. Louisbourg may be well off the main Baddeck-Cape Breton Highlands National Park itinerary of many visitors, but it gets a steady flow of visitors through summer and has limited accommodations, so plan accordingly.

★ Fortress of Louisbourg National Historic Site

The **Fortress of Louisbourg National Historic Site** (259 Park Service Rd., 902/733-3552; mid-May-Oct. daily 9:30am-5pm; adult $17.60, senior $15, child $8.80) is a fantastic re-creation of the original French fort. Parks Canada has reconstructed 50 of the original 80 buildings, right down to the last window, nail, and shingle, based on historical records.

Louisbourg reveals itself slowly. The seaport covers 10 hectares, and you can spend the better part of a day exploring. From the Visitor Reception Centre, it's a brief bus ride across fields and marsh to the back of the fortress. The reconstructed fortress and town open a window on New France; they are designed to reflect Louisbourg on a spring day in 1744, the year preceding England's first attack, when the seaport hummed with activity. The houses, fortifications, ramparts, and other structures—as authentically 18th-century French as anything you will find in France—were conceived as a statement of grandeur and power in the New World. The fancy houses lining cobbled lanes belonged to the elite, who ate sumptuous meals on fine china and drank the finest French wines. The simpler houses are the rustic cottages of the working class. Guides and reenactors—portraying soldiers, merchants, workers, and craftspeople—are on hand to answer questions and demonstrate military exercises, blacksmithing, lace making, and other skills. The historical feel flows through to three dining rooms. Hungry visitors can feast on a slice of heavy bread and a chunk of cheese at the **King's Bakery;** at **Hotel de la Marine** servers dish up simple fare in big wooden bowls; while over in **Grandchamps Inn** the "wealthy" can dine on exquisite European cuisine served up on the finest china.

The site is open and fully staffed June to mid-October. In May and through the last two weeks of October, access is by guided tour only (departs daily 10am and 2pm). There are no services during these periods, and so admission is reduced (adult $7.50, senior $6.25, child $4.25). The grounds are closed the rest of the year.

Be prepared for walking, and bring a sweater or jacket in case of breezy or wet weather. Louisbourg's reconstructed buildings stretch from the bus stop to the harbor. Remaining ruins lying beyond the re-creation are marked by trails. You can wander on your own or join a the Fortress of Louisbourg National Historic Site

tour—usually 10am and 2pm for English tours and 1pm for the French-language tour.

Accommodations and Camping

Accommodations in Louisbourg are limited, so it's wise to make reservations.

Overlooking the harbor is **Stacey House** (7438 Main St., 902/733-2317 or 866/924-2242; June–mid-Oct.; $65-95 s or d). It offers four rooms, two with private baths, and an antique-filled parlor within walking distance of town. Rates include a cooked breakfast.

Perfectly situated on a headland with sweeping views of the fortress, ★ **Point of View Suites** (15 Commercial St., 902/733-2080 or 888/374-8439, www.louisbourgpointofview.com; mid-May-Oct.; $125-199 s or d) is Louisbourg's finest accommodation. The sun-filled suites (some with ocean views) and much larger apartments look as if they are straight out of a glossy architectural magazine with their crisp color schemes, hardwood floors, and sliding doors that open to balconies with ocean views. At the edge of the property is a private beach, and each evening at 6pm guests are invited to a Beggar's Banquet in the adjacent restaurant.

Louisbourg RV Park (24 Harbourfront Cres., 902/733-3631 or 866/733-3631; June–mid-Oct.; $23-29) enjoys a downtown waterfront setting. Amenities include showers, 30-amp hookups, and wireless Internet.

The wilderness camping nearest to Louisbourg is at **Mira River Provincial Park** (mid-June-early Sept.), 17 kilometers before town off Highway 22. The park has showers, fire pits and firewood sales, and canoe rentals. Sites scattered through the forest or along the river are all $26 per night.

Food

Wander Louisbourg's main street and you'll find numerous dining choices. My favorite is ★ **Grubstake Restaurant** (7499 Main St., 902/733-2308; daily noon-8:30pm; $13-25), which has been open since the 1970s but offers an up-to-date menu of seafood, with such offerings as linguine topped with shrimp, scallops, haddock, and salmon in a cream sauce. If you want to take a break from seafood, this is the place to do so—the meatloaf with mashed potatoes and vegetables is delicious.

Getting There

Louisbourg is 30 kilometers (25 minutes) southeast of Sydney along Highway 22. It's 440 kilometers from Halifax.

Background

The Land 187
Flora and Fauna 189
History 194
Economy and Government 199
People and Culture 201

The Land

Nova Scotia is predominantly rocky and thinly covered with soil, making it less conducive to farmland than to forests, and thick woodlands blanket the province. The Atlantic coast is rugged, edged with granite, and flanked with sandy beaches, salt marshes, and bogs. The Fundy Coast, from Yarmouth to Cape Split, is rimmed by basalt bedrock mixed with tidal flats. Along this coast, Annapolis Valley, famed for its fruit orchards, is a geological oddity; scoured out by glaciers at the end of the last ice age, the valley is sheltered by mountains north and south, creating a hothouse of warmth and humidity. Along the Northumberland Strait seacoast, rolling terrain with fertile farmlands rises to picturesque high hills and plateaus in Pictou and Antigonish counties.

Cape Breton Island is joined to mainland Nova Scotia by the 1.4-kilometer Canso Causeway. Cape Breton's smaller, eastern section consists of lowlands and rolling hills, with deeply indented Sydney Harbour on its northern coast. The western part of the island rises gradually from sea level to soaring headlands and highlands, culminating at Cape Breton Highlands National Park near the northern tip. Much of the island's center is taken up by the expansive saltwater Bras d'Or Lakes.

Known as the Graveyard of the Atlantic, the province's shores and treacherous shoals are littered with scores of shipwrecks.

In the Beginning

Nova Scotia was under a shallow sea until 500 million years ago. Then pressurized sand and clay oozed to the surface, where it cooled and hardened to create a landscape of sandstone, quartzite, and slate. Molten granite later emerged the same way, heaved, and broke apart. You can see these primordial extrusions at Peggy's Cove near Halifax, where the coast is strewn with oddly placed mammoth boulders.

As the earth's surface heaved and shuddered, the land's contours and seacoasts were formed. Between 405 million and 190 million years ago, the turbulent earth devoured its own creations; evidence is visible at Joggins on the upper Fundy's Chignecto Bay, where upright trees were enfolded into cliff edges. Archaeologists date these fossils at 280 million to 345 million years old.

Glaciation

Glaciation and eons of erosion, however, have ground down the once-mammoth summits such as 532-meter **White Hill**, in Cape Breton Highlands National Park, which is Nova Scotia's highest point. One of the reasons for this was glacial ice, uncountable trillions of tons of it, formed in the last four ice ages. Glaciers up to an estimated three kilometers (two miles) thick weighed down on the elastic bedrock as recently as 14,000 years ago, submerging the coasts and counteracting the inexorable thrust of tectonic uplift.

The last ice sheet retreated and took what remained of prehistory with it. The ice had scoured the earth's surface as it raked back and forth, and this too can be seen at Peggy's Cove, where the ancient scratches are etched in the granite boulders.

As the ice sheet moved, it bulldozed glacial debris into drumlins, large islands of fine soil piled up in places on the predominantly rocky land. The best known of these drumlins is the steep hill upon which the Halifax Citadel sits, but to see drumlins

BACKGROUND
THE LAND

without the manmade distractions, plan to visit Kejimkujik National Park.

Water

More than any other province, Nova Scotia is defined by water—it is nearly completely surrounded by ocean. The 7,400-kilometer-long coastline is a study in contrasts. While the Atlantic Ocean laps the entire east coast, the planet's mightiest tides surge through the Bay of Fundy; the unexpectedly warm Northumberland Strait creates a broad blue parenthesis dividing Prince Edward Island from Nova Scotia; and the wild and wooly Cabot Strait separates Nova Scotia's Cape Breton Island and the island of Newfoundland.

CLIMATE

Nova Scotia's climate comprises distinct seasons, with mild winters and cool summers. Mainland Nova Scotia's climate differs noticeably from Cape Breton's, where more extreme weather patterns occur. Average annual precipitation amounts to 130 centimeters, falling mainly as rain during autumn and as snow in winter. Frost-free periods vary from 120 days on Cape Breton to 145 days in the sheltered Annapolis Valley.

Spring high temperatures range from -2.5°C (27.5°F) to 9°C (48°F), although the days begin to warm up toward the end of March. **Summer** weather varies. Daytime temperatures average up to 30°C (86°F). Nights are usually cool at around 12°C (54°F) but can dip to 5°C (41°F) in late summer. Inland areas are generally five degrees warmer. The coasts often bask in morning fog, which is later dispersed by sea breezes and the warming sun. Late in the season, most hurricanes, having spent their force farther south, limp through the region, bringing to the northwestern Atlantic short spells of rain and wind. On occasion, the province is hit by much harder storms, such as in September 2003, when Hurricane Juan touched land in Halifax, bringing winds gusting up to 185 kilometers per hour.

In **autumn,** the evenings start to cool, but warm days can continue until the end of September at up to 18°C (64°F). The days are cool to frosty October through mid-November. **Winter** lasts from late November through early March, with high temperatures averaging -10°C (14°F) to 4°C (39°F).

Environment Canada (www.weather.gc.ca) has weeklong weather forecasts for towns across the province.

Bay of Fundy

Water Temperatures

The ocean water off Nova Scotia is far from hot, but water temperatures in some areas can be pleasantly warm. Conditions vary on the four seas and in each region. The warmest seas during August are found around Cape Breton's northern tip and along the Northumberland Strait—in both places temperatures reach 18°C (64°F). The Atlantic is a cool 10-15°C (50-59°F) at Mahone Bay and warms a bit as you head up the coast to the northeast; hence the popularity of swimming and surfing at Martinique and Lawrencetown Beaches. Generally, Cape Breton's coastal waters range 14-17°C (57-63°F). The Bay of Fundy is always cool to cold, although it be comes bearable where low tide leaves shallow pools that warm up.

ENVIRONMENTAL ISSUES

Humans have been exploiting Nova Scotia's abundant natural resources for thousands of years. Indigenous hunting and fishing had little effect on ecological integrity, but the arrival of Europeans, who came especially to harvest cod in local waters as early as the 1500s, did. Today, the state of local fisheries, most notably the collapse of cod stocks, is the most important environmental issue facing the province. The beginning of the end was the arrival of "factory ships" in the 1960s, which could harvest up to 200 tons of cod per hour. By the late 1980s, the cod stock had been mostly obliterated, and in the early 1990s a moratorium was put in place until the fishery had recovered. Unfortunately, what was not fully understood at that time was that overfishing was only a part of the problem. Cod are a groundfish, and the factory ships had been bottom-trawling—scooping up the cod in nets with an opening up to one kilometer wide that dragged along the sea floor and devastated the very ecosystem that was a breeding ground for the fish. It is widely thought that the cod stock will never fully recover, although it is currently in better shape than in the waters off Newfoundland.

Contacts

An excellent website for learning more about sustainable seafood is www.seachoice.org. For information on general environmental issues in Nova Scotia, contact the following organizations: **Canadian Parks and Wilderness Society Nova Scotia** (www.cpawsns.org), **Greenpeace** (www.greenpeace.ca), and **Ecology Action Centre** (www.ecologyaction.ca).

Flora and Fauna

To a great extent, it was the land's natural resources—and the potential riches they represented—that attracted Europeans to Canada over the centuries. Since time immemorial, mammals, fish, and varied plant species had, of course, fed and clothed the indigenous peoples of Nova Scotia, who harvested only enough to sustain themselves. But the very abundance of the wildlife seemed to fuel the rapacity of the newcomers, driving them to a sort of madness of consumption—and hastening the exploration and settlement of the newfound continent. Luckily for today's visitor, much remains, in sometimes astonishing abundance and variety, thanks to each species' own unique genius for survival, blind luck, the shifting vagaries of public tastes, and even the occasional glimmer of human enlightenment.

FLORA

The receding glaciers of the last ice age scoured the land and left lifeless mud and rubble in their wake. Overall, the climate then was considerably cooler than it is today, and the first life forms to recolonize in the shadow of the glaciers were hardy mosses, lichens, and other cold-tolerant plants. Junipers and other shrubs later took root, and afterward came coniferous trees—hardy fast-growing spruce and fir—that could thrive here despite the harsh climate and relatively brief growing season. In the boggy interior sprouted moisture-loving willows and tamaracks. As the climate warmed and the soil grew richer, broadleaf deciduous trees arrived. Today, 80 percent of Nova Scotia is thickly blanketed by typical Acadian forest of mixed hardwoods and conifers. Common trees include hemlock, spruce, balsam fir, yellow and paper birches, cedar, maple, ash, and oak. In autumn, the brilliant hues of the changing leaves are one of the province's most cherished attractions.

Large tracts are set aside in the province at Kejimkujik and Cape Breton Highlands National Parks, which protect areas of unique plant habitat. In the Cape Breton Highlands, for example, stands of 300-year-old maples (believed to be the oldest in the country) have survived, and unusual wild orchid species thrive as well. In the highlands' highest elevations, the stunted taiga and alpine-arctic plant communities have been included in an international biological preserve. Bogs in the national parks nourish insectivorous pitcher plants, more orchids, and other specially adapted species.

Along the Atlantic Coast

Along the Atlantic coast, familiar plants—spruces, hardy cinnamon ferns, northern juniper—take on a stunted, gnarled look from contending with the unmitigated elements. It can take endurance and adaptation to survive here amid often harsh conditions. Trees and bushes lie cropped close to the ground or lean permanently swept back by the wind, as if with a giant hairbrush. Taylor Head Provincial Park, along the Marine Drive, is a good place to view this phenomenon. Living on or near the beach requires specialization, too. Marram grass, also called American beach grass, is abundant all along the Atlantic coast. Its extensive root systems help to stabilize the sand dunes on which it grows. Beach pea, seaside goldenrod, dusty miller, and sea rocket are a few of the other plants that can

manage on the less-than-fertile soils just above the high-tide line. Lower down grow cord grass and glasswort, whose systems can tolerate regular soakings of salt water.

Wildflowers

Common wildflowers throughout Nova Scotia—easily seen along roadsides in summertime—include lupine, Queen Anne's lace, yarrow, pearly everlasting, and a variety of daisies. Everywhere, the showy spikes of purple loosestrife, a pretty but aggressive and unwelcome pest, flourish. Bayberry bushes and wild roses bloom in the northeast corner of Nova Scotia during June. The bayberry bush grows clusters of dimpled fruits close along woody stems and releases a pleasant spicy aroma popular in potpourris and Christmas candles. The provincial flower is the trailing arbutus (mayflower), which blooms in early spring in woodlands and higher-elevation barrens.

The yellow beach heather colors the Northumberland Strait dunes and sandy plains, and the rhodora (miniature rhododendron) brightens coastal marshes. Another dune resident, the beach plum, grows snowy white to pinkish flowers in June, which produce fruit welcomed by birds, beasts, and man in late summer and early fall.

LAND MAMMALS

Nova Scotia is home to 70 different mammals. Some, such as beavers, are common. Others, such as the lynx, are endangered, while the presence of cougars is unproven, and species such as woodland caribou have disappeared completely. But it's not all bad news—wildlife-viewing opportunities present themselves throughout the province.

Moose

The giant of the deer family is the moose, an awkward-looking mammal that appears to have been designed by a cartoonist. It has the largest antlers of any animal in the world, stands up to 1.8 meters (six feet) at the shoulder, and weighs up to 500 kilograms (1,100

Was That a Cougar?

Probably not. Cougars (called mountain lions or pumas elsewhere in North America) may still be common on Canada's west coast, but in Nova Scotia their presence is a bit of a mystery.

These large members of the cat family can grow to more than two meters in length and weigh up to 90 kilograms. Elsewhere in Canada, their fur varies in color from light brown to a reddish-tinged gray, but one thing many local sightings have in common is reports of much darker fur. They are incredibly agile creatures. They can spring forward more than 8 meters from a standstill, leap 4 meters into the air, and safely jump from a height of 20 meters (66 feet).

Once widespread through the province, they were hunted to supposed extinction by 1900. Today, there are a few sightings every year, many in the remote backcountry of Nova Scotia's Marine Drive. Because they are solitary animals, cunning and cautious, sightings are generally fleeting.

pounds). Its body is dark brown, and it has a prominent nose, long spindly legs, small eyes, big ears, and an odd flap of skin called a bell dangling beneath its chin. Apart from all that, it's good-looking. Each spring the bull begins to grow palm-shaped antlers that by August will be fully grown. Moose are solitary animals, preferring marshy areas and weedy lakes, but they are known to wander to higher elevations searching out open spaces in summer. They forage in and around ponds on willows, aspen, birch, grasses, and all aquatic vegetation. Although they may appear docile, moose will attack humans if they feel threatened.

While Nova Scotia's moose population has fluctuated greatly since the arrival of Europeans, it is today mostly stable at around 6,000. The densest populations find a home in Cape Breton Highlands National Park as well as in and around Kejimkujik National Park.

White-Tailed Deer

Populations of deer are not particularly high in Nova Scotia; they were practically nonexistent by the late 1800s but came back in the ensuing years. The color of the white-tailed deer varies with the season, but it is generally light brown in summer, turning dirty gray

white-tailed deer

in winter. The white-tailed deer's tail is dark on top, but when the animal runs, it holds its tail erect, revealing an all-white underside. White-tails frequent thickets along the rivers and lakes of interior forests.

Black Bears

Black bears are the only bears present in Nova Scotia. But black bears are not always black (they can be brown), causing them to be called brown bears when in fact they are not. Black bears are widespread through the province but are not particularly common, numbering about 3,000 of Canada's total estimate of 360,000. Their weight varies considerably; males average 150 kilograms (330 pounds), and females 100 kilograms (220 pounds). Their diet is omnivorous, consisting primarily of grasses and berries and supplemented by small mammals. They are not true hibernators, but in winter they can sleep for up to a month at a time before changing position. During this time, their heart rate drops to 10 beats per minute, their body temperature drops, and they lose up to 30 percent of their body weight. Females reach reproductive maturity after five years; cubs, usually two, are born in late winter while the mother is still asleep.

Lynx

The elusive lynx is an endangered species in Nova Scotia and is present only within the remote interior of Cape Breton Highlands National Park. Easily identifiable by its pointy black ear tufts and an oversize, tabby cat appearance, the animal has broad padded paws that distribute its weight, allowing it to float on a surface of snow. It weighs up to 10 kilograms (22 pounds) but appears much larger because of its coat of long thick fur. The lynx is a solitary creature that prefers the cover of forest, feeding mostly at night on small mammals.

Beavers

One of the animal kingdom's most industrious mammals is the beaver. Growing to a length of 50 centimeters (20 inches) and tipping the scales at around 20 kilograms (44 pounds), it has a flat, rudder-like tail and webbed back feet that enable it to swim at speeds of up to 10 kilometers (six miles) per hour. Once hunted for their fur, beavers can be found in flat, forested areas throughout the province. They build their dam walls and lodges of twigs, branches, sticks of felled trees, and mud. They eat the bark and smaller twigs of deciduous plants and store branches underwater near the lodge as a winter food supply.

Black bears are widespread throughout Nova Scotia.

SEA LIFE

Although the province is just 560 kilometers from north to south, Nova Scotia's coastline is 7,400 kilometers long. The surrounding fertile seas nurture an astonishing abundance and variety of sea creatures, from tiny uncounted single-celled organisms up through the convoluted links of the food chain to the earth's largest beings—the great whales.

Tidal Zones

Along the shores, the same conditions that provide for rich and diverse plants—rocky indented coasts, dramatic tidal variations— also create ideal habitats for varied animal communities in the tidal zone. Between the highest and lowest tides, the Maritime shore is divided into six zones, each determined by the amount of time it is exposed to air. The black zone, just above the highest high-water mark, gets its name from the dark band of primitive blue-green algae that grows there. The next zone is called the periwinkle zone, for the small marine snails that proliferate within it. Able to survive prolonged exposure to air, periwinkles can leave the water to graze on the algae. The barnacle zone, encrusted with the tenacious crustaceans, while also exposed several hours daily during low tides, receives the brutal pounding of breaking waves. Next is the rockweed zone—home to mussels, limpets, and hermit crabs (which commandeer the shells of dead periwinkles)— and the comparatively placid Irish moss zone, which shelters and feeds sea urchins, starfish, sea anemones, crabs, and myriad other animals familiar to anyone who has peered into the miniature world of a tide pool. Last is the laminarian zone, where lobsters, sponges, and fishes thrive in the forests of kelp growing in the deep, churning water.

Fish

Beyond the tidal zones lie the waters of the continental shelf, and then the open sea. Flowing south from the Arctic, cold, oxygen-laden currents also carry loads of silica, ground out of the continental granite by the glaciers and poured into the sea by coastal rivers. Oxygen and silica together create an ideal environment for the growth of diatoms, the microscopic one-celled plants that form the bedrock of the ocean's food chain. In the sunlight of long summer days in these northern latitudes, the numbers of diatoms increase exponentially. They are the food source for shrimp and herring, which in turn support larger fish, such as mackerel, Atlantic salmon, and tuna.

Fisheries have been the economic engine driving exploration and development of these northeastern Atlantic coasts for centuries. In days past, codfish were said to carpet the sea floor of the shallow Grand Banks, and the men who caught them—first with lines from small dories, then with nets, and finally from great trawlers that scour the sea—have hauled in untold millions of tons of not only cod but also flounder, salmon, pollack, haddock, anchovies, and dozens of other species. But the fish are in serious trouble, and so, too, inexorably, are the people and communities whose lives have revolved around them.

Whales

The whales that frequent Nova Scotia arrive from the Caribbean between June and mid-July and remain through October. Watching the whales cavort is one of summer's great visitor delights; whale-watching boats leave from Brier Island on the Bay of Fundy and Cape Breton's Chéticamp. The Fundy is especially rich in whales, and the fast incoming tides bring in the mammoth mammals in pursuit of herring schools. Among the 20 species that summer offshore, the most frequently sighted are minkes, pilots, fins, orcas, and humpbacks. The Atlantic right whale is a treasured August visitor.

Seals

Gray and harbor seals inhabit Nova Scotian waters at various times of the year. Whale-watching tours often include a stop at an offshore seal colony, although you may also spot one unexpectedly, such as while dining

Look for harbour seals in all protected ocean waterways.

at a waterfront restaurant in Halifax or in the ocean far below while walking the trail to Cape Chignecto. Harp seals, Arctic dwellers that fatten themselves on fish off the Labrador and Greenland coasts, are occasionally sighted around Cape Breton Island.

BIRDS

About 280 bird species have been reported in Nova Scotia. The province is best known for its bald eagles; about 250 pairs nest here, the second-largest population on North America's east coast after Florida. The season for eagle-watching is July and August. Some of the prime viewing areas are the Lake Ainslie and St. Ann's Bay coastlines; the village of Iona, where Bras d'Or Lakes meets St. Andrews Channel on Cape Breton Island;

and the St. George's Bay coastline. Ospreys nest on McNabs Island in Halifax Harbour. Other raptors may be seen at Brier Island on the Bay of Fundy.

As Nova Scotia lies on the Atlantic flyway, many migratory species can be spotted, including common and arctic terns, kittiwakes, great and double-crested cormorants, Leach's storm petrels, Atlantic puffins, guillemots, and various gulls, ducks, and geese.

Bird-Watching

The **Nova Scotia Bird Society** (www.nsbirdsociety.ca) can direct you to prime birding sites and answer even the most esoteric questions about the province's many and varied species. Its website has bird lists, a schedule of field trips, and links to local contacts.

History

THE EARLIEST INHABITANTS

The earliest evidence of human habitation in Nova Scotia dates from about 8600 BC. and is found at the present site of Debert, northwest

of Truro. Here, at one of the northernmost Paleo-Indian sites in North America, archaeologists have uncovered a wealth of artifacts, including telltale Clovis-like spear tips. The people who once set up camp here were descendants of *Homo sapiens* who migrated from northeast Asia across a land bridge spanning the Bering Strait starting 15,000 years ago. At the time, the northern latitudes of North America were covered by an ice cap, forcing them to travel south down the west coast before fanning out across the ice-free southern latitudes. As the ice cap receded northward, the people drifted north also, perhaps only a few kilometers in an entire generation, and began crossing the 49th parallel, which roughly follows the present U.S.-Canadian border, about 12,000 years ago.

Mi'kmaq

Culturally and linguistically related to Algonquian people, the largest language group in Canada, the Mi'kmaq made a home throughout present-day Nova Scotia as well as northern New Brunswick and as far west as Québec. They were coastal dwellers who fished with spears and hook and line while also collecting shellfish from the shoreline. Hunting was of lesser importance for food but earned one a great degree of status among other members of the group. Canoes with sails were built for summer travel, while in winter toboggans (*toboggan* originates from the Mi'kmaq word *topaghan*) and snowshoes were essential.

Like other aboriginal peoples across North America, the Mi'kmaq practiced a kind of spiritual animism, deeply tied to the land. The trees, animals, and landforms were respected and blessed. Before food could be consumed or a tree felled, for example, it was appreciated for its life-sustaining sacrifice. Mythology also played an important part in spiritual life, along with rituals, shamanism, and potlatch ceremonies.

The name Mi'kmaq (also Micmac) is thought to have derived from the word *nikmaq*, meaning "my kin-friends," which early French settlers used as a greeting for the tribe. Mi'kmaq historically referred to themselves as Lnu (meaning "human being" or "the people").

ACADIA

Nova Scotia's tie to Europe began in 1497, when the explorer John Cabot sighted Cape Breton Island and claimed it for England. A few decades later, explorer Jacques Cartier also claimed much of the same coastline. For France, the region was choice property, a potential New France in the New World. On the other hand, England's colonial aspirations centered farther south, where colonization had begun at Virginia and Massachusetts. England didn't *need* what is now Nova Scotia, though the region offered much with its rich fisheries, but it was a place to confront the expansion of the French, England's most contentious enemy in Europe.

Colonization

England's claim notwithstanding, France eyed the area for colonization and dispatched explorer Samuel de Champlain to the region in 1604. After a tough winter on an island on the St. Croix River (which today forms the New Brunswick-Maine border), the encampment moved across the Bay of Fundy, where the fortified Port-Royal was established near what is now Annapolis Royal. The French named the region—encompassing what is now Nova Scotia, New Brunswick, and Prince Edward Island—Acadia (Peaceful Land). Not to be outdone, England's James I named the same region Nova Scotia (New Scotland) and granted it to Sir William Alexander in 1621.

After a 1632 peace treaty forced England to surrender Nova Scotia to the French, Acadian settlements quickly spread beyond the Port-Royal area to the Fundy and Minas Basin coastlines. The merchant Nicholas Denys, whose name is entwined with France's early exploration, established a fortified settlement on Cape Breton Island at St. Peters and also at Guysborough in 1653. So many Acadians settled at Grand-Pré that it became the largest

Acadian Deportation

In the mid-1700s, decades of war between England and France were winding down in England's favor. The British demanded unqualified oaths of allegiance from the Acadians, who refused and claimed neutrality. Rather than compromise their principles, they fled Nova Scotia for Acadia's more peaceful north. The British followed, burning villages and crops as they went. The Acadian deportation began in 1755, when about 1,100 Acadians were deported to England's other colonies in South Carolina, Georgia, and Pennsylvania. Guerrilla warfare raged as the Acadians fought for their lives and then fled to the hinterlands.

Refugee camps sprang up, the most well-known of which were Beaubears Island, now a national historic site on the Miramichi River, and the nearby swatch of land today home to Enclosure Park (at Derby Junction, five kilometers west of Miramichi), one of the province's most important archaeological sites. Many Acadians died of scurvy and starvation.

The Peace of Paris in 1763 ushered in an uneasy truce. France surrendered its mainland possessions, but during the ensuing decades about 3,800 Acadians returned to the region. The deportation officially finished in 1816.

settlement and hub of villages along the Fundy Coast. Other settlements were established across Acadia on Cape Breton Island, the Cobequid Bay and Cape Chignecto coastlines, and in what is now New Brunswick. The villagers cultivated grains and forage crops on wetlands reclaimed by dikes and planted the region's first orchards.

Through Acadian expansion, bitter military confrontations continued. The two powers had different strategies: France first built settlements, then used its military to defend them. England, boasting a superior military savvy, fought its battles first, then used settlements to stabilize areas. As it turned out, England had the edge, and it was on this advantage that Nova Scotia's history frequently turned during the following century and a half.

Treaty of Utrecht

Hostilities between England and France in the New World mirrored political events in Europe. Fighting ebbed and flowed across the

Port-Royal National Historic Site, the first permanent settlement north of Florida region as the powers jockeyed for control on the European continent. Queen Anne's War (1701-1713), the War of Austrian Succession (1745-1748), and the Seven Years' War (1756-1763) were all fought in Europe, but corresponding battles between the English and French took place in North America as well (where they were known collectively as the French and Indian Wars).

The Treaty of Utrecht in 1713 settled Queen Anne's War in Europe. Under the terms of the treaty, England fell heir to all of French Acadia (though the borders were vague), which became an English colony. Nova Scotia (New Scotland) rose on the ashes of New France and the fallen Port-Royal; the British took the fort in 1710, renamed it Fort Anne, and renamed the settlement Annapolis Royal. The town was designated the colony's first capital, remaining as such until Halifax was established and became the capital in 1749.

ONGOING CONFLICT

The French military regrouped after the fall of Port-Royal. It fled from the region and began to build the Fortress of Louisbourg on Cape Breton Island in 1719. Once again, the French envisioned the fortification as a New Paris and France's major naval base, port city, and trading center in North America.

The British quickly responded. A fort at Grassy Island on Chedabucto Bay was their first effort, a site close enough to the Fortress of Louisbourg to watch the arrivals and departures of the French fleets. By 1745, Louisbourg represented a formidable threat to England, so the Brits seized the fortress and deported the inhabitants. But no sooner had they changed the flag than the French were moving back in again. The War of Austrian Succession in Europe ended with the Treaty of Aix-la-Chapelle in 1748, which, among other things, returned Louisbourg to France.

Full-Fledged War

In 1749 a British convoy sailed into Halifax Harbour, established England's military hub in the North Atlantic in the capacious harbor, and named Halifax the capital of Nova Scotia. Seven years later, the Seven Years' War broke out in Europe, and once more both powers geared for confrontation across the Atlantic Ocean. In 1758 the British again seized the Fortress of Louisbourg and toppled Port la Joye, renaming it Fort Amherst. In the ultimate act of revenge, the British troops returned to Louisbourg in 1760 and demolished the fortress stone by stone so it would never rise again against England.

Fort Edward, on the Fundy Coast, went up in the midst of an Acadian area and guarded the overland route from Halifax. Fort Lawrence on the Chignecto Isthmus, between Nova Scotia and New Brunswick, was built to defend the route to the mainland.

BRITISH SETTLEMENT

After the Acadian deportation, the British began peopling the territory with pro-Crown settlers. Lunenburg began with 2,000 German, Swiss, and French "foreign Protestants." In 1760 England resettled the prime Fundy Coast once farmed by the Acadians with 12 shiploads of farmers from its colonies farther south. The Crown officially regained the region, including Cape Breton Island, with the Peace of Paris in 1763. After the American Revolution, 25,000 British Loyalists poured into Nova Scotia.

SCOTTISH HERITAGE

Nova Scotia's Scottish heritage originated with a shipload of immigrants who arrived at Pictou in 1773, followed by hundreds of settlers to New Glasgow in the 1780s and the Arisaig area in the next decade.

It was during the early 1800s, however, that the region's decidedly Scottish complexion was firmly established. England and France were engaged in the Napoleonic War, and the French had blocked British ports. England desperately needed food and began the Highland Clearances, in which poor tenant farmers in Scotland were turned off their land, their homes burned, and the farmlands

Cable to Canso

On the outskirts of tiny Canso, at the northeastern end of the Marine Drive, is **Hazel Hill Cable Station,** an imposing but crumbling brick building that has important ties to the history of communications. The first cable link between Europe and North America came ashore in Newfoundland, and the company that established the link was given landing rights for 50 years. With problems providing a reliable link between Newfoundland and New York, the Commercial Cable Company laid its own cable, which came ashore at Canso and then continued south to Boston and New York. Completed in 1884, the Hazel Hill Cable Station was a state-of-the-art facility, helping transmit messages from one side of the Atlantic to the other in less than one minute. The distress signal from the sinking *Titanic* and news of the 1929 stock market crash were transmitted through the station before the final message was sent in 1962.

converted to sheep and cattle pastures. The Clearances continued for almost two decades. Thousands of Scots died of starvation and disease, while thousands more took the Crown up on its offer of free land in Nova Scotia. They left their beloved Highlands forever and re-created their old home in a new land. Intense emotional ties to the region remain to this day, and the Scots' heritage is kept alive with festivals commemorating their history and culture.

NOVA SCOTIA TAKES SHAPE

In the late 18th century, Nova Scotia was defined as a distinct colony. Cape Breton Island, for a while a separate colony, was reannexed to Nova Scotia in 1820. Fortunes were founded on trade. Halifax's Samuel Cunard started a shipping empire based on steamship service to England in 1839. During the Great Age of Sail, shipbuilding seaports thrived. In 1878 Yarmouth ranked as Canada's second-largest port. Coal mining began in 1872 at Springhill, near Amherst, where the 1,220-meter shaft was Canada's deepest.

Confederation

In 1864, Nova Scotia sent five delegates across to neighboring Prince Edward Island for a landmark event in Canada's history. The "Fathers of the Confederation"—from Nova Scotia as well as New Brunswick, Prince Edward Island, Ontario, and Québec—met at

Province House in Charlottetown to discuss the joint dominion that followed. England gave the union its blessing and signed the British North America Act (now known as the Constitution Act). Confederation was not popular with all Nova Scotians, but it offered economic inducements, including the rail connections to central Canada that Nova

Scotia wanted. Finally, the Dominion of Canada was born on July 1, 1867, as a confederation of Québec, Ontario, New Brunswick, and Nova Scotia united under a parliamentary government, with the other provinces of today joining between 1870 and 1949 (neighboring Newfoundland and Labrador was last to join).

Economy and Government

ECONOMY

Traditionally, Nova Scotia's economy revolved around resource-based industries such as fishing, forestry, and mining. Although communities established around fishing and farming areas continue to thrive, the economy today is a lot more diverse. In addition to all the stalwarts discussed below, other growing sectors include information technology, the medical field (Nova Scotia is a world leader in multiorgan transplants), and the film industry.

In 2014, Nova Scotia's gross domestic product was a little more than $39 billion, with ocean industries generating the largest segment ($3.1 billion). Second most important to the economy is manufacturing ($2.1 billion).

Ocean Industries

Fishing, the traditional stalwart of the Nova Scotia economy, has decreased greatly in importance dollar-wise in the last two decades. Poor resource management and overfishing have destroyed its once-bounteous supplies. Cod stocks especially have declined greatly, and quotas have been put in place in an effort to protect and rebuild existing stocks. Even so, fisheries and fish-processing remain an important contributor to Nova Scotia's gross domestic product, and cod, haddock, herring, and lobster are caught inshore and off the Atlantic's Scotian Shelf. The province is the world's largest lobster exporter.

The government has put a positive spin on the decline of the fishing industry by claiming

that the "ocean industries" sector is growing. It may be, but only because other industry is being added to the fishing equation, including aquaculture, boatbuilding, offshore gas and oil drilling, ocean-related tourism, sea-based government services, and transportation. Regardless of how you approach the issue, the ocean is extremely important to the Nova Scotian economy, generating $3.1 billion dollars annually.

Tourism

Tourism ranks as the third most important component of the provincial economic pie, generating $1.9 billion annually. It is also the fastest-growing sector of the economy, having doubled in worth during the last decade and currently employing over 45,000 people. Most visitors (36 percent) are from the neighboring provinces, while the rest of Canada contributes 30 percent, and the United States adds almost 25 percent. Of the 1.8 million people who arrive annually, around three-quarters are returning visitors.

Agriculture and Forestry

Although just 8 percent of Nova Scotia's land is arable, agriculture contributes heavily to the economy, producing fruits (including Annapolis Valley apples), dairy products, poultry, hogs, and the world's largest share of blueberries.

Although fishing gets all the attention, forestry has historically been an important component of the provincial economy. In the

1800s, local lumber was used in shipbuilding, but today the pulp and paper industries use the great majority of harvested wood. About 37,000 square kilometers of Nova Scotia is deemed to be productive forest, and most of it is owned by private companies. Nova Scotia also exports 1.7 million Christmas trees each year.

Military

Nova Scotia is the region's federal civil service and military center. Halifax has served as a naval center since its founding in 1749 as headquarters for the Royal Navy. The city is now Maritime Command headquarters for the Canadian Armed Forces. Other in-province military installations are at Shearwater, Cornwallis, and Greenwood; training stations are at Barrington, Mill Cove, Shelburne, and Sydney.

Mining

Offshore deposits of oil and gas below the Scotian Shelf near Sable Island, 250 kilometers from the mainland, have been drilled since the early 1990s. It is estimated that two billion barrels of oil and up to 40 trillion cubic feet of natural gas remain. Important salt deposits are mined along the Northumberland Strait, including at Pugwash. Nova Scotia is the leading Canadian supplier of gypsum, which is exported to the United States. Historically, coal was the most important mineral product, with mines on Cape Breton Island supplying coal to power stations and used to produce iron and steel. The last of these mines closed in 2001, creating an economic catastrophe for Cape Bretoners.

GOVERNMENT

Canada is a constitutional monarchy. The federation of 10 provinces and three territories operates under a parliamentary democracy in which power is shared between the federal government, based in Ottawa, and the provincial governments. Canada's three nonprovincial territories, Nunavut, Yukon, and the Northwest Territories, exercise delegated—rather than constitutionally guaranteed—authority. The power to make, enforce, and interpret laws rests in the legislative, executive, and judicial branches of government, respectively.

Federal Government

Under Canada's constitutional monarchy, the formal head of state is the queen of England, who appoints a governor-general to represent her for a five-year term. The governor-general stays out of party politics and performs largely ceremonial duties, such as opening and closing parliamentary sessions, signing and approving state documents on the queen's behalf, and appointing a temporary replacement if the prime ministry is vacated without warning. The head of government is the prime minister, who is the leader of the majority party or party coalition in the House of Commons.

The country's legislative branch, the Parliament, comprises two houses. The House of Commons, with 308 members, is apportioned by provincial population and elected by plurality from the country's districts (11 members are from Nova Scotia). The Senate comprises 105 members appointed by the governor-general on the advice of the prime minister. Legislation must be passed by both houses and signed by the governor-general to become law.

National elections are held whenever the majority party is voted down in the House of Commons or every five years, whichever comes first. Historically, it has been unusual for a government to last its full term.

Provincial and Local Governments

Whereas the federal government has authority over defense, criminal law, trade, banking, and other affairs of national interest, Canada's 10 provincial governments bear responsibility for civil services, health, education, natural resources, and local government. As in the other provinces, Nova Scotia's Legislative

Assembly consists of a one-house legislative body with members elected every four years. The nominal head of the provincial government is the lieutenant governor, appointed by the governor-general of Canada. Executive power, however, rests with the cabinet, headed by a premier, the leader of the majority party.

As elsewhere, local government in Nova Scotia has always been top-heavy with bureaucracy, and so in the 1990s the number of incorporated towns was trimmed by creating regional municipalities. One of these was Cape Breton Regional Municipality, formed by amalgamating six incorporated towns and one existing county. The main population base lives in Halifax Regional Municipality, which was created through the amalgamation of the cities of Halifax and Dartmouth and the town of Bedford.

People and Culture

While the rugged topography of Nova Scotia has tended to separate people and isolate them in scattered settlements, centuries of sometimes turbulent history have bound the Nova Scotians together: the mutual grief of the early wars, the Acadian deportation, immigration upheavals, and the abiding hardships common to resource-based economies.

DEMOGRAPHY

Nova Scotia's population is 941,000. It is the seventh-most populous province and is home to 2.7 percent of Canada's total population (35 million). The population density is 18 people per square kilometer. Distribution is closely divided between urban and rural, with a full third of Nova Scotians concentrated in and around Halifax.

Almost four of five Nova Scotians trace their lineage to the British Isles. Forty-nine original Scottish families, from Archibald to Yuill, are still on the rolls of the Scottish Societies Association of Nova Scotia, which does genealogical surveys.

After the American Revolution, 25,000 United Empire Loyalists poured into Nova Scotia. Several thousand African Americans arrived during the War of 1812, followed by Irish immigrants from 1815 to 1850. Recent worldwide immigration has added more than 50 other ethnic groups (including Poles, Ukrainians, Germans, Swiss, Africans, and Lebanese) to the province's cultural milieu, making it the most cosmopolitan in the region. About 8,000 Black people live in Nova Scotia today, many of them descendants of immigrants from colonial America.

Mi'kmaq

For thousands of years before the arrival of Europeans, the Mi'kmaq people had lived off the land's abundant natural resources. As the Mi'kmaq were forced to sign treaties, they gave up traditional land and settled on reserves (known as reservations in the United States). They were no longer free, they no longer hunted or fought, their medicine men could do nothing to stop the spread of the white man's diseases, and, slowly, they lost their pride. The first Indian Act, drafted in 1876, attempted to prepare natives for "European" society, but it only ended up isolating them from the rest of society.

Today, a total of 45 reserves and bands create affiliation for 6,000 Mi'kmaq. The total number of aboriginal people in Nova Scotia is quoted at 26,000; many of the remaining 20,000 live off reserves but on traditional lands.

Various names are used to describe aboriginal Canadians, and all can be correct in context. The government still uses the term "Indian," despite its links to Christopher Columbus and the misconception he had landed in India. "Native" is generally considered acceptable only when used in conjunction with "people," "communities," or "leaders." "Indigenous" or "aboriginal" can have insulting connotations when used in certain contexts. The Mi'kmaq themselves most often refer to themselves and others by none of the above, preferring to use band names.

Métis

The progeny of native people and Caucasians, the Métis (named for an old French word meaning "mixed") form a diverse and complex group throughout Canada. They date from the time of earliest European contact; in Nova Scotia, unions between European fishermen and Mi'kmaq women—sometimes casual, sometimes formal—produced Métis offspring by the early 1600s. In the 17th century, the French government encouraged this mixing, seeing it as conducive to converting the native people to Christianity and to more speedily increasing the population of New France. Samuel de Champlain said, "Our young men will marry your daughters, and we shall be one people." That policy had changed by the 1700s, however, and France then *discouraged* mixed unions, in part because of the increased presence of white women in North America.

Today, Métis culture in Nova Scotia remains strongest along the Fundy Coast.

LANGUAGE AND RELIGION

Although Canada is constitutionally bilingual, English is the language of choice for the majority of Nova Scotians. (French is the mother tongue of about 22 percent of Canadians, while the figure in Québec is 88 percent.) The Official Languages Acts of 1969 and 1988 established French and English as equal official languages and designated rights for minority-language speakers throughout the country. Still, there has been no shortage of acrimony between francophone Québec and the rest of the country over the issue of language (as well as broader cultural distinctions), which has led to constitutional crisis and nearly to the secession of Québec from the confederation.

English is spoken by 94 percent of Nova Scotians, while 6 percent are bilingual. French has gained appeal as a second language, and one in four primary schoolchildren in Halifax is enrolled in French immersion classes. Francophones are a small minority in Nova Scotia (4 percent). The French spoken here is not a patois; it's closely tied to the language that was brought to the continent by the original settlers from France. Visitors who have studied standard Parisian French may have a little trouble with the accent, syntax, and vocabulary (the differences are not unlike those between American and British English).

Canada, Eh!

Canadian English is subtly different from American English, not only in pronunciation but also in lexicon. For instance, Canadians may say "serviette," "depot," and "chesterfield" when Americans would say "napkin," "station," and "couch." Spelling is a bit different as well, as Canadians have kept many British spellings—for example, *colour, kilometre, centre, and cheque.* "Eh?" is a common lilt derived from British and Gaelic, in which each sentence ends on a high note, as though a question had been asked. At the same time, Canadian English has been profoundly influenced by its neighbor to the south. Nevertheless, language variations pose no serious threat to communication.

Religion

Although the domination of organized religions over the lives of Canadians has waned substantially since the 1960s, church affiliation in Nova Scotia is higher than elsewhere in the country.

Nova Scotia's cultural diversity is reflected in religion. Protestants and Roman Catholics make up 58 and 37 percent of the mainland population, respectively, while on Cape Breton Catholics are in the majority. Anglicans account for almost 16 percent of the mainland

and 10 percent of Cape Breton. Other denominations include the United Church of Canada and the Baptist and Presbyterian churches, as well as small populations of Jews, Buddhists, and Hindus, living mainly in Halifax.

THE ARTS

The Canada Council gives grants to theaters, dance troupes, orchestras, and arts councils to promote and keep the arts alive. The provincial tourism office (902/425-5781 or 800/565-0000, www.novascotia.com) can tell you what's going on, or you can check out the local paper. See each travel chapter for specific listings detailing nightlife, theater, dance, and music options.

Halifax attracts concerts and major events to the Halifax Metro Centre. Farther up the hillside, the Neptune Theatre hosts year-round repertory theater, as does Dalhousie University's Rebecca Cohn Auditorium, which doubles as the home of the Symphony of Nova Scotia. Dozens of nightclubs and other venues around the capital city showcase established and up-and-coming local bands, such as Sloan, which are earning the province, and especially Halifax, a reputation as an influential breeding ground for pop, rock, and alternative music.

Dancing the Jig

Through the first half of the 18th century, life in the northeast and Highlands of Scotland was becoming more and more difficult. Not only was there discontent over the union with England, the Scots were facing ever-decreasing resources, the dismantling of clans, and the confiscation of property. After the defeat of Bonnie Prince Charlie in 1745, thousands of these Gaelic speakers migrated to the New World, with many of them settling in Nova Scotia. They brought with them their farming skills, their language, and their music. Centuries later, these Celtic traditions remain a strong part of life in Nova Scotia.

Music is the best-known part of the Celtic culture, especially fiddle music, which creates the perfect rhythm for step dancing. While this style of music is all but forgotten in Scotland, it thrives in Nova Scotia. Many cherished songs describing life on the land have been passed down through the generations, while a new wave of lively tunes (known as jigs and reels) creates a spirited mix of music heard throughout the region and beyond.

The world's largest fiddle is on the Sydney harborfront.

Cape Breton-born **Natalie MacMaster** has the highest profile of Nova Scotia's fiddlers. Her energetic performances, in which she steps the dances while playing, bring crowds around the world to their feet. Born and raised on the west coast of Cape Breton Island, five siblings make up **The Rankins,** who infuse a variety of musical styles into their music. The fiddle, mandolin, and percussion instruments keep the traditional vibe going, while the songs vary from country to folk. The fiddle is central to the music performed by **Ashley MacIsaac,** but his shows are anything but traditional. Described by some as "grunge fiddle," his music crosses from Celtic to garage rock to heavy metal, and he's a unique nonconformist who performs in sold-out shows across North America. In addition to the big names, bands such as the **Irish Descendants** (from Newfoundland, but often performing in Nova Scotia) are worth watching for, while bands churning out lively foot-stomping, beer-drinking tunes can be heard in pubs throughout the province.

Cape Breton is renowned for its contributions to folk music. Not surprisingly, Scottish and Irish fiddle tunes form much of the source material, but Cape Breton musicians have taken that extremely rich foundation and made something with a uniquely Maritime flavor: frisky jigs and reels for dancing, as well as ballads, often centering on the theme of fishing and the ubiquitous sea.

Museums

With an ethnic heritage as varied as Nova Scotia's, it's no wonder that its museums are among the country's best. Some museums are moving tributes to the people, such as the Grand Pré National Historic Site, while others, such as the Fortress of Louisbourg National Historic Site, re-create early Anglo years with authentic buildings and demonstrations.

On a smaller scale, county and town museums document regional historic, cultural, and economic subjects. Municipal or privately operated museums in towns and villages put the emphasis on local history or specialties.

Grand Pré National Historic Site

Essentials

Getting There 206

Getting Around 208

Recreation 209

Accommodations and Food 215

Travel Tips 221

Health and Safety 223

Information and Services 225

Getting There

Visitors to Nova Scotia have the option of arriving by road, rail, ferry, or air. The main gateway city for flights from North America and Europe is the capital, Halifax. Ferries cross to Yarmouth from Maine and to Digby from New Brunswick, while the main rail line enters the region from New Brunswick and terminates at Halifax.

Unless otherwise noted, telephone numbers given in this section are the local (North American) contacts.

AIR

Most long-haul international and domestic flights into eastern Canada set down at Toronto, Ottawa, or Montréal, with connecting or ongoing flights to Halifax.

Air Canada

Air Canada (888/247-2262, www.aircanada. com) is one of the world's largest airlines, serving five continents. The company has one of the world's easiest-to-understand fare systems, with five fare levels and multiple ways of searching for online flights and fares. It offers direct flights to Halifax from Fredericton, Saint John, Moncton, St. John's, Montréal, Ottawa, Toronto, Calgary, and Boston. All other flights from North America are routed through Toronto, Ottawa, or Montréal, where connections can be made to Halifax. From Europe, Air Canada flies from London to Halifax. From the South Pacific, Air Canada operates flights from Sydney to Vancouver for onward connections to Halifax. Asian cities served by direct Air Canada flights include Beijing, Hong Kong, Nagoya, Osaka, Seoul, Shanghai, Taipei, and Tokyo. All terminate in Vancouver. Air Canada's flights

originating in South America are all routed through Toronto.

WestJet

Canada's second-largest airline, **WestJet** (403/250-5839 or 888/937-8538, www.westjet. com), is the main competition to Air Canada. Based in Calgary, its flights extend as far east as St. John's, with flights routed through Toronto to Halifax.

U.S. Airlines

Air Canada offers direct daily flights from Boston to Halifax, but the city is also served by **Delta** (800/221-1212, www.delta.com) from New York (LGA); **US Airways** (800/428-4322, www.usairways.com) from Philadelphia; and **United** (800/538-2929, www.united.com) from Chicago and Newark.

RAIL

Amtrak (800/872-8725, www.amtrak.com) has service from New York City to Toronto (via Buffalo), and from New York City to Montréal.

VIA Rail

Once you're in Canada, rail travel is handled by **VIA Rail** (416/366-8411 or 888/842-7245, www.viarail.ca). Best known for the transcontinental rail route, the spectacular journey from Vancouver to Toronto through the Canadian Rockies. VIA Rail has replicated the transcontinental route's deluxe trappings and service with its Sleeper Plus class aboard the *Ocean.* The *Ocean* departs Montréal, follows the St. Lawrence River's southern shore to northern New Brunswick, cuts across the province to Moncton, speeds into Nova

---

Previous: Halifax International Airport; oceanfront camping.

Air Taxes

The Canadian government collects a variety of "departure taxes" on all flights originating from Canada. These taxes are generally not in the advertised fare, but they will all be included in the ticket purchase price. First up is the **Air Travellers Security Charge,** $5-10 each way for flights within North America and $25 round-trip for international flights. **NAV Canada** also dips its hand in your pocket, collecting $10-20 per flight for maintaining the country's navigational systems. Additionally, passengers departing Halifax International Airport must pay an **Airport Improvement Fee** of $25, while those departing Sydney also pay $25 (these are among the highest AIFs in Canada). Additionally, if your flight transits through Toronto, you pay a $4 improvement fee for that airport.

Scotia via Amherst and Truro, and finishes at Halifax. The trip takes 21 hours. The train has a variety of classes, but it is the Sleeper Plus class that gets all the attention. These luxuriously appointed carriages include a domed car with three small salons (one of which is a replica of the transcontinental's mural lounge), a dining car with art deco trappings, and a more informal car designed for lighter dining. Fares from Montreal to Halifax range from $180 each way in Economy class to $625 in Sleeper Plus class, the latter including sleeping-car accommodations and all meals.

BUS

North America's main bus line, **Greyhound** (800/231-2222, www.greyhound.ca or www.greyhound.com), doesn't provide service to Nova Scotia. Instead, you will need to get yourself to Riviere-du-Loup in Quebec and connect with **Maritime Bus** (902/429-2029 or 800/575-1807, www.maritimebus.com), which provides service from these three cities to locations throughout Nova Scotia.

FERRY

From Toronto, the most direct driving route to Halifax includes a ferry trip across the Bay of Fundy.

From New Brunswick

Bay Ferries (902/245-2116 or 888/249-7245, www.ferries.ca) handles the busy Bay of Fundy crossing between Saint John (New Brunswick) and Digby (a three-hour drive from Halifax), a shortcut that saves drivers a few hours of driving time. Operating once or twice daily year-round, one-way high-season fares are adult $44, senior and youth $34, child under five $5, vehicle $88 plus a $20 fuel surcharge. Reservations are essential through summer.

From Maine

Yarmouth, 310 kilometers southwest of Halifax, is the Canadian terminus for **Nova Star Cruises** (866/864-6295, www.novastarcruises.com; May-Oct.), which departs Portland Maine daily in the evening between May and October. Fares for the 11-hour crossing are adult $139, vehicle also $139, and children under 18 free.

CAR
Principal Routes into Nova Scotia

The majority of visitors drive to Nova Scotia. From the United States, Highway 9 heads east from Bangor, Maine, and enters New Brunswick—Atlantic Canada's principal land gateway—at St. Stephen. From this point, the options are to continue north via Moncton to Nova Scotia, or to jump aboard the ferry at Saint John. The TransCanada Highway from central Canada is more roundabout, following the St. Lawrence River through Québec, and then passing through northern New Brunswick to enter Nova Scotia at Amherst.

Getting Around

Driving, whether it be your own vehicle or a rental car, is by far the best way to get around Nova Scotia. This section talks about driving in Canada as well as the public transportation options.

AIR

While Halifax International Airport, 35 kilometers from Halifax, serves as Atlantic Canada's principal air hub, there is a just a single intraprovincial flight within Nova Scotia—the daily **Air Canada** (888/247-2262, www.aircanada.com) link between Halifax and Sydney.

BUS

Getting around Nova Scotia by bus is made possible by **Maritime Bus** (902/429-2029 or 800/575-1807, www.maritimebus.com), which links all major cities and towns as well as many minor ones (although there is no service along the South Shore or Fundy Coast). It operates seven days a week year-round.

Halifax has an extensive public transportation system that revolves around scheduled bus service. If you have a day on your hands and no other plans, consider an early morning bus to an unexplored area, and a late afternoon or early evening return to the city. Few outsiders do it, but mixing among the locals on a bus circuit is a terrific way to explore the capital.

DRIVING IN CANADA

United States and international driver's licenses are valid in Canada. All highway signs give distances in kilometers and speeds in kilometers per hour. Unless otherwise posted, the maximum speed limit on the highways is 100 kilometers per hour (62 miles per hour).

Infants weighing up to nine kilograms must be strapped into a "bucket" style car seat. Use of a child car seat for larger children weighing 9-18 kilograms is also required.

Before venturing north of the 49th parallel, U.S. residents should ask their vehicle insurance company for a Canadian Non-resident Inter-provincial Motor Vehicle Liability Insurance Card. You may also be asked to prove vehicle ownership, so be sure you have your vehicle registration form.

If you're a member in good standing of an automobile association, take your membership card—the Canadian AA provides members of related associations full services, including free maps, itineraries, excellent tour books, road- and weather-condition information, accommodations reservations, travel agency services, and emergency road services. For more information, contact the **Canadian Automobile Association** (613/247-0117, www.caa.ca).

Note: **Drinking and driving** (with a blood alcohol level of 0.08 percent or higher) in Nova Scotia can get you imprisoned for up to five years on a first offense and will cost you your license for at least 12 months. Those caught driving with a blood alcohol level between 0.05 and 0.08 percent automatically lose their license for seven days.

Note: Like most Canadian provinces, Nova Scotia has a **distracted driving** law that prohibits drivers from using handheld cell phones while operating a motor vehicle.

Highways and Byways

Long distances notwithstanding, the province has a superb system of roads, classified by numbers. For example, the TransCanada (Highway 104) enters at Amherst, zips east across the mainland, and finishes at North Sydney. The highway is one of the new 100-series roads designed for rapid transit. Similar highways connect major towns in the central region and rim the heavily traveled southwest region's seacoast along the Fundy.

The highways numbered 1-99 often parallel the 100-series expressways and connect major cities and towns. Roads numbered 200-399 are paved, rambling, two-lane routes that take visitors to all the interesting out-of-the-way places. These roads often work as diversionary routes off major sightseeing highways such as Highway 316, which departs the Marine Drive's Highway 7 and meanders through Canso and Guysborough on its way to the Canso Strait. The Cabot Trail around western Cape Breton is the exception. It is unnumbered and ranks as a special scenic highway.

Car Rental

All major car rental companies have outlets at Halifax International Airport, in downtown Halifax, and in major towns across the province. Try to book well in advance, especially in summer. Expect to pay from $50 a day and $250 a week for a small economy car with unlimited kilometers.

Major rental companies with outlets in Halifax include:

- **Avis** (800/331-1212, www.avis.ca)
- **Budget** (800/268-8900, www.budget.ca)
- **Discount** (800/263-2355, www.discountcar.com)
- **Enterprise** (800/261-7331, www.enterprise.com)

- **Hertz** (800/654-3131, www.hertz.ca)
- **National** (877/222-9058, www.nationalcar.com)
- **Rent-a-Wreck** (800/327-0116, www.rentawreck.ca)
- **Thrifty** (800/847-4389, www.thrifty.com)

RV and Camper Rental

You might want to consider renting a campervan or other recreational vehicle for your trip. With one of these apartments-on-wheels, you won't need to worry about finding accommodations each night. Even the smallest units aren't cheap, but they can be a good deal for longer-term travel or for families or two couples traveling together. The smallest vans, capable of sleeping two people, start at $175 per day with 100 free kilometers (62 miles) per day. Standard extra charges include insurance, a preparation fee (usually around $60 per rental), a linen/cutlery charge (around $60 per person per trip), and taxes. Major agencies with rental outlets in Halifax include **Cruise Canada** (800/671-8042, www.cruisecanada.com) and **Canadream** (888/480-9726, www.canadream.com). Both of these companies also have rental outlets across the country.

ESSENTIALS
RECREATION

Recreation

In Nova Scotia's great outdoors, just about every form of recreation is feasible and first-rate: bicycling, hiking, scuba diving, canoeing, sea kayaking, stand-up paddleboarding, sailing, rockhounding, bird-watching, surfing, fishing, golfing, and downhill skiing—you name it. Many outfitters around the province rent bikes, boats, and other equipment and can equip you for wilderness expeditions and all sorts of other activities.

PARKS

The province's national and provincial parks come in a wide range of personalities and offer an equally eclectic array of activities and facilities, from searching for gemstones at Blomidon Provincial Park to lounging in luxury at Cape Breton Highlands' Keltic Lodge resort.

National Parks

Nova Scotia has three of Canada's 45 national parks. Nova Scotians dote on **Kejimkujik National Park** (kedgie-muh-KOO-jick), which combines interesting ice-age topography with an interior network of lakes ideal for canoeing. Visiting **Sable Island National Park** is an expensive affair as access is by air charter, but it remains an almost mythical destination for its population of wild horses. But it is **Cape Breton Highlands National Park** that ranks as a showstopper among all of Canada's national parks. It's more than twice as large as Kejimkujik, and whereas that park can be uncrowded even in summer, the Highlands park attracts hordes of visitors for its ocean scenery, abundant wildlife, and network of hiking trails.

Permits are required for entry into all Canadian national parks. These are sold at park gates, at all park information centers, and at campground fee stations. Day passes (under $10 per person) are the best deal for short visits, but if you're planning to visit both Nova Scotia parks, as well as those in other provinces, consider an annual **Parks Canada Discovery Pass,** good for entry into all of Canada's national parks and national historic sites for one year from the date of purchase. The cost is adult $67.70, senior $57.90, child $33.30, up to a maximum of $136.40 per vehicle. For more information on park passes, check the Parks Canada website (www.pc.gc.ca).

Provincial Parks

The **Department of Natural Resources** (902/662-3030, www.novascotiaparks.ca) manages a system of 205 provincial parks, 84 wilderness areas, and 138 natural reserves within the province. Of the provincial parks, most are day-use areas (formerly called "picnic parks"—you'll see this designation on some signs) with picnic facilities and often hiking trails and along coastal areas beaches for clam digging and swimming. Many boast sensational views; Blomidon Provincial Park, for example, north of Wolfville, provides access to a hiking trail atop towering red cliffs that jut into the Bay of Fundy and overlook the foaming sea. In addition, some of Nova Scotia's best beach scenes are found at the day-use parks; some have lifeguards, but otherwise facilities are limited. The best of the provincial park beaches are **Risser's Beach** near Lunenburg and **Clam Harbour** northeast of

Halifax, which often has sand-sculpture contests. Naturalists go for **Martinique Beach** near Musquodoboit Harbour because of its dunes, salt marshes, and the nearby bird sanctuary; and **Taylors Head** near Spry Bay, which has boardwalk-laced dunes, a beach, and peninsula hiking trails. A good number of provincial parks have campgrounds and summer interpretive programs. Camping fees are $18-26, with many campgrounds having flush toilets and showers but no hookups. Most campgrounds are open mid-June to mid-October, with a few of the more popular facilities opening in mid-May.

HIKING AND WALKING

Hiking is one of the most popular activities in Nova Scotia. Not only are there hundreds of trails to explore, it's free and anyone can do it. The hiking season spans spring to fall. Coastal areas are generally free of pesky insects, but insect repellent is wise inland from May to September. As national and provincial parks protect the most spectacular scenery, it'll be no surprise that this is where you find the best hiking. One standout is **Cape Breton Highlands National Park** on Cape Breton Island. Here you can find anything from short interpretive trails along raised boardwalks to strenuous slogs that end at high ocean lookouts. Nova Scotia's provincial parks generally lack long trails, but short walks often lead to local natural landmarks. Brochures on these walking trails are widely available at information centers, or check the Department of Natural Resources website (www.novascotiaparks.ca).

FISHING

Neighboring New Brunswick and Newfoundland and Labrador get most of the attention by anglers, but Nova Scotia has a wide range of fishing experiences and a diverse number of species.

Salmon

Just one species of salmon is native to the tidal waters of Nova Scotia—the Atlantic salmon.

It is anadromous, spending its time in both freshwater and salt water. The fish spend up to three years in local rivers before undergoing massive internal changes that allow them to survive in salt water. They then spend between two and three years in the open water, traveling as far as Greenland. After reaching maturity, they begin the epic journey back to their birthplace, to the exact patch of gravel on the same river from where they emerged. It is the returning salmon that are most sought after by anglers, with Cape Breton Island's Margaree River the focus for serious anglers. Atlantic salmon grow to 36 kilograms (79 pounds), although their landlocked relatives rarely exceed 10 kilograms (22 pounds).

Deep-Sea Fishing

Deep-sea fishing's star attraction is the giant bluefin tuna; its season runs September-November. In 1979, a bluefin weighing a record 679 kilograms (1,497 pounds) was caught off St. Georges Bay. The bay ranks as the top tuna area, while the Fundy coast off Yarmouth from Cape St. Mary to Wedgeport is another prime fishing area. Expect to pay $160-300 per person per day for a tuna charter. In addition to tuna, other deep-sea catches include pollack, mackerel, striped bass, sea trout, and bottom dwellers such as haddock, cod, and halibut.

Freshwater Fish

Speckled trout (also known as brook trout) are widespread throughout the region and are fun to catch and tasty to eat. They tend to gravitate to cooler water, such as spring-fed streams, and can be caught on spinners or flies. A 3.4-kilogram (7.5-pound) specimen, one of the largest ever caught, is on display in Halifax's Museum of Natural History (the record is one that weighed in at 4.1 kilograms, which was reeled in from Porters Lake, east of Halifax). Introduced in the late 1800s, **rainbow trout** are in lakes and rivers across Nova Scotia. Sherbrooke Lake and Dollar Lake, both near Halifax, have healthy populations of **lake trout. Brown trout** are found in some streams and larger lakes.

Long and lean, **striped bass** inhabit rivers and estuaries throughout the region. There is a definite art to catching the species—it is estimated it takes an average of 40-50 hours of fishing to catch one. **Smallmouth bass** are a popular sport fish introduced to the waterways of southwestern Nova Scotia. They live in clear, calm water that usually has a gravelly bottom. Common throughout North

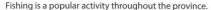

Fishing is a popular activity throughout the province.

A Photographer's Dream

Peggy's Cove Lighthouse is often called "the world's most photographed lighthouse."

Nova Scotia has incredible light for photography. The sky turns from a Wedgwood color to sapphire blue—a beautiful background for seacoast photographs. Rise at dawn to take advantage of the first rays of sunlight hitting picturesque east coast villages such as popular **Peggy's Cove** and **Fisherman's Cove,** both within an hour's drive of Halifax, as well as delightful seaside gems such as **Blue Rocks,** beyond Lunenburg. The town of Lunenburg itself attracts photographers for its harbor front panorama of colorful buildings (best in the late afternoon).

While photography is simplest when the weather is favorable—and that's more often than not—don't pass up a morning basking in thick mist, as bright sun illuminates the sky behind the thick clouds. The fog breaks apart gradually, and when it does, the sun radiates like a spotlight, illuminating the sparkling dampness that briefly clings to the landscape.

America, **whitefish** are easily caught in most rivers and lakes, although they rarely exceed 15 centimeters (6 inches) in length. **Atlantic whitefish** (also called Acadian whitefish) are endemic to southwestern Nova Scotia. As they are a protected species, angling for them is prohibited, so carry an identification chart if fishing these waters. **Yellow perch** (also known as lake perch) are identified by wide vertical stripes. Most often caught in shallow rivers and lakes throughout Nova Scotia, they are great fun for children to reel in.

Around 1.7 million fingerlings from two hatcheries are released at 400 easily accessible lakes and rivers across the province each year. Most are speckled trout because they are easy to raise and adapt to varying conditions; other

stocking fish are rainbow and brown trout. You can catch them on artificial flies, small spinners, or spoons.

Fishing Licenses and Regulations

Before casting a line, make yourself aware of provincial regulations. The recreational fishery is managed by the **Department of Fisheries and Aquaculture** (www.novascotia.ca/snsmr/paal/ndxfish.asp). A freshwater license for nonresidents costs $13 for one day, $34 for seven days, or $62 per year. Residents pay $27 for an annual license. No license is required for ocean fishing.

Fishing in national parks requires a separate license, which is available from park offices and some sport shops—$9.80 for a seven-day license, $34.30 for an annual license.

CYCLING AND MOUNTAIN BIKING

Reasonably good roads and gorgeous scenery make Nova Scotia excellent road-biking territory, while mountain biking has caught on among the adventurous as a way to explore more remote areas of the region. Except on main arteries, particularly the TransCanada Highway, car traffic is generally light. Cyclists, nonetheless, should remain vigilant: Narrow lanes and shoulders are common, and in some areas, drivers may be unaccustomed to sharing the road with bicycles. The premier bike-touring route is the **Cabot Trail** through Cape Breton Highlands National Park.

Many shops rent decent- to good-quality road and mountain bikes. But if you plan to do some serious riding, you'll probably want to bring your own; most airlines will let you bring a bike for little or no extra charge. An outstanding information resource is **Bicycle Nova Scotia** (902/425-5454, www.bicycle. ns.ca), which handles cycling information and publishes *Nova Scotia by Bicycle,* detailing 4,000 kilometers of roads along 20 detailed routes. Also contact **Atlantic Canada Cycling** (902/423-2453, www.atlanticcana-dacycling.com), which publishes extensive information on cycling routes (including descriptions and ratings of highways and byways throughout the province), tours, races, clubs, and equipment.

Guided Tours

Halifax-based **Freewheeling Adventures** (902/857-3600 or 800/672-0775, www.free-wheeling.ca) leads agreeable arrangements of guided trips in small groups, each accompanied by a support van to carry the luggage and, if necessary, the weary biker. Owners Cathy and Philip Guest plan everything—snacks, picnics, and meals at restaurants en route, as well as overnight stays at country inns. Expect to pay around $250-300 per person per day for the all-inclusive tour. The trips pass through some of Nova Scotia's prettiest countryside, including the South Shore, the Annapolis Valley, and Cape Breton Island.

GOLFING

Nova Scotia has more than 80 golf courses and a season that extends from mid-April to late October. Greens fees are generally very reasonable, with rates at less than $20 at some

Highlands Links ranks as one of Canada's best golf courses.

municipal courses. Where you really see a difference in fees is at better courses such as **Chester Golf Club,** a mature seaside layout kept in pristine condition, where the high-season rate is just $63. The best-known courses are on Cape Breton Island, including **Highlands Links,** considered one of the world's finest, yet costing just $100 per round, while nearby **Cabot Links** opened in 2012 to rave reviews as one of North America's only true links courses. A limited number of resort-style courses have been developed in the last decade, with the most upscale being **Fox Harb'r Golf Resort and Spa,** along Northumberland Strait, where greens fees are over $200.

The provincial governing body is the **Nova Scotia Golf Association** (902/468-8844, www.nsga.ns.ca), which provides a listing of all courses with contact numbers and fees. **Golf Nova Scotia** (877/894-3982, www.golf-novascotia.com) promotes a selection of the province's better courses.

WATER SPORTS

This ocean-bound province has no shortage of beaches, and most waterside provincial parks have a supervised **swimming** area. The warmest beaches are found along the Northumberland Strait. The Bay of Fundy and Atlantic shores tend to be much cooler, although conditions vary considerably throughout the region.

With so much water surrounding and flowing through the province, **boating** opportunities are nearly infinite. Sailing is popular in the Bay of Fundy, in spacious Halifax and Sydney harbors, and in protected inland areas such as Bras d'Or Lakes.

Canoeing, Kayaking, and Stand-Up Paddleboarding

If you bring your own canoe, kayak, or stand-up paddleboard, you can slip into any body of water whenever you please, taking in the scenery and viewing wildlife from water level. Canoeing is a traditional form of transportation that remains extremely popular

throughout Nova Scotia. You can rent canoes at many of the more popular lakes, including those protected by Kejimkujik National Park.

Coastal kayaking is another adventure, especially around picturesque South Shore fishing villages, along the remote coast near Tangier, and along Cape Breton Island's Atlantic coast. Expect to pay around $100 per person for a full day of kayaking. The tour cost always includes kayak and wetsuit rental, and usually also lunch.

Tidal-Bore Rafting

Instead of white-water rafting, Nova Scotia is known for wild and wooly trips on the tidal bore created by the world's highest tides in the Bay of Fundy. Between May and October, **Tidal Bore Rafting Park** (902/758-4032, www.tidalboreraftingpark.com) offers trips for varying levels of adrenaline rushes in motorized Zodiacs, riding the bore as it rushes upriver before blasting back across its face. Trips last two or four hours and cost from $60 and $95 per person respectively. This company is based a one-hour drive north of Halifax.

Whale-Watching

Today's lucrative whaling industry is based not on butchering but on simply bringing curious onlookers to observe the wonderful animals up close. Prime whale-watching areas are the Bay of Fundy (commercial operators are based along Digby Neck and on Brier Island) and off the west coast of Cape Breton Island. Minke, pilot, finback, orca, and humpback whales are the most populous species, and Atlantic right whales are spotted during a short window of time (August) in the Bay of Fundy.

Surfing

Nova Scotia is home to a small but dedicated population of surfers who hit the waves of the province's east coast year-round. **Lawrencetown Beach,** less than an hour's drive north of Halifax, is the best-known spot, with beach breaks along the long stretch of sand and a right-hander breaking off the rocky point. Other surf spots are scattered along the province's east coast. Water temperatures rarely rise above 16°C (61°F), meaning a 4/3 mm or 3/2 mm wetsuit is necessary, even in midsummer.

Boards and wetsuits can be rented in Dartmouth at **DaCane Surf Shop** (300 Prince Albert Rd., Dartmouth, 855/434-8900, www.dacanesurfshop.com; daily 9am-5pm); from **Kannon Beach** (4144 Lawrencetown Rd., 902/471-0025; Mon.-Fri. 9am-6pm, Sat. 9am-5pm) ideally located within walking distance of Lawrencetown Beach; and from **Rossignol Surf Shop** (White Point Beach Resort, 902/354-7100, www.surfnovascotia.com) on the South Shore.

WINTER SPORTS

Winter is definitely low season for travel to Nova Scotia. Outdoor recreation is severely limited by the weather, although snow-related sports are popular with the locals. In addition to downhill skiing and boarding, skating on frozen ponds is a hit, while locals cheer for minor-league ice-hockey teams scattered throughout the region.

Skiing and Snowboarding

The three alpine resorts of Nova Scotia may lack the vertical rise of their western counterparts, but snowfall is high and outsiders will be greeted with open arms wherever they choose to ski or board. Day passes top out at $45, and each resort has day lodge facilities and rentals. Vertical rises range from 180 to 300 meters (590-980 feet), and the season generally runs from Christmas to late March. Closest to Halifax is **Ski Martock,** south of the Annapolis Valley; **Wentworth** is near the New Brunswick border; and **Ski Cape Smokey,** with sweeping ocean views, sits at the north end of Cape Breton Island, although the latter has been opening on a limited basis in recent years.

Cross-Country Skiing

The province's two mainland national parks stay open year-round. In winter, hiking routes are transformed by snow into excellent cross-country ski trails, many of which are groomed by local ski clubs that charge a nominal fee for their use. **Ski Tuonela,** on Cape Breton Island (902/929-2144, www.skituonela.com), is one of North America's only lift-served telemark hills. In addition to a rope tow, the resort has 20 kilometers of groomed trails, a day lodge, and overnight accommodations.

Organizations with handy websites loaded with information and links to ski clubs are **Canada Trails** (www.canadatrails.ca) and **Cross Country Canada** (www.cccski.com).

SPECTATOR SPORTS

Windsor, Nova Scotia, claims its place in history as the birthplace of ice hockey (known simply as "hockey" in Canada). Although the region is home to no National Hockey League (NHL) teams, the exploits of the Toronto Maple Leafs, Montréal Canadiens, and other NHL franchises are passionately followed here. You can also see lively play from the Québec Major Junior Hockey League's Halifax Mooseheads (www.halifaxmooseheads.ca), as well as high-quality college and amateur teams in cities and towns throughout the region. The season runs October-March; check with local tourist information offices for game schedules and ticket information.

Accommodations and Food

Nova Scotia has all the chain hotels you know, as well as a range of accommodations that showcase the region—historic B&Bs, grand resorts, waterfront cottage complexes, and rustic campgrounds. This section will give you a taste of the choices and some hints on reserving a room. (Throughout the travel chapters of this book, I detail my favorites in all price ranges.)

To make reservations at any of the chain properties, simply phone their toll-free reservation centers or book online using their websites. Another option is a province-sponsored free reservation system, which is online at www.novascotia.com.

HOTELS, MOTELS, AND RESORTS

International, Canadian, and regional lodging chains are represented in Nova Scotia. At the more expensive properties, expect all the requisite amenities and services—swimming pools, air-conditioning, high-speed Internet access, room service, toiletries, restaurants, and bars. This type of accommodation can be found in central locations in Halifax, Sydney, and major tourist areas. Rates at four-star hotels start at $180 s or d in high season. Prices for a basic motel room in a small town start at $70 s, $80 d, rising to $120 for a room in a chain hotel within walking distance of a major city's downtown core.

The chains you know are represented in Nova Scotia, as well as the following you may not be familiar with.

Best Western

Presumably you have heard of the world's largest motel chain, but the website www.bestwesternatlantic.com is helpful in providing direct links to local properties.

Choice Hotels Canada

Over 300 properties across Canada are marketed under the Choice Hotels (800/424-6423, www.choicehotels.ca) banner. It operates 10 brands, including Sleep, with smallish but clean, comfortable, and inexpensive rooms;

Getting a Good Deal on Accommodations

Rates quoted through this guidebook are for a standard double room in the high season (usually July and August, but sometimes as early as June and as late as September). Almost all accommodations are less expensive outside of these busy months, with some discounting their rates by up to 50 percent. You'll enjoy the biggest seasonal discounts at properties that rely on summer tourists, such as those in Lunenburg or along the Northumberland Strait. The same applies in Halifax on weekends—many of the big downtown hotels rely on business and convention travelers to fill the bulk of their rooms; when the end of the week rolls around, the hotels are left with rooms to fill at discounted rates Friday, Saturday, and Sunday nights.

While you have no influence on the seasonal and weekday/weekend pricing differences detailed above, *how* you reserve a room *can* make a difference in how much you pay. First and foremost, when it comes to searching out actual rates, the Internet is an invaluable tool. All hotel websites listed in *Moon Nova Scotia* show rates, and many have online reservation forms. Use these websites to search out specials, many of which are available only on the Internet. Don't be afraid to negotiate during slower times. Even if the desk clerk has no control over rates, there's no harm in asking for a bigger room or one with a better view. Just look for a vacancy sign hanging out front.

Most hotels offer auto association members an automatic 10 percent discount, and whereas senior discounts apply only to those older than 60 or 65 on public transportation and at attractions, most hotels offer discounts to those age 50 and older, with chains such as Best Western also allowing senior travelers a late checkout. "Corporate Rates" are a lot more flexible than in years past; some hotels require nothing more than the flash of a business card for a 10-20 percent discount.

When it comes to frequent-flyer programs, you really do need to be a frequent flyer to achieve free flights, but the various loyalty programs offered by hotels often provide benefits simply for signing up.

Comfort, where guests enjoy a light breakfast and newspaper with a no-frills room; Quality, a notch up in quality with a restaurant and lounge; and Econo Lodge, older properties that have been renovated to Choice's standard and often have a pool and restaurant.

Delta Hotels and Resorts

This Canadian-owned company (506/443-3401 or 888/890-3222, www.deltahotels.com) is a class operation; expect 40-plus fine hotels with splendid facilities in notable settings. Nova Scotia locations include two in Halifax. Check the Delta website for package deals offered year-round.

Maritime Inns and Resorts

With package deals and locations in Antigonish, Port Hawkesbury, and the Cape

Breton resort town of Baddeck, these properties (902/863-4001 or 888/662-7484, www.maritimeinns.com) are popular with holidaying locals. Generally, packages include meals and activities such as golfing from about $120 per person per day.

Signature Resorts

Nova Scotia's provincial government owns three older but impressive lodges. They appeal to the carriage trade—travelers who like the understated ambience of a resort lodge with a tony rustic setting and furnishings, gourmet dining, a remote location with manicured grounds, and the genteel sports of golf or fly-fishing. Provincial resorts in Nova Scotia are the Pines Resort at Digby; the Keltic Lodge at Ingonish Beach, Cape Breton; and Liscombe Lodge at Liscomb Mills. The website www.signatureresorts.com has links to all three.

BED-AND-BREAKFASTS

Nova Scotia is blessed with hundreds of B&Bs. Concentrations are in Halifax, Mahone Bay, Lunenburg, the Annapolis Valley, and Baddeck. Styles run the gamut from historic mansions to rustic farmhouses, and as a result, amenities can also vary greatly. Regardless, guests can expect hearty home cooking, a peaceful atmosphere, personal service, knowledgeable hosts, and conversation with like-minded travelers. They are usually private residences, with hosts who live on-site and up to eight guest rooms. As the name suggests, breakfast is included in quoted rates; ask before booking whether it is a cooked or continental breakfast. Rates fluctuate enormously—from $60 s, $70 d for a spare room in an otherwise regular family home to $200 in a grandly restored Victorian mansion.

Finding and Reserving a Room

My favorite B&Bs are recommended throughout the travel chapters of this book. You can also use the provincial accommodation guide (www.novascotia.com) and local information centers to find out about individual properties. **Select Atlantic Inns** (www.

one of Nova Scotia's historic homes with overnight accommodations selectinns.ca) is an organization of mid- to top-end B&Bs, with online reservations and lots of information on specific properties. The **Canadian Bed and Breakfast Guide** (www.canadianbandbguide.ca) is a regularly updated database, although listings aren't recommendations as such. Finally, **Bed and Breakfast Online** (www.bbcanada.com) doesn't take bookings, but links are provided and its search engine helps you find the accommodation that best fits your needs.

Before reserving a room, it is important to ask a number of questions of your hosts. The two obvious ones are whether or not you'll have your own bathroom and how payment can be made (many establishments don't accept debit cards or all credit cards).

BACKPACKER ACCOMMODATIONS

As accommodation prices are reasonable throughout Nova Scotia, there is less of a need to find a dorm bed than in other parts of North America. Privately operated backpacker lodges are limited (those at Mahone Bay and Brier Island are both excellent) and **Hostelling International** operates five hostels around the province.

Hostelling International

The curfews and chores are long gone in this worldwide nonprofit organization of over 4,000 hostels in 60 countries. Hostelling International Canada has hostels in Nova Scotia at Halifax, Springhill, Wentworth, and two on Cape Breton Island. For a dorm bed, members of Hostelling International pay $22-30 per night, nonmembers pay $26-34. Generally, you need to provide your own sleeping bag or linen, but most hostels supply extra bedding (if needed) at no charge. Accommodations are in dormitories (2-10 beds), although single and double rooms are often available for an additional charge. All also offer a communal kitchen, lounge area, and laundry facilities, while some have Internet access, bike rentals, and organized tours.

You don't *have* to be a member to stay in an affiliated hostel of Hostelling International,

but membership pays for itself after only a few nights of discounted lodging. Aside from discounted rates, benefits of membership vary from country to country but often include discounted air, rail, and bus travel; discounts on car rental; and discounts on some attractions and commercial activities. For Canadians, the membership charge is $35 annually, or $175 for lifetime membership. For more information, contact HI-Canada (800/663-5777, www.hihostels.ca). Joining the Hostelling International affiliate of your home country entitles you to reciprocal rights in Canada, as well as around the world; click through the links at www.hihostels.com to your country of choice.

CAMPING

Camping out is a popular summer activity across Nova Scotia, and you'll find campgrounds in both national parks, many provincial parks, on the outskirts of cities and towns, and in most resort areas. Facilities at park campgrounds vary considerably, but most commercial operations have showers and water, electricity, and sewer hookups.

National parks provide some of the nicest surroundings for camping. All sites have picnic tables, fire grates, toilets, and fresh drinking water, although only some provide showers. Prices range $18-38, depending on facilities and services. A percentage of sites can be reserved through the **Parks Canada Campground Reservation Service** (877/737-3783, www.reservation.pc.gc.ca). Backcountry camping in a national park costs $8 per person per night.

The reservation line for provincial park campground reservations (519/826-5301 or 888/544-3434, www.novascotiaparks.ca) opens in early April. The reservation fee is $9 per booking. Most provincial parks, however, do not accept reservations, but instead assign sites on a first-come, first-served basis. At those parks, it's best to arrive before noon to assure yourself a spot. Most provincial parks are open mid-May to mid-October.

Most privately owned campsites accept

reservations, although some have started to charge up to $10 for the privilege of reserving a site.

FOOD AND DRINK

Thankfully, the Nova Scotian cuisine promoted today is very different from what locals traditionally dined on. In what was a difficult environment, generations past were happy eating salt pork, salt cod, hardtack (a type of vegetable), and vegetables that were boiled longer than necessary. Locals have traditionally shunned hot spices and go lightly on other condiments. While country-style cooking embodies the essence of provincial style in the smaller towns and seaports, dining in Halifax offers more sophisticated global fare.

If you travel on your stomach, look for the Taste of Nova Scotia (www.tasteofnovascotia.com) emblem affixed to restaurants' front windows or doors. The emblem is awarded to dining places judged noteworthy by the province.

Highlights

Regardless of cooking styles, seafood, red meat, and produce abound. Local lamb originates in Pictou County. Fruits and vegetables are fresh and are often picked from backyard inn and restaurant gardens. Local delicacies include wild chanterelle mushrooms, smoked mackerel pâté, and seafood from lobster to locally caught Digby scallops and Solomon Gundy (pickled herring). Preserves are generally homemade. Soups vary from lobster chowder thickened with whipped cream to pea soup brimming with corned-beef chunks.

Salmon is often cooked on a cedar board plank before an open fire, as the Mi'kmaq historically prepared it. Desserts know no limit and vary from trifles rich with raspberry jam and sherry, to cheesecakes concocted of local cheese and cream, to molded flans embellished with fruit toppings.

Acadian

While Anglo cuisine features red meats, Acadian fare is based on seafood. Common Acadian-style dishes include seafood chowder, shellfish (shrimp and crab), and fish (especially mackerel, herring, and cod). For variety, Acadian menus might offer chicken *fricot* (chicken stew), *poutine râpé* (boiled or deep-fried pork and grated raw potatoes, rolled into a ball and dipped in corn or maple syrup or molasses), and rappie pie (filled with a mixture of clams or chicken with grated potatoes as translucent as pearls). Desserts

Head to Rapure Acadienne on the La Côte Acadienne for traditional rappie pie.

Two Traditional Acadian Recipes

RAPPIE PIE

This traditional recipe is unique for the texture of the potato filling, and one succulent bite will make you a convert. (For best results, read the recipe all the way through before starting.)

> 5-6 lbs. chicken
> 6 large onions
> 2 tsp. salt or 2 tbsp. salted (preserved) onions
> 1 tsp. pepper
> 1 pail (10 lbs.) of big potatoes

1. Cut chicken in pieces, place in large pot, and cover with water. Bring to a boil. Add three large chopped onions, salt, and pepper. (While chicken is cooking, continue with the following steps.) When chicken is cooked, remove it from the pot, remove meat from bones, and break pieces into desired size. Keep broth simmering to be used later.

2. Chop the remaining onions and sauté in butter or margarine until tender but not brown. Set aside to be used later.

3. Peel, rinse, and grate potatoes in a large bowl. Take note of how much grated potato you have, because later you will use this same large bowl to scald the potatoes after they are squeezed, and you should have the same amount of potato mixture then as you have grated potatoes now.

4. Squeeze potatoes (about two cups at a time) in a fine cotton bag or cloth until quite dry. Place the squeezed potatoes in a second bowl as you go, and transfer them back into the large bowl when done. Add the sautéed onions.

5. Scald the squeezed potatoes by adding the boiling chicken broth gradually and stirring constantly. Remember, you must end up with the same amount of scalded potato mixture in this bowl as you had grated potatoes before. If you do not have enough broth, add boiling water. When you're through scalding, the mixture should be slightly thicker and darker. Add salt and pepper to taste.

6. Grease a 17-by-12-inch pan and dust with flour. Spread half of the potato mixture in the pan. Spread chicken meat evenly over this. Cover with other half of potato mixture. Bake at 400°F for 2.5 hours. It should come out brown, crusty, and delicious! The more often you make it, the better it gets.

CHICKEN FRICOT

A cross between a soup and a stew, this dish is especially appreciated on a cold winter evening.

> 2 lbs. chicken (cut in small pieces)
> 2 large onions, diced
> 2 tsp. salted (preserved) onions (or 1 tsp. salt)
> ½ tsp. pepper
> 8 medium-size potatoes, diced and rinsed
> 2 medium-size potatoes, grated

In a soup pot, put chicken pieces, diced onions, salted onions, and pepper. Add 12 cups of water and bring to a boil. Cook for 30 minutes on medium heat. Add diced potatoes and continue to boil until cooked. To thicken *fricot,* lower heat to simmer and add grated potatoes. Cook a few minutes more. Serve hot in bowls.

Courtesy of Imelda Chiasson, lifetime resident of Nova Scotia, from the village of Concession, La Côte Acadienne.

beer from a local brewery

along La Côte Acadienne (Fundy Coast) and in Chéticamp (Cape Breton Island).

Drinks

All the popular Canadian and American beers are available at bars and liquor stores, but you should be drinking the Halifax-brewed **Keith's** if you want to look like a local. Halifax also has a number of microbreweries.

Nova Scotia has 70 grape growers and 550 acres of commercially harvested grapes. Local wines are prominently displayed on wine lists throughout the province, especially those from Jost Vineyards, along the Northumberland Strait. Most grapes are French hybrids, but the local specialty is **ice wine,** made by a process in which the grapes aren't harvested until *after* the first frost; the frost splits the skins and the fermentation process begins with the grapes still on the vine. These concentrated juices create a super sweet wine. Ice wine is generally marketed in a distinctively narrow 375-milliliter bottle and promoted as a dessert wine. The website www.winesofnovascotia.ca is a good source of information.

The legal drinking age in Nova Scotia is 19, the same as all other Canadian provinces except Québec, Manitoba, and Alberta (where it is 18).

include sugar pie, apple dumplings, and cinnamon buns. Acadian cooking may be terribly hard on the waistline, but it's delicious. The best places to sample Acadian cuisine are

Travel Tips

EMPLOYMENT AND STUDY

International visitors wishing to work or study in Canada must obtain authorization *before* entering the country. Authorization to work will only be granted if no qualified Canadians are available for the work in question. Applications for work and study are available from all Canadian embassies and must be submitted with a nonrefundable processing fee. The Canadian government has a reciprocal agreement with Australia for a limited number of **holiday work visas** to be

issued each year. Australian citizens aged 30 and younger are eligible; contact your nearest Canadian embassy or consulate. For general information on immigrating to Canada, check the **Citizenship and Immigration Canada** website (www.cic.gc.ca).

VISITORS WITH DISABILITIES

A lack of mobility should not deter you from traveling to Nova Scotia, but you should definitely do some research before leaving home.

If you haven't traveled extensively, start

by doing some research at the website of the **Access-Able Travel Source** (www.access-able.com), where you will find databases of specialist travel agencies and lodgings in Canada that cater to travelers with disabilities. **Flying Wheels Travel** (612/381-1622 or 877/451-5006, www.flyingwheelstravel.com) caters solely to the needs of travelers with disabilities. The **Society for Accessible Travel and Hospitality** (212/447-7284, www.sath.org) supplies information on tour operators, vehicle rentals, specific destinations, and companion services. For frequent travelers, the membership fee (US$49 per year) is well worth it. *Emerging Horizons* (www.emerginghorizons.com) is a U.S. quarterly online magazine dedicated to travelers with special needs.

Access to Travel (www.accesstotravel.gc.ca) is an initiative of the Canadian government that includes information on travel within and between Canadian cities. For vision-impaired visitors, **CNIB** (www.cnib.ca) offers a wide range of services from its Halifax office (902/453-1480 or 800/563-2642). Finally, the **Canadian Paraplegic Association** (www.thespine.ca) is another good source of information; the provincial head office is in Halifax (902/423-1277).

FAMILY TRAVEL

Regardless of whether you're traveling with toddlers or teens, you will come upon decisions affecting everything from where you stay to your choice of activities. Luckily for you, Nova Scotia is very family-friendly, with a variety of indoor and outdoor attractions aimed specifically at the younger generation, such as Shubenacadie Wildlife Park, north of Halifax, and Upper Clements Parks, near Annapolis Royal. The Annapolis Valley is also home to a number of campgrounds where the emphasis is on keeping the kids busy rather than being simply somewhere to stay the night. The best of these in this region are South Mountain Park and Look-Off Family Camping.

Admission prices for children are included throughout the travel chapters of this book. As a general rule, reduced prices are for 6- to 16-year-olds. For two adults and two-plus children, always ask about family tickets. Children younger than six nearly always get in free. Most hotels and motels will happily accommodate children, but always try to reserve your room and let the reservations desk know the ages of your brood. Often, children stay free in major hotels, and in the case of some major chains—such as Holiday Inn—eat free also. Generally, B&Bs aren't suitable for children and in some cases don't accept kids at all. Ask ahead.

When it comes to traveling with children, let them help you plan the trip, looking at websites and reading up on Nova Scotia together. To make your vacation more enjoyable

What to Pack

You'll find little use for a suit and tie in Nova Scotia. Instead, pack for the outdoors. At the top of your must-bring list should be walking or **hiking boots.** Even in summer you should be geared up for a variety of weather conditions, especially at the change of seasons or if you'll be spending time along the coast. Do this by preparing to **dress in layers,** including at least one pair of fleece pants and a heavy long-sleeved top. For breezy coastal sightseeing, a sweater or windbreaker, hat, sunscreen, and comfortable shoes with rubber soles will come in handy. For dining out, **casual dress** is accepted at all but the most upscale restaurants.

Electrical appliances from the United States work in Canada, but those from other parts of the world will require a **current converter** (transformer) to bring the voltage down. Many travel-size shavers, hair dryers, and irons have built-in converters.

if you'll be spending a lot of time on the road, rent a minivan (all major rental agencies have a supply). Don't forget to bring along favorite toys and games from home—whatever you think will keep your kids entertained when the joys of sightseeing wear off.

The provincial tourism website (www. novascotia.com) has a section devoted to children's activities. Another handy source of online information is **Traveling Internationally with Your Kids** (www. travelwithyourkids.com).

Health and Safety

Nova Scotia is a healthy place. To visit, you don't need to get any vaccinations or booster shots. And when you arrive you can drink the water from the faucet and eat the food without worry.

If you need an ambulance, call 911 or the number listed on the inside front cover of local telephone directories. Halifax and most of the large towns have hospitals (look in the travel chapters of this book for locations and telephone numbers).

INSURANCE AND PRESCRIPTIONS

Intraprovincial agreements cover the medical costs of Canadians traveling across the nation. As a rule, the usual health insurance plans from other countries do not include medical-care costs incurred while traveling; ask your insurance company or agent if supplemental health coverage is available, and if it is not, arrange for coverage with an independent carrier before departure. Hospital charges vary from place to place but can be as much as $3,000 a day, and some facilities impose a surcharge for nonresidents. Some Canadian companies offer coverage specifically aimed at visitors.

If you're on medication, bring adequate supplies with you, and get a prescription from your doctor to cover the time you will be away. You may not be able to get a prescription filled at Canadian pharmacies without visiting a Canadian doctor, so don't wait till you've almost run out. If you wear glasses or contact lenses, ask your optometrist for a

spare prescription in case you break or lose your lenses, and stock up on your usual cleaning supplies.

GIARDIA

Giardiasis, also known as beaver fever, is a real concern for those who drink water from backcountry water sources. It's caused by an intestinal parasite, *Giardia lamblia*, that lives in lakes, rivers, and streams. Once ingested, its effects, although not instantaneous, can be dramatic: severe diarrhea, cramps, and nausea are the most common. Preventive measures should always be taken and include boiling all water for at least 10 minutes, treating all water with iodine, or filtering all water using a filter with a small-enough pore size to block the *Giardia* cysts.

WINTER TRAVEL

Travel through Nova Scotia during winter should not be undertaken lightly. Before setting out in a vehicle, check antifreeze levels, and always carry a spare tire and blankets or sleeping bags.

Frostbite can occur in a matter of seconds if the temperature falls below freezing and if the wind is blowing. Layer your clothing for the best insulation against the cold, and don't forget gloves and, most important, a warm hat, which can offer the best protection against heat loss. Frostbite occurs in varying degrees. Most often it leaves a numbing, bruised sensation and the skin turns white. Exposed areas of skin such as the nose and ears are most susceptible, particularly when

Tracing Family Roots

If you are interested in tracing family ties, the place to start is with **Nova Scotia Archives** (6016 University Ave., Halifax, 902/424-6060, www.novascotia.ca/archives; Mon.-Fri. 8:30am-4:30pm, Sat. 9am-5pm). It's possible to take advantage of the department's resources without visiting in person. Its website is an excellent starting point—helpful for everyone from those searching out long-lost relatives to professional genealogists.

Ancestries originating on Cape Breton can be traced at the **Beaton Institute** (Cape Breton University, Glace Bay, 902/563-1329, www.cbu.ca/beaton).

cold temperatures are accompanied by high winds.

Hypothermia occurs when the body fails to produce heat as fast as it loses it. Cold weather combined with hunger, fatigue, and dampness creates a recipe for disaster. Symptoms are not always apparent to the victim. The early signs are numbness, shivering, slurring of words, dizzy spells; in extreme cases, these can progress to violent behavior, unconsciousness, and even death. The best treatment is to get the patient out of the cold, replace wet clothing with dry, slowly give hot liquids and sugary foods, and place the victim in a sleeping bag. Prevention is a better strategy; dress for cold in layers, including a waterproof outer layer, and wear a warm wool cap or other headgear.

CRIME

Nova Scotia enjoys one of the country's lowest crime rates. Violent crimes are infrequent; the most common crime is petty theft. If you must leave valuable items in your car unattended, keep them out of sight, preferably locked in the vehicle's trunk. Women have few difficulties traveling alone throughout the region.

Remember that Halifax is an international port with seamy (albeit interesting) bars and taverns at or near the working area of the waterfront; keep your wits about you here, especially late at night. Better yet, leave these night scenes to the sailors and others who frequent the areas.

Both possession and sale of illicit drugs are considered serious crimes and are punishable with jail time, severe fines, or both. Furthermore, Canadians consider drinking while driving equally serious; the penalty on the first conviction is jail, a heavy fine, or both. A conviction here or in your home country can even be grounds for exclusion from Canada.

Royal Canadian Mounted Police (RCMP)

Despite the romantic image of the staid red-jacketed officer on horseback, Mounties (as they are most often called) nowadays favor the squad car as their mount of choice and a less colorful uniform. They are as ubiquitous a symbol of the country as the maple leaf and are similar to the highway patrol or state police in the United States. They operate throughout all the country's provinces and territories (except Ontario and Québec), complementing the work of local police.

Information and Services

MONEY

Unless noted otherwise, prices quoted in this guide are in Canadian currency.

Canadian currency is based on dollars and cents, with 100 cents equal to one dollar. Coins come in denominations of 1, 5, 10, and 25 cents, and one and two dollars. The 11-sided, gold-colored, one-dollar coin is known as a "loonie" for the bird featured on it. The unique two-dollar coin is silver with a gold-colored insert. The most common notes are $5, $10, $20, and $50. A $100 bill does exist but is uncommon.

Credit and debit cards are readily accepted throughout Nova Scotia. By using these cards you eliminate the necessity of thinking about the exchange rate—the transaction and rate of exchange on the day of the transaction will automatically be reflected in the bill from your bank or credit-card company. On the downside, you'll always get a better exchange rate when dealing directly with a bank. You should always carry some cash, as places like farmers' markets and some bed and breakfasts do not accept debit or credit cards.

Costs

The cost of living in Nova Scotia is similar to that in the surrounding provinces but lower than elsewhere in the country. By planning carefully, having a tent, or traveling in the shoulder seasons, it is possible to get by on about $100 per person per day or less. If you will be staying in hotels or motels, accommodations will be your biggest expense. Gasoline is sold in liters (3.78 liters equals one U.S. gallon) and is generally $1.30-1.50 a liter for regular unleaded.

Tipping charges are not usually added to your bill. You are expected to add a tip of 15 percent to the total amount for waiters and waitresses, barbers and hairdressers, taxi drivers, and other such service providers.

Bellhops, doormen, and porters generally receive $1 per item of baggage.

Harmonized Sales Tax (HST)

The 13 percent Harmonized Sales Tax is a tax levied on most goods and services purchased in Nova Scotia. All residents must pay the tax, as must visitors.

SHOPPING
Export Details

Americans can bring $400 worth of duty-free goods back into the United States after a 48-hour stay in Canada; $25 is the duty-free limit after stays of less than 48 hours. Gifts sent by mail and worth a total of $50 or less are duty-free also.

If you are interested in shopping for exotic wares, such as whalebone carvings or bearskin rugs, beware of customs regulations prohibiting the export of these types of items; hundreds of animals and their by-products are on the Convention on International Trade in Endangered Species of Wild Fauna and Flora list, which is online at www.cites.org. For a list of imports banned in your home country, contact your nearest customs office before departure.

Business Hours

Shopping hours are generally Monday-Saturday 9am-6pm Late shopping in most areas is available until 9pm on Thursday and Friday, and supermarkets open 24 hours have begun to appear in a few towns. Generally, banks are open Monday-Wednesday 10am-4pm and Thursday-Friday 10am-5pm A few banks may open on Saturday, but all are closed on Sunday. Nova Scotia is the only Canadian province that disallows Sunday shopping, although exceptions are made for essential services such as gas stations and in "tourist areas" such as the Halifax waterfront.

MAPS AND INFORMATION

Maps

Driving maps such as those published by **MapArt** (www.mapart.com) and **Rand McNally** (www.randmcnally.com) are available at bookstores, gas stations, and even some grocery stores across the province. In Halifax, **Maps and Ducks** (1601 Lower Water St., 902/422-7106) and the **Trail Shop** (6210 Quinpool Rd., 902/423-8736) are specialty map stores. The most detailed atlas to the province is the *Nova Scotia Atlas,* produced by Formac Publishing.

Nautical maps are handled by the **Canada Hydrographic Service,** a division of Fisheries and Oceans Canada, but it doesn't sell directly to the public. To request a map catalog and a list of dealers, call 613/995-4413 or check www.charts.gc.ca. This department also distributes *Sailing Directions,* a composite of general navigational information, port facility descriptions, and sailing conditions (in English or French) for Nova Scotia and the Gulf of St. Lawrence.

Tourism Information

Begin planning your trip by contacting the government tourist office: **Tourism Nova Scotia** (902/425-5781 or 800/565-0000, www. novascotia.com). Its literature and a provincial map can be downloaded from the website or ordered by phone. This organization also operates **Provincial Visitor Centres** at major gateways, including one at Halifax International Airport (902/873-1223; year-round daily 9am-9pm) and another along the downtown waterfront (1655 Lower Water St., 902/424-4248; year-round daily 9am-5pm, until 8pm in summer). Other locations are Yarmouth (mid-May-Oct.), Digby (mid-May-Oct.), Amherst (year-round), and Pictou (May-mid-Dec.).

Every town of any size in Nova Scotia has a locally operated **Visitor Information Centre** (hours vary, but most are open mid-May-mid-Oct.).

COMMUNICATIONS

Postal Services

Canada Post (www.canadapost.ca) issues postage stamps that must be used on all mail posted in Canada. First-class letters and postcards sent within Canada are $0.85, to the United States $1.20, to other foreign destinations $2.50. Prices increase with the weight of the mailing. You can buy stamps at post offices (closed weekends), some hotel lobbies, airports, many retail outlets, and some newsstands.

Phone

The country code for Canada is 1, the same as the United States, and the area code for all of Nova Scotia is **902.** This prefix must be dialed for all long-distance calls. Toll-free numbers have the 800, 888, 877, or 866 prefix, and may be good for Nova Scotia, the Maritimes, Canada, North America, or, in the case of major hotel chains and car rental companies, will work worldwide.

To make an international call from Canada, dial the prefix 011 before the country code or dial 0 for operator assistance.

Public phones accept 5-, 10-, and 25-cent coins; local calls are $0.35 and most long-distance calls cost at least $2.50 for the first

Heading Farther Afield?

- **Tourism New Brunswick** (800/561-0123, www.tourismnewbrunswick.ca)

- **Tourism Prince Edward Island** (902/368-4444 or 800/463-4734, www. tourismpei.com)

- **Tourisme Québec** (514/873-2015 or 877/266-5687, www.bonjourquebec. com)

- **Newfoundland and Labrador Tourism** (709/729-2830 or 800/563-6353, www.newfoundlandlabrador.com)

- **Maine Office of Tourism** (888/624-6345, www.visitmaine.com)

minute. The least expensive way to make long-distance calls from a public phone is with a **phone card.** These are available from convenience stores, newsstands, and gas stations.

Internet Access

If your Internet provider doesn't allow you to access your email away from your home computer, open an email account with **Gmail** (www.gmail.com), **Hotmail** (www.hotmail.com), or **Yahoo!** (www.yahoo.com)—or use **Facebook** (www.facebook.com) to keep in touch with friends and family.

Free public Internet access is available throughout Nova Scotia through the **Community Access Program (CAP).** To find out addresses and hours of the 400-odd locations across the province, call 866/569-8428 or go to www.nscap.ca.

Almost all hotels and motels, and most B&Bs have wireless access from guest rooms. You'll also find wireless access at most libraries, visitor centers, and cafes.

WEIGHTS AND MEASURES

Canada uses the metric system, with temperature measured in degrees Celsius, liquid measurements in liters, solid weights in kilograms and metric tons, land areas in hectares, and distances in kilometers, meters, and centimeters. This system hasn't completely taken hold everywhere, and many Nova Scotians still think in terms of the imperial system; expect to hear a lobster described in pounds, local distances given in miles, and the temperature expressed in Fahrenheit degrees.

The electrical voltage is 120 volts. The standard electrical plug configuration is the same as that used in the United States—two flat blades, often with a round third pin for grounding.

Time Zones

Even though Nova Scotia was home to Sir Sandford Fleming, the man who devised time zones, the province didn't receive any special favors. It is on **Atlantic Standard Time (AST),** the same as New Brunswick and Prince Edward Island. **Newfoundland Standard Time (NST),** 30 minutes ahead of Atlantic Standard Time, is used in Newfoundland and Labrador.

Atlantic Standard Time is one hour ahead of Eastern Standard Time and four hours ahead of Pacific Standard Time.

ESSENTIALS
INFORMATION AND SERVICES

Resources

Suggested Reading

NATURAL HISTORY

Dawson, Joan. *The Mapmaker's Eye: Nova Scotia Through Early Maps*. Halifax: Nova Scotia Museum, 1988. Nova Scotia evolved through the centuries, as did the art of mapping. This illustrated book is a cartographer's dream.

Grescoe, Taras. *Bottomfeeder*. Toronto: HarperCollins, 2008. An insight into the fisheries industry made more readable by the author's firsthand accounts of visits to the world's most important fisheries, including Nova Scotia.

Hare, F. K., and M. K. Thomas. *Climate Canada*. Toronto: John Wiley & Sons, 1974. One of the most extensive works on Canada's climate ever written. Includes a chapter on how the climate is changing.

Lyell, Charles. *Geological Observations on the U.S., Canada, and Nova Scotia*. New York: Arno Press, 1978. During an early 1840s visit, Lyell thought enough of Nova Scotia's unusual landscape and geology to give it equal space among the nations in this insightful account.

MacAskill, Wallace R. *MacAskill Seascapes and Sailing Ships*. Halifax: Nimbus Publishing. Cape Breton's famed photographer captures the misty moods of fishermen, schooners, seaports, and seacoasts.

Natural History of Nova Scotia. Halifax: Departments of Education and Lands and Forests, two volumes. Everything on land or beneath the nearby seas is comprehensively detailed here with illustrations.

Primrose, Mary and Marian Munro. Wildflowers of Nova Scotia, New Brunswick & Prince Edward Island. Halifax: Formac Publishing, 2006. A glorious combination of text by Munro and stunning color photography by Primrose—a must for every naturalist who revels in wildflowers.

Saunders, Gary. *Discover Nova Scotia: The Ultimate Nature Guide*. Halifax: Nimbus Publishing, 2001. Perfect for a daypack, this handy guide includes maps, trail descriptions, and the natural wonders of Nova Scotia's parks.

Thurston, Harry. *Tidal Life: A Natural History of the Bay of Fundy*. Halifax: Nimbus Publishing, 1998. The lavishly illustrated contents describe natural habitats formed by the Fundy.

Towers, Julie, and Anne Camozzi. *Discover Nova Scotia: Wildlife Viewing Sites*. Halifax: Nimbus Publishing, 1999. Another of Nimbus's popular "Discover Nova Scotia" titles, this one gives detailed directions to more than 100 sites.

Tufts, Robbie. *Birds of Nova Scotia*. Halifax: Nimbus Publishing, 2007. The authoritative guide since 1961. The most recent edition includes color plates, detailed illustrations, a provincial map, and all the descriptive information bird-watchers will need to find and identify species across the province.

Wagg, Len (photographer). *Nova Scotia Landmarks*. Halifax: Formac Publishing, 2004. Filled with stunning aerial photography, this coffee-table book pinpoints natural highlights across the province. A great souvenir.

HUMAN HISTORY

Boileau, John. *Half-Hearted Enemies*. Halifax: Formac Publishing, 2005. Examines the intriguing story of how Nova Scotia and New England continued to trade through the War of 1812.

Brasseaux, Carl A. *The Founding of New Acadia*. New Orleans: Louisiana State University Press, 1997. A little academic, but this book will make interesting reading for anyone from the South who wants to learn about the links between Cajuns and the Acadians of Nova Scotia.

Bruce, Harry. *An Illustrated History of Nova Scotia*. Halifax: Nimbus Publishing, 1998. Primarily aimed at the younger set, this book is highly readable and well worth a look, even for adults.

Campey, Lucille H. *After the Hector: The Scottish Pioneers of Nova Scotia and Cape Breton 1733–1852*. Edinburgh: Birlinn Publishing, 2005. An account of those who arrived in Pictou aboard the Hector and how their Scottish Highlands heritage helped them adapt and thrive in the New World.

Crooker, William. *Oak Island Gold*. Halifax: Nimbus Publishing, 2011. One of many books devoted to the world's longest treasure hunt, this one does a noble job of unraveling the story—and even suggests an explanation to the secrets of the island.

Crowell, Clement W. *Novascotiaman*. Halifax: Nova Scotia Museum, 1979. A sea captain's correspondence forms the basis for a retelling of the story of Nova Scotia's Great Age of Sail.

Daigle, Jean, ed. *Acadians of the Maritimes*. Moncton, New Brunswick: Chaire d'Études Acadiennes, Université de Moncton, 1995. The history of the Acadians in Atlantic Canada is a tangled tale of upheaval and survival, cultural clashes and passions. Daigle's collection of Acadian literature is among the best on the bookshelves.

Duivenvoorden Mitic, Trudy. *Pier 21: Gateway that Changed Canada*. Halifax: Nimbus Publishing, 2011. As a child of parents who emigrated through Pier 21 who was employed as a director with Employment and Immigration Canada, Duivenvoorden Mitic is well qualified to author a book on this important Halifax site.

Faragher, John Mack. *A Great and Noble Scheme: The Tragic Story of the Expulsion of the French Acadians from Their American Homeland*. New York: W. W. Norton, 2005. In this hefty 560-page book, Faragher describes the evolution of Acadia, the horrors of the deportation, and the resulting pockets of Acadian culture that thrive to this day.

Irwin, Rip. *Lighthouses and Lights of Nova Scotia*. Halifax: Nimbus Publishing, 2011. Nova Scotia is renowned for its photogenic lighthouses—and this new edition details all 164, complete with historical facts.

Lawrence, Ian. *Historic Annapolis Royal*. Halifax: Nimbus Publishing, 2002. Filled with historic photographs, this book details the history of the oldest town north of St. Augustine, Florida.

Ledger, Don. *Swissair Down*. Halifax: Nimbus Publishing, 2000. The story of the September 1998 crash of a Swissair jetliner off the village of Peggy's Cove from a pilot's point of view.

Lyell, Charles. *Travels in North America in the Years 1841–2*. New York: Arno Press, 1978. The author included Nova Scotia in his 19th-century travel observations.

Nunn, Bruce. *History with a Twist*. Halifax: Nimbus Publishing, 2002. Light yet interesting reading that covers a few dozen tales from Nova Scotia's past. And if you're looking for more, there's *More History with a Twist* by the same author, as well as a third volume released in 2008.

Oickle, Vernon. *Busted: Nova Scotia's War on Drugs*. Halifax: Nimbus Publishing, 1997. Stories of local lawmen and their struggle to curb the trade of illicit drugs along Nova Scotia's remote coastline.

Poliandri, Simone. *First Nations, Identity, and Reserve Life: The Mi'kmaq of Nova Scotia*. Lincoln, Nebraska: University of Nebraska Press, 2011. A big, beautiful book that tells the story of the Mi'kmaq from their arrival in the province.

Raddall, Thomas. *Halifax: Warden of the North*. Halifax: Nimbus Publishing, 2007. One of the best historical accounts of the provincial capital, although the focus is on its military past.

Sanderberg, Anders, and Peter Clancy. *Against the Grain: Foresters and Politics in Nova Scotia*. Vancouver: University of British Columbia Press, 2000. A detailed look at the province's forestry practices and the viability of the industry in this millennium.

Vacon, Shirley Irene. *Giants of Nova Scotia: The Lives of Anna Swan and Angus McAskill*. East Lawrencetown, Nova Scotia: Pottersfield Press, 2008. The remarkable story of two Nova Scotians who toured the world as the "world's tallest couple" in the 1800s.

SPORTS, CULTURE, AND CRAFTS

Buist, Ron. *Tales from Under the Rim: The Making of Tim Hortons*. Fredericton: Goose Lane Edition, 2011. Although non-Canadians may not be familiar with the Tim Hortons chain of fast-food restaurants, you'll see them everywhere on your Nova Scotia travels, which makes this book an interesting read for those interested in a local marketing success story.

Elliot, Elaine. *The Chowder Trail Cookbook*. Halifax: Formac Publishing, 2014. One of the best-loved meals in Atlantic Canada is seafood chowder. This hardcover book takes readers on a journey through Nova Scotia, searching out the best ingredients and recipes.

Harper, Marjory. *Myth, Migration and the Making of Memory: Scotia and Nova Scotia*. Halifax: John Donald Publishers, 2000. Explores Nova Scotia's Scottish heritage and the importance of the province's links to Scotland through the years.

Hollingsworth, Paul. *Sidney Crosby: The Story of a Champion*. Halifax: Nimbus Publishing, 2011. Hockey's current superstar has already been the subject of many books, but this one, published by a local company, includes much detail of growing up in Nova Scotia's Cole Harbour.

Lief, Charles. *Taste of Nova Scotia Cookbook*. Halifax: Nimbus Publishing, 2011. An indepth look at local cuisine, including many traditional dishes, with recipes supplied by local restaurants, inns, and bed and breakfasts.

Parsons, Catriona. *Gaidhlig Troimh Chomhradh (Gaelic Through Conversation)*. South Gut St. Ann's, Nova Scotia: Gaelic College of Celtic Arts and Crafts. The college's mission is to keep the language alive, and it does so with this text and accompanying cassette tapes, as well as a number of other books and varied literature.

Penney, Allen. *Houses of Nova Scotia: An Illustrated Guide to Architectural Style Recognition*. Halifax: Nova Scotia Museum and Formac Publishing, 1989. Penney, a professor of architecture, sums up provincial architectural styles and explains how to identify styles by dates, similarities, and differences.

Pilsworth, Graham. *Nova Scotia Drink-o-pedia*. Halifax: Nimbus Publishing, 2008. Local author Pilsworth takes a detailed yet humorous look into the culture of drinking in Nova Scotia, from the days of rum running to the success of Alexander Keith's brewery.

RECREATION GUIDES AND GUIDEBOOKS

Doers and Dreamers Guide. Free annual publication from Tourism Nova Scotia. Lists accommodations, campgrounds, and some attractions. Order online at www.novascotia.com or by calling 902/425-5781 or 800/565-0000.

Friends of McNabs Island Society. *Discover McNabs Island*. Halifax: Friends of McNabs Island Society, 1997. This island in Halifax Harbour has become a provincial park since this book was published, but it is an essential reference guide and well worth buying even if you're just visiting for the day.

Gadd, Ben. *The Canadian Hiker's and Backpacker's Handbook*. Vancouver: Whitecap Books, 2008. Authored by a renowned expert, this is the best book for reading up on your backcountry and hiking skills.

Haynes, Michael. *Hiking Trails of Mainland Nova Scotia*. Fredericton, New Brunswick: Goose Lane Editions, 2012. The ninth edition of this comprehensive yet compact guide details about 50 trails throughout the

province. Each description, up to five pages long, is accompanied by a map.

Haynes, Michael. *Trails of Halifax Regional Municipality*. Fredericton, New Brunswick: Goose Lane Editions, 2010. This comprehensive guide to hiking trails in and around Halifax includes maps, photos, GPS co-ordinates, and useful offerings such as cellphone coverage for each trail.

Hempstead, Andrew. *Moon Atlantic Canada*. Berkeley, California: Avalon Travel, 2015. For those traveling beyond Nova Scotia.

Lawley, David. *A Nature and Hiking Guide to Cape Breton's Cabot Trail*. Halifax: Nimbus Publishing, 1994. The first half of this 200-page book covers all major trails along the Cabot Trail. The second half delves into the region's natural history, complete with descriptions of all flora and fauna.

Nightingale, Marie. *Out of Old Nova Scotia Kitchens*. Halifax: Nimbus Publishing, 2011. Beloved by Nova Scotians for decades, this is a reprint of a classic known for its simple approach to preparing comfort food with locally available ingredients.

MAGAZINES, MAPS, AND ATLASES

Canadian Geographic. Ottawa: Royal Canadian Geographical Society (www.canadiangeographic.ca). Bimonthly publication pertaining to Canada's natural and human histories and resources.

Explore. Toronto. Bimonthly publication of adventure travel throughout Canada (www.explore-mag.com).

Hamilton, William B. *Place Names of Atlantic Canada*. Toronto: University of Toronto, 1996. Although no book is devoted to the toponymy of Nova Scotia, this tome includes definitions of all the province's most unusual and interesting place-names.

MapArt. Driving maps for all of Canada, a Halifax-Dartmouth street atlas, and folded maps of Atlantic Canada and Nova Scotia (www.mapart.com).

Nature Canada Newsletter. Ottawa. Seasonal e-newsletter of Nature Canada (www.naturecanada.ca).

Nova Scotia Atlas. Halifax: Formac Publishing, 2006. This comprehensive atlas breaks the province down into 90 topographical-style maps, including geographical features and all public roads. The back matter includes an index of 14,500 place-names and a short description of all provincial and national parks.

Rand McNally. Products include the *Atlantic Canada Road Atlas* and *Halifax* and *Nova Scotia Communities StreetFinder,* as well as folded maps of Nova Scotia, Halifax, and Cape Breton Island (www.randmcnally.com).

Internet Resources

TRAVEL PLANNING
Canadian Tourism Commission
www.canadatourism.com
Official tourism website for all of Canada.

Destination Halifax
www.destinationhalifax.com
In addition to all the usual travel information, use this website to order free literature, learn about current festivals and events, and read up on Halifax trivia.

Economic and Rural Development and Tourism
www.novascotia.com
The first place to go when planning your trip to Nova Scotia. This site includes a distance calculator, order forms for brochures, and detailed events calendars.

PARKS
Nova Scotia Provincial Parks
www.novascotiaparks.ca
This government website details seasons, fees, and the campsite reservation process, and has a handy search tool to make help finding parks easy, and .

Parks Canada
www.pc.gc.ca
Official website of the agency that manages Canada's national parks and national historic sites, of which two and 16 respectively are located in Nova Scotia.

Parks Canada Campground Reservation Service
www.pccamping.ca
Use this website to make reservations for campsites in Kejimkujik and Cape Breton Highlands National Parks.

GOVERNMENT
Citizenship and Immigration Canada
www.cic.gc.ca
Check this government website for anything related to entry into Canada.

Environment Canada
www.weather.gc.ca
Seven-day forecasts from across Canada, including over 50 locations in Nova Scotia. Includes weather archives such as seasonal trends, hurricane history, and sea ice movement.

Government of Canada
www.gc.ca
The official website of the Canadian government.

Halifax Regional Municipality
www.halifax.ca
Official website of the Halifax Regional Municipality. Has links to transit schedules as well as information on visiting the city for business and local government issues.

Nova Scotia Museum
www.museum.novascotia.ca
A network of 27 museums managed by the Nova Scotia Department of Communities, Culture, and Heritage. This website includes details on each site, as well as passes for those planning on extensive touring.

ACCOMMODATIONS
Bed and Breakfast Online
www.bbcanada.com
Easy-to-use tools for finding and reserving B&Bs that suit your budget and interests.

Hostelling International–Canada
www.hihostels.ca
Canadian arm of the worldwide organization.

Select Atlantic Inns
www.selectinns.ca
A loosely affiliated group of mid- to top-end B&Bs use this online presence to promote their properties and take bookings.

Signature Resorts
www.signatureresorts.com
Upscale lodging chain owned and operated by the Government of Nova Scotia. Locations include Digby, Liscomb Mills, and Ingonish Beach.

TRANSPORTATION
Air Canada
www.aircanada.ca
Canada's national airline.

Halifax International Airport
www.hiaa.ca
The official airport website, which includes images of departure and arrival boards, tools to help reach Halifax using the most direct flights, and virtual flight maps that show the location of all incoming and outgoing flights.

Maritime Bus
www.maritimebus.com
Where Greyhound buses terminate, Maritime takes over, with inexpensive service throughout Nova Scotia.

Northumberland Ferries
www.ferries.ca
Provides a link between Saint John, New Brunswick, and Digby, Nova Scotia.

VIA Rail
www.viarail.ca
Passenger rail service across Canada, including Montreal to Halifax.

WestJet
www.westjet.com
Before booking with Air Canada, check out this airline for flights into Halifax from throughout Canada.

CONSERVATION
Canadian Parks and Wilderness Society (Nova Scotia Chapter)
www.cpawsns.org
Particularly active local chapter of a non-profit organization that is instrumental in highlighting conservation issues throughout Canada.

Ducks Unlimited Canada
www.ducks.ca
Respected organization responsible for the protection of over 30,000 hectares of wetland throughout Nova Scotia.

Nova Scotia Nature Trust
www.nsnt.ca
Provincial nonprofit organization that has been instrumental in land protection through the purchase and donation of land.

Sable Island Green Horse Society
www.greenhorsesociety.com
A group of individuals interested in Sable Island and its unique environmental issues.

OTHER INTERNET RESOURCES

Dill's Atlantic Giant
www.howarddill.com
Dill, the world's preeminent super-sized pumpkin grower, sells his record-breaking seeds through this website. He also gives growing tips and uploads photos of his massive vegetables.

Nimbus Publishing
www.nimbus.ca
While all the best books on Nova Scotia are detailed under *Suggested Reading,* check the website of this prolific Nova Scotia publisher for the latest titles.

Pugwash Conferences on Science and World Affairs
www.pugwash.org
This is the official website of a Nobel Prize-winning peace movement that had its beginnings in Pugwash, Nova Scotia.

Titanic in Nova Scotia
www.novascotia.ca/titanic
Maintained by the Government of Nova Scotia, this website includes everything from full passenger lists to local links as obscure as a plaque in the Halifax YCMA that commemorates the sinking with the wrong date.

Index

A

Acadian Coast: 22, 102-105
Acadian culture: Acadian Museum 172; Amherst 139; Annapolis Royal 111; cuisine 219-220; deportation 196; Festival de l'Escaouette 172; Fort Edward National Historic Site 126; Grand Pré 125; Grosses Coques 105; Historic Gardens 112; history 195-197; La Vieille Maison 102
Acadian Museum: 172
accommodations: 215-219; see also specific place
Admiral Digby Museum: 105
Adventure Park: 114
Advocate Harbour. 138
African American history: 37
Africville Park: 31, 37
agriculture: 199
air travel: 62, 206, 208
Alexander Graham Bell National Historic Site: 18, 160, 167
Alexander Keith's Brewery: 14, 18, 24, 32, 47
Amherst: 139-140
Amherst Point Migratory Bird Sanctuary: 139
Amherst Shore Provincial Park: 141
An Drochaid: 164
animals: 190-194
Annapolis Royal: 15, 18, 111-116, 118
Annapolis Tidal Station: 111
Annapolis Valley: 118-121
Anne Murray Centre: 139
Antigonish: 149
Antigonish Heritage Museum: 149
Antigonish Highland Games: 149
architecture: Amherst 139; Bridgetown 118; Dartmouth Heritage Museum 40; Haliburton House 126; Historic Gardens 112; Lunenburg 77; Mahone Bay churches 73; Main Street Wolfville 121; Pictou 144; Province House 32; Shand House 127; Shelburne Historic District 91; St. John's Anglican Church 79-80; St. Mary's Church 104; Yarmouth 94
Arisaig: 130, 148
Arisaig Provincial Park: 148
art galleries: Acadia University Art Gallery 121; Art Gallery of Nova Scotia 31;; Chéticamp 172; deGarthe Gallery 69; Halifax 48; La Galerie Comeau 103; Pictou 145; Wolfville 121
Art Gallery of Nova Scotia: 20, 31
Atlantica Oak Island Resort: 16, 76
Atlantic Canada Aviation Museum: 38

Atlantic Film Festival: 47
Atlantic Fringe Festival: 47
aviation museums: 38, 40

B

backpacker accommodations: 217; see also specific place
backpacking: 138, 176
Baddeck: 12, 19, 166-172
Balancing Rock: 19, 100, 109
Ballantynes Cove: 148
Balmoral Grist Mill: 130, 143
banks: 61
Barrington: 93
Bay of Fundy: 11, 18, 110
Bay of Fundy tides: 19, 132, 134, 214
beaches: Cabot's Landing Provincial Park 176; Cape Sable Island 94; Crescent Beach 66, 87-88; Five Islands Provincial Park 137; Gulf Shore Picnic Park 142; Ingonish Beach 178; Kejimkujik National Park Seaside Adjunct 90; Lawrencetown 150; Mavillette Beach Provincial Park 102; McNabs Island 39; Port Joli 90; Queensland Beach 70; Sand Hills Beach Provincial Park 93; Summerville Beach Provincial Park 89; Taylor Head Provincial Park 153; Tidnish 141; Tor Bay Provincial Park 155; White Point Beach Resort 89
Bear River: 105
bed-and-breakfasts: 216-217; see also accommodations
Bedford Basin: 31
Bedford Institute of Oceanography: 40
Bell, Alexander Graham: 167
Bell Island: 88
Benjie's Lake Trail: 176
berry-picking: 155
Bickerton Lighthouse Interpretive Centre: 155
Big Pond: 163
Big Tancook Island: 70
biking: general discussion 213; Cape Breton Highlands National Park 174; Cape George 148; Halifax 40, 41; Thomas Raddall Provincial Park 90
Bird Islands: 180
bird-watching: Amherst Point Migratory Bird Sanctuary 139; Bird Islands 180; Cape Breton Highlands National Park 174, 176; Kejimkujik National Park 116; Kejimkujik National Park

Seaside Adjunct 90; McNabs Island 39; Queensland Beach 70; Robie Tufts Nature Centre 121; Westport 110
Black Brook Cove: 19, 176
Blomidon Estate Winery: 119
Blomidon Peninsula: 119-121
Blomidon Provincial Park: 120
Bluenose II: 18, 43, 56, 66, 81
Blue Rocks: 66, 80
boating: *Bluenose II* 81; Bras d'Or Lakes 168; Halifax Harbour cruises 43; Lunenburg 81; tidal bore riding 130, 132, 214
Bras d'Or Lakes scenic drive: 19, 163
Bridgetown: 118
Bridgewater: 86
Brier Island: 19, 110
Bus Island: 88
bus travel: 62, 207, 208

C

Cabot's Landing Provincial Park: 176
Cabot Trail: 12, 15, 17, 160, 171, 175, 213
Calvary Temple Pentecostal: 73
camping: 217; *see also specific place*
Canadian Museum of Immigration at Pier 21: 33
Canning: 118, 119
canoeing and kayaking: general discussion 214; Halifax 42; Kejimkujik National Park 116, 117; Liscombe Lodge Resort 153; Shubie Park 40; Tangier 152; Webber Lakeside Park 151
Canso: 156-157, 198
Canso Islands National Historic Site: 17, 130, 156-157
Cape Breton Highlands National Park: 12, 174-178
Cape Breton Island: 12, 15, 17, 158-186; Baddeck 166-172; Cape Breton Highlands National Park 174-178; Chéticamp 172-173; highlights 160; historical tour 18; Ingonish 178-181; maps 161; northeast 182-185; planning tips 159; Port Hastings to Baddeck 162-166
Cape Breton Miners' Museum: 184
Cape Chignecto Provincial Park: 138
Cape Forchu: 95
Cape George: 148; scenic drive 147
Cape Lighthouse: 94
Cape North: 175
Cape Sable Island: 94
Cape Smokey: 180
Cape Split: 120
Captain Mark's: 176
car travel: 61, 63, 207
Causeway Beach: 94
caves: 80, 103
Ceilidh Trail: 164
Celtic Colours International Festival: 160, 181
Celtic culture: 160, 164

Central Nova Scotia: 11, 128-157; Glooscap Trail 136-141; Halifax to Truro 132-136; highlights 130; historical tour 18; maps 131; Marine Drive 150-157; Pictou 144-147; Pictou to Cape Breton Island 147-149; planning tips 129; Sunrise Coast 141-143
Centreville: 109
Chester: 22, 70-72
Chéticamp: 12, 17, 171, 172-173, 175
Chowder House: 16, 180
Christmas Craft Village: 48
Church Point: 103
Citadel Hill: 34-36, 52-53
clam digging: Cabot's Landing Provincial Park 176; Cape Sable Island 94; Grosses Coques 105; Murphy's Camping on the Ocean 152
Clam Harbour Provincial Park: 152
climate: 188-189
Cobequid Bay: 135
Colchester Society Museum: 134
Cole Harbour Heritage Farm Museum: 40
Comeauville: 103
Cossit House: 182
Country Harbour: 155
crafts: Christmas Craft Village 48; Festival de l'Escaouette 172; Gaelic College of Celtic Arts and Crafts 181; Gaspereau Valley Fibres 121; Halifax 48; hooked rugs 172; Mahone Bay 74; Nova Scotia Centre for Craft and Design 33
Crescent Beach: 22, 66, 87-88
crime: 224
cross-country skiing: general discussion 215; Halifax 42; Kejimkujik National Park 116
Crystal Crescent Beach Provincial Park: 42
cultural attractions: Antigonish Highland Games 149; Ceilidh Trail 164; Celtic Colours International Festival 160, 181; Gaelic College of Celtic Arts and Crafts 181; Lunenburg Folk Harbour Festival 82; Nova Scotia Multicultural Festival 47; Pictou's Scottish 144; Rossignol Cultural Centre 88; *see also* Acadian culture
Cumberland Basin: 140
Cumberland County Museum: 139
Customs House Inn: 19, 146

DE

Dartmouth: 39-40, 60
Dartmouth Heritage Museum: 40
deCoste: 145
deep-sea fishing: 211
Delap's Cove Wilderness Trail: 113
DesBrisay Museum: 86
Digby: 19, 105-111
Digby Neck: 19, 109
Digby Scallop Days: 106
Digby scallops: 106, 107

Dingle Tower: 39
disabilities, travelers with: 61
Dock Street: 91
Dory Shop Museum: 92
downtown Halifax: accommodations 50-52; food 55-58; sights 28-34
driving: 207, 208
Dunromin Waterfront Campground and Cabins: 16, 114
Eastern Passage: 40-41
economy: 199-200
Economy Shoe Shop: 28, 57
Église de Sainte-Marie (St. Mary's Church): 100, 104
electricity, tidal: 112
emergency services: 61
environmental issues: 189
Evergreen House: 40

F

Fairview Cemetery: 18, 24, 26, 28, 37
family activities: Alexander Graham Bell National Historic Site 167; Annapolis Royal amusement parks 114; Cole Harbour Heritage Farm Museum 40; Look-Off Family Camping 120; Murphy's Camping on the Ocean 152; road trip itinerary 16; Seafoam 143; Shubenacadie Wildlife Park 132-133; South Mountain Park 119; travel tips 222
farmers' markets: Halifax 16, 20, 49; Lunenburg Folk Harbour Festival 82; Wolfville 123
fauna: 190-194
ferries: 16, 207; see also specific place
Festival Antigonish: 149
Festival de l'Escaouette: 172
Firefighters' Museum of Nova Scotia: 95
First Baptist Church: 139, 140
Fisheries Museum of the Atlantic: 79
Fisherman's Cove: 24, 41, 54, 60
Fisherman's Life Museum: 152
fishing: general discussion 210-213; Cape Sable Island 94; Kejimkujik National Park 116; Margaree River Valley 170; South Mountain Park 119
fishing industry: general discussion 199; Bridgewater villages 86; Dory Shop Museum 92; Fisheries Museum of the Atlantic 79; Fisherman's Cove 41; Lunenburg 78; Westport 110
Five Islands Provincial Park: 137
flora: 189-190
folk festivals: 82, 157
Fort Anne National Historic Site: 15, 18, 100, 112
Fort Edward National Historic Site: 126
Fort Ives: 39
Fort McNab: 39

Fort Needham Memorial Park: 36, 37
Fort Petrie: 183-184
Fortress of Louisbourg National Historic Site: 18, 160, 184
fossils: Arisaig 148; Joggins Fossil Cliffs 138; Parrsboro 137
French Mountain: 175
Freshwater Lake Loop: 178
Fundy Coast: 11, 19, 98-127; Annapolis Royal 111-116; Annapolis Valley 118-121; Digby 105-111; highlights 100; historical tour 18; La Côte Acadienne (Acadian Coast) 102-105; maps 101; planning tips 99; Wolfville 121-127
Fundy Geological Museum: 137
Fundy tides: 11, 19, 132, 134, 214

G

Gaelic College of Celtic Arts and Crafts: 160
Gaelic culture: 181
gardens: Cole Harbour Heritage Farm Museum 40; Grand Pré National Historic Site 125-126; Historic Gardens 112; Prescott House Museum 119; Public Gardens 35; Ross-Thomson House and Store Museum 92; Victoria Park 134
geography: 187
geology: general discussion 187; Arisaig Provincial Park 148; Fundy Geological Museum 137
Gilbert's Cove: 105
Glace Bay: 184
Glenora Inn and Distillery: 17, 160, 164
Glooscap Trail: 136-141
gold mining: 80, 154
golf: general discussion 213-214; Chester Golf Club 70; Dundee Resort 163; Fox Harb'r Golf Resort and Spa 142; Halifax 42; Highlands Links 160, 178; South Mountain Park 119; White Point Beach Resort 89
government: 200-201
Grand Anse River: 174
Grand Pré: 125
Grand Pré National Historic Site: 16, 100, 125
Grassy Island: 156
Graves Island Provincial Park: 71
Grosses Coques: 105
Gulf Shore Picnic Park: 142
Gulf Shore Road: 142

HIJK

Haliburton House: 18, 126
Halifax: 14, 17; accommodations 50-55; entertainment and events 44-48; food 55-60; harbor 31, 43; highlights 24; historical tour 18; history 25-27; information and services 60-61; itinerary 28; maps 25, 29; orientation

27; planning tips 10, 23; recreation 41-44; shopping 48-50; sights 28-41; transportation 61-63
Halifax Citadel National Historic Site: 14, 18, 24, 28, 34
Halifax Explosion: 36, 37
Halifax Harbour: 31
Halifax International Busker Festival: 47
Halifax Jazz Festival: 47
Halifax Mooseheads: 43
Harbour Hopper Tours: 16, 43
Hawk Beach: 94
Hazel Hill Cable Station: 198
health: 223-224
Heather Beach Provincial Park: 141
Hector: 18, 145
Hector Heritage Quay: 16, 130, 144
Hemlock Ravine Park: 37, 41
Highland Games (Antigonish): 149
Highlands Links: 15, 19, 160, 178
Highland Village Museum: 166
Highway 19: 164
Highway 28: 183
Highway 105: 165
Highway 331: 87
Highway 366: 141
hiking: Amherst Shore Provincial Park 141; Annapolis Royal 113; Battery Provincial Park 163; Blomidon Provincial Park 120; Cape Breton Highlands National Park 174, 176; Cape Chignecto Provincial Park 138; Cape Smokey 180; Five Islands Provincial Park 137; Halifax 41; Kejimkujik National Park 116, 117; Liscombe Lodge Resort 153; Mabou Highlands 164; McNabs Island 39; Partridge Island 137; Shubie Park 40; Taylor Head Provincial Park 153; Uniacke Estate Museum Park 38; Victoria Park 134
Hines, Sherman: 88
Historic Downtown Lunenburg: 66, 79
Historic Gardens: 112
Historic Properties of Halifax: 24, 30
history: 72, 194-199
hotels: 216; *see also* accommodations
Hubbards: 70
Hunts Point Beach Cottages: 89
Ingonish: 12, 15, 17, 171, 176, 178-181
Ingonish Beach: 178
Internet access: 227
Inverness: 165
Iona: 165
Isaacs Harbour: 155
Isle Madame: 162
itineraries: 11, 14-21
James House Museum: 118
Joggins: 138
Joggins Fossil Centre: 139
Joggins Fossil Cliffs: 138
Jost Vineyards: 142
Kannon Beach: 150
Kejimkujik National Park: 15, 116-118
Kejimkujik National Park Seaside Adjunct: 90
Kentville: 119
Kidston Island: 166, 168
King's County Museum: 119
kite surfing: 88

L
La Côte Acadienne (Acadian Coast): 18, 22, 102-105
LaHave Islands: 88
La Vieille Maison (Old House Museum): 103
Lawrence House Museum: 133
Lawrencetown Beach: 17, 150
LeHave Island: 88
Leif Ericson Picnic Park: 96
Le Musée Sainte-Marie: 104
Lennox Passage: 162-163
LeNoir Forge Museum: 163
Les Trois Pignons: 172
licenses, fishing: 212
lighthouses: Ballantynes Cove 148; Bickerton Lighthouse Interpretive Centre 155; Cape Forchu 95; Cape Sable Island 94; Gilbert's Cove 105; Kidston Island 168; Peggy's Cove 68
Liscomb Mills: 153
Liverpool: 88-89
lobster suppers: 170
Longfellow, Henry Wadsworth: 125
Long Island: 109
Louisbourg: 184
Lunenburg: 10, 14, 18, 22, 28, 77-85
Lunenburg Academy: 80
Lunenburg Folk Harbour Festival: 82

M
Mabou: 164
Mabou Highlands: 164
MacAskill House Museum: 163
MacDonald Bridge: 31
MacKay Bridges: 31
MacKenzie Mountain: 175
Mahone Bay: 14, 22, 28, 72-73
Mahone Bay churches: 10, 66, 73
Mahone Bay Settler's Museum: 72
Main Street Wolfville: 121
Maitland: 133
Margaree Forks: 171
Margaree River Valley: 170
Margaree Salmon Museum: 170
Marine Drive: 11, 17, 150-157

Maritime Command Museum: 37
Maritime Fall Fair: 48
Maritime Museum of the Atlantic: 18, 24, 26, 28, 30
Martinique Beach Provincial Park: 151
Mauger's Beach: 39
Mavillette Beach Provincial Park: 102
McCulloch Heritage Centre: 145
McNabs Island: 31, 39, 41
Memorial Tower: 31
Meteghan: 103
Meteghan River: 103
Métis: 202
Mi'kmaq people: 195, 201
military sights: Fort Anne National Historic Site 112; Fortress of Louisbourg National Historic Site 184; Halifax Citadel National Historic Site 34; Maritime Command Museum 37; Prince of Wales Martello Tower 34; Royal Nova Scotia International Tattoo 47; York Redoubt National Historic Site 39
mining: Cape Breton Miners' Museum 184; economy 200; gold 80, 154; Inverness 165
Mink Cove: 109
money: 225-227
Mont Blanc explosion: 36
motels: 216; see also accommodations
mountain biking: 213
Mount Olivet Cemetery: 26
Muir-Cox Shipyard: 92
Murphy Cove: 152
Museum of Natural History: 16, 35
music: Anne Murray Centre 139; ceilidh 164; Celtic Colours International Festival 181; Festival de l'Escaouette 172; Halifax 46, 47; Hank Snow Home Town Museum 88-89; Lunenburg Folk Harbour Festival 82; Scottish 204; Stan Rogers Folk Festival 157
Musquodoboit Harbour: 150
Musquodoboit Railway Museum: 150

NO

Narrows, The: 31
Natal Day: 47
national parks: 209-210; day pass 175; see also specific park
Ned Macdonald Museum: 165
nightlife: Halifax 45-46; Lunenburg 81-82
North Mountain: 175
Northport Beach Provincial Park: 19, 141
Northumberland Fisheries Museum: 145
Northumberland Strait: 11, 129, 141
Nova Scotia: Cape Breton Island 158-186; Central Nova Scotia 128-157; Fundy Coast 98-127; Halifax 22-63; South Shore 64-97
Nova Scotia Archives: 26

Nova Scotia Centre for Craft and Design: 20, 33
Nova Scotia Multicultural Festival: 47
Nova Scotian crystal: 20, 28, 48
Oak Island: 74
Old Burying Ground: 32
Old House Museum: 103
Old Meeting House Museum: 93
Old Town Clock: 34
orchards: 118, 125-126
Ottawa House Museum: 137
Ovens Natural Park: 80, 84
Oyster Pond: 152

PQ

packing tips: 222
panning for gold: 80
parks: 209-210; see also specific place
Parrsboro: 137
Parrsboro Rock and Mineral Shop and Museum: 137
Partridge Island: 137
Peggy's Cove: 10, 14, 22, 28, 66, 68-70
performing arts: 46, 70
Perkins House: 88
phone services: 226
photography: 163, 212
Pictou: 18, 19, 144-149
Pictou Lodge Beach Resort: 16, 146
Pirate Festival: 16, 66, 74
plants: 189-190
Pleasant Bay: 175
Pointe de l'Église (Church Point): 103
Point Pleasant Park: 24, 31, 33, 41
police: 224
Pondville Beach: 163
Port Hastings: 162
Port Joli: 90-91
Port of Privateers: 88
Port-Royal National Historic Site: 15, 100, 113
postal services: 226
Prescott House Museum: 119
Prince of Wales Martello Tower: 34
Privateer Days: 89
Province House: 32
provincial parks: 210; see also specific park
Psyche Cove: 153
Public Gardens: 14, 24, 28, 35, 41
public transportation: 63; see also specific place
Pugwash: 141
Quaker House: 40
Queensland Beach: 70

R

rafting, tidal bore: 130, 132
rail travel: 62, 206

Rainbow Haven Provincial Park: 42
Randall House Museum: 121
rappie pie: 220
recreation: 209-215; *see also specific place*
resorts: 216; *see also* accommodations
Rissers Beach Provincial Park: 88
Robie Tufts Nature Centre: 121
rodeos: 48
Rogers Brook: 117
Rossignol Cultural Centre: 88
Ross-Thomson House and Store Museum: 92
Royal Canadian Mounted Police (RCMP): 224
Royal Nova Scotia International Tattoo: 47
Rum Runners Rum Cake Factory: 28
RV rentals: 209

S
Sable Island: 151
salmon fishing: 170, 210-211
Salmon River: 135
Salmon River Bridge: 151
Salty's: 16, 28, 31, 56
sand dunes: Crescent Beach 88; Lawrencetown
    Beach 150; Sand Hills Beach Provincial Park 93
Sand Hills Beach Provincial Park: 93
Sandy Cove: 109
scallops: 11, 106, 107
scenic drives: Bras d'Or Lakes 163; Cabot Trail 160,
    171, 175; Cape Forchu 95; Cape George 147;
    Marine Drive 150
Scotia Festival of Music: 47
Scotia Trawler Shipyard: 79
Scottish culture: Antigonish Highland Games 149;
    Great Hall of the Clans 181; Pictou 144
Seafoam: 19, 143
seafood: Baddeck lobster suppers 227; Digby
    scallops 107; Halifax 10, 49; J. Willy Krauch and
    Sons 152; Nova Lobster 103
Shand House: 127
Shearwater Aviation Museum: 40
Shelburne: 10, 22, 91-94
Shelburne County Museum: 91
Shelburne Historic District: 18, 66, 91
Sherbrooke: 154, 155
Sherbrooke Village: 130, 154
shipbuilding: Mahone Bay Settler's Museum 72;
    Maitland 133; Meteghan River 103; Muir-Cox
    Shipyard 92
Shubenacadie: 132
Shubenacadie River: 132
Shubenacadie Wildlife Park: 16, 132-133
Shubie Park: 40
Silver Dart: 167
Sir Sandford Fleming Park: 38-39, 41
skiing: 42, 215
Ski Martock: 42

Skyline Loop Trail: 176
Smuggler's Cove Provincial Park: 102
snowboarding: 42, 215
South Mountain Park: 119
South Shore: 64-97; Halifax to Mahone Bay 68-72;
    highlights 66; historical tour 18; Lunenburg
    77-85; Lunenburg to Shelburne 86-91;
    Mahone Bay 72-77; maps 67; planning tips 10;
    Shelburne 91-94; Yarmouth 94-97
South Side Beach: 94
Spring Garden Road: 58
Springhill: 139
Spry Bay: 153
stand-up paddleboarding: 214
St. Ann's: 171, 180
Stan Rogers Folk Festival: 157
Starr's Point: 119
St. Francis Xavier University: 149
St. George's Anglican Church: 26
St. George's Round Church: 36
St. James Anglican Church: 73
St. John's Anglican Church: 79-80
St. John's Lutheran: 73
St. Mary's Cathedral Basilica: 32
St. Mary's Catholic Church: 26
St. Mary's Church (Church Point): 104
Stoney Island Beach: 94
St. Patrick's Church Museum: 182
St. Paul's Anglican Church: 26, 32, 36
St. Peters: 163
St. Pierre Catholic Church: 172
Summerville Beach Provincial Park: 89
Sunrise Coast: 141-143
surfing: 94, 150, 214
swimming: Black Brook Cove 176; Cape Sable
    Island 94; Crescent Beach 88; Halifax 42;
    Ingonish Beach 178; Kejimkujik National
    Park 116; Sand Hills Beach Provincial Park 93;
    Tidnish 141; Webber Lakeside Park 151; White
    Point Beach Resort 89
Sydney: 182-183

TUV
Tangier: 17, 152
Taylor Head Provincial Park: 17, 130, 152
telephone services: 226
tennis: Liscombe Lodge Resort 153; South
    Mountain Park 119; White Point Beach Resort
    89
Thomas Raddall Provincial Park: 90
Tidal Bore Rafting Park: 132
tidal bore riding: 130, 132, 214
tidal bore watching: 134
tide pools: 39, 193
Tidnish: 141
Tidnish Dock Provincial Park: 141

time zones: 227
Titanic: general discussion 26; Bedford Institute of Oceanography 40; Fairview Cemetery 37
Tiverton: 109
Tor Bay: 155
Tor Bay Provincial Park: 155
tourist information: 61, 226
train travel: 62, 206
transportation: 13, 206-209; *see also specific place*
Treaty of Utrecht: 196
Trinity United Church: 73
Truro: 134-136
UNESCO World Heritage Sites: Historic Downtown Lunenburg 10, 79; Joggins Fossil Cliffs 138
Uniacke Estate Museum Park: 38
United Baptist Church: 73
Upper Clements Parks: 114
Valleyview Provincial Park: 118
Victoria Park (Truro): 134

WXYZ

walking paths: Ballantynes Cove 148; Big Tancook Island 70; Halifax 41; Keltic Lodge 178; Kidston Island 168; Thomas Raddall Provincial Park 90; Tor Bay Provincial Park 155; Waterfront Wolfville 121

waterfalls: 134
Waterfront Wolfville: 121
water sports: 214-215
Webber Lakeside Park: 151
Westport: 110
whale-watching: general discussion 214; Bay of Fundy 19, 100, 110; Cape Breton Highlands National Park 176-177; Chéticamp 172; Lunenburg Whale Watching Tours 81; Pleasant Bay 16, 175; Westport 110
whiskey distilleries: 164
White Point: 89
Whycocomagh: 171
wildflowers: 110, 190
wildlife: 190-194
wildlife-viewing: Cabot Trail 12, 171; Cape Breton Highlands National Park 174; Cape Sable Island 94; Kejimkujik National Park 116
Wile Carding Mill: 86
Windsor: 126-127
wine and wineries: Blomidon Estate Winery 119; Grand Pré Wines 125; Jost Vineyards 142
Wolfville: 121-127
Yarmouth: 94-97
Yarmouth County Museum: 95
York Redoubt National Historic Site: 39
zip lines: 114
zoos: 132-133

List of Maps

Front map
Nova Scotia: 2-3

Discover Nova Scotia
chapter divisions map: 10

Halifax
Halifax: 25
Downtown Halifax: 29

South Shore
South Shore: 67
Halifax to Mahone Bay: 69
Chester: 71
Mahone Bay: 73
Lunenburg: 78
Shelburne: 91
Yarmouth: 95

Fundy Coast
Fundy Coast: 101
Digby: 106
Annapolis Royal: 111
Kejimkujik National Park: 117
Wolfville: 122

Central Nova Scotia
Central Nova Scotia: 131
Truro: 134
Glooscap Trail: 136
Pictou: 144

Cape Breton Island
Cape Breton Island: 161
Baddeck: 166
Cape Breton Highlands National Park: 174
Sydney: 182

Photo Credits

MAP SYMBOLS

≡≡≡≡	Expressway	○	City/Town	✈	Airport	⚑	Golf Course
≡≡≡	Primary Road	◉	State Capital	✕	Airfield	🅿	Parking Area
≡≡	Secondary Road	⊛	National Capital	▲	Mountain	≜	Archaeological Site
∙∙∙∙∙∙	Unpaved Road	★	Point of Interest	✦	Unique Natural Feature	♦	Church
——	Feature Trail	•	Accommodation				
- - - -	Other Trail			🦢	Waterfall	⬛	Gas Station
∙∙∙∙∙∙∙	Ferry	▼	Restaurant/Bar	▲	Park	◉	Glacier
≡≡≡	Pedestrian Walkway	■	Other Location	⬛	Trailhead	▨	Mangrove
▥▥▥	Stairs	▲	Campground	⛷	Skiing Area	⬛	Reef
						⬛	Swamp

CONVERSION TABLES

°C = (°F - 32) / 1.8
°F = (°C x 1.8) + 32
1 inch = 2.54 centimeters (cm)
1 foot = 0.304 meters (m)
1 yard = 0.914 meters
1 mile = 1.6093 kilometers (km)
1 km = 0.6214 miles
1 fathom = 1.8288 m
1 chain = 20.1168 m
1 furlong = 201.168 m
1 acre = 0.4047 hectares
1 sq km = 100 hectares
1 sq mile = 2.59 square km
1 ounce = 28.35 grams
1 pound = 0.4536 kilograms
1 short ton = 0.90718 metric ton
1 short ton = 2,000 pounds
1 long ton = 1.016 metric tons
1 long ton = 2,240 pounds
1 metric ton = 1,000 kilograms
1 quart = 0.94635 liters
1 US gallon = 3.7854 liters
1 Imperial gallon = 4.5459 liters
1 nautical mile = 1.852 km

MOON NOVA SCOTIA
Avalon Travel
a member of the Perseus Books Group
1700 Fourth Street
Berkeley, CA 94710, USA
www.moon.com

Editor: Leah Gordon
Series Manager: Kathryn Ettinger
Copy Editor: Kristie Reilly
Graphics Coordinators: Kathryn Osgood,
    Elizabeth Jang
Production Coordinator: Elizabeth Jang
Cover Design: Faceout Studios, Charles Brock
Moon Logo: Tim McGrath
Map Editor: Kat Bennett
Cartographers: Brian Shotwell, Stephanie Poulain
Indexer: Rachel Kuhn

ISBN-13: 978-1-63121-039-6
ISSN: 1930-1502

Printing History
1st Edition — 2006
4th Edition — May 2015
5 4 3 2 1

Text © 2015 by Andrew Hempstead.
Maps © 2015 by Avalon Travel.
All rights reserved.

Front cover photo: historic sailing vessel, Halifax
© Robert George Young/Getty Images

Back cover photo: lighthouse at Peggy's Cove at
sunset © Natalia Bratslavsky/123rf.com

Printed in Canada by Friesens

KEEPING CURRENT

If you have a favorite gem you'd like to see included in the next edition, or see anything that needs updating, clarification, or correction, please drop us a line. Send your comments via email to feedback@moon.com, or use the address above.